A Suffragette in America

Miss Sylvia Pankhurst

Artist, Prison Reformer, Suffrage Advocate

American Tour, January, February, 1912

UNDER DIRECTION OF WILLIAM B. FEAKINS
(Successor to Civic Forum Lecture Bureau)
23 WEST 44TH STREET, NEW YORK
TELEPHONE: BRYANT, 4897

PLEASE NOTE
CHANGE OF ADDRESS
21 WEST 44TH STREET
TELEPHONE: BRYANT, 8317

A Suffragette in America

Reflections on Prisoners, Pickets and Political Change

E. Sylvia Pankhurst

Edited and with an Introduction
by Katherine Connelly

PLUTO PRESS

First published 2019 by Pluto Press
345 Archway Road, London N6 5AA

www.plutobooks.com

British Library Cataloguing in Publication Data
A catalogue record for this book is available from the British Library

ISBN   978 0 7453 3937 5   Hardback
ISBN   978 0 7453 3936 8   Paperback
ISBN   978 1 7868 0454 9   PDF eBook
ISBN   978 1 7868 0456 3   Kindle eBook
ISBN   978 1 7868 0455 6   EPUB eBook

This book is printed on paper suitable for recycling and made from fully
managed and sustained forest sources. Logging, pulping and manufacturing
processes are expected to conform to the environmental standards of the
country of origin.

Typeset by Stanford DTP Services, Northampton, England

Simultaneously printed in the United Kingdom and United States of America

Contents

Photographs

Dedicated to the memory of Sylvia Pankhurst's son,
Professor Richard Pankhurst (1927–2017)

Acknowledgements

First, I owe a huge debt of thanks to Helen Pankhurst for kindly granting me the rights to publish Sylvia Pankhurst's manuscript and for being so warmly supportive throughout. Helen, I hope that you and the Pankhurst family enjoy the book.

Thank you to the staff at Pluto Press, especially to Neda Tehrani for thoughtful and constructive comments on the manuscript, and to David Castle and Robert Webb for your enthusiasm for this project and for guiding it through to publication. Thank you also to Ros Connelly, Morgan Daniels, Elaine Graham-Leigh and Dana Mills for invaluable help reading and commenting on the introductory writing. Sincere thanks to Jeanne Brady for so diligently copy-editing the text.

Rachel Holmes, whose own writing on Sylvia Pankhurst I eagerly await, provided comradely support throughout, which meant a great deal to me; Jacqueline Mulhallen, always supportive and generous, provided me with the transcript for Sylvia's article in *The London Magazine* and William Alderson kindly sent the photographed text; Professor Joan Sangster shared her knowledge of Pankhurst connections in Canada; thanks too to Joan Ashworth for an inspiring conversation about this part of Sylvia's life.

The organisers of the 'Women's Suffrage and Political Activism' conference at Cambridge University and the 'Women's Suffrage and Beyond: Local, National and International Contexts' conference at Oxford University allowed me to explore my ideas with other suffrage scholars. Maggie Cohen invited me to speak on Sylvia and America at the Working Class Movement Library, enabling me to discuss this material with others who share a deep knowledge of socialist and feminist history.

For assistance with archival research, I would like to thank all the staff at the International Institute of Social History in Amsterdam; the British Library; the Women's Library at the LSE, and the Special Collections at Senate House Library. For assistance with archival research in America, I would like to thank all the staff at the Manuscript Division of the Library of Congress in Washington, DC; the National Archives and Records Administration in Washington, DC; the staff at the New

York Public Library, especially John Calhoun at the Billy Rose Theatre Division who helped locate the Neighborhood Playhouse material; Arlene Yu, Collections Manager at the Jerome Robbins Dance Division, and those in the Periodicals and Microforms Room in the Schwarzman Building; the staff at the University of Wisconsin-Milwaukee, particularly Heidi Anoszko, the reference and instruction archivist, who gave so much of her time to help me; the staff at the Central Milwaukee Public Library, especially Casey Lapworth and Daniel Lee; to Susan Kruger at the Wisconsin Historical Society, and to all the staff at the North Dakota State University archives, especially John Halberg and Katrina Burch.

Thank you to Katie Vogel, public historian at the Henry Street Settlement in New York, for meeting with me and affording me the incredibly special experience of being shown around Lillian Wald's Settlement building. Chris Segedy, senior house manager at the Pabst Theatre Group, was kind enough to give me a tour of the beautiful theatre where Sylvia spoke in 1912, allowing another treasured glimpse into Sylvia's America. In the course of this project, I was incredibly lucky to start working with Christine Hoenigs at Lawrence University's London centre who kindly put me in contact with Erin Dix, the archivist at Lawrence University, Appleton, Wisconsin. Thanks to Erin for delving into the college's history to find evidence of Sylvia's visit in 1912. Archival advice was also provided by Thai Jones, at the Rare Books and Manuscripts Library at Columbia University; Professor Cathy Moran Hajo, editor and director of the Jane Addams Papers Project; Julianna Jenkins, at UCLA Public Services Library Special Collection; Linnea M. Anderson, archivist at the Social Welfare History Archives at the University of Minnesota, and Eisha Neely, at the Research Services Division of Rare and Manuscript Collections at Cornell University in Ithaca, New York.

The geographical scale of the research would have been impossible to attempt without a huge amount of generosity and imagination. It is my privilege to be sharing my life with someone who possesses both qualities in abundance. Thank you so very much to my partner Morgan Daniels for planning the route across America, thank you for transforming a research trip into a wonder-filled adventure, for sharing in every discovery, everything that was magical and inspiring, bleak and strange. Your generosity is reflected in your friendships – and it is an additional good fortune for me that so many of those happen to be in America! I am extremely grateful to a friendship group united by a passion for a band based in Dayton, Ohio, and I thank all of you for opening your homes so generously to this outsider who was made to feel entirely welcomed: to comrade Steve Panovich, Andy Cline, Emily Robinson and Mike Jueneman, Ryan and Stephanie Brush, and to Matthew Cutter, Maureen Creedon Cutter, Patrick, Abby and Maeve – thank you for letting us join your family, and special thanks to Patrick who so kindly gave us his room. Thank you also to Dan Sayer, who helped us out (not for the first time) at short notice.

Many thanks to Nancy and Barry Libecki who looked after us in Milwaukee and to Nancy for telling me about Milwaukee's past, which helped bring the research to life. Thank you to Andrew Faas for the introduction.

I owe a lifetime of thanks to my parents, Ros and Paul Connelly, and my sister, Ruth Keogh Connelly. Your constant love, support and encouragement help me every day. Thank you from the bottom of my heart to Morgan for your love, for inspiring me and for everything you did to help me to realise this book.

For many years, I was lucky enough to experience the kindness of Sylvia Pankhurst's son, Professor Richard Pankhurst. Committed to the continuation of and research into his mother's work, he afforded me advice and support when I was writing her biography. We discussed how interesting the American material was and I mentioned my hope to write an article about it, an idea that he was characteristically supportive of. That idea eventually developed into this project to bring Sylvia's own writing about America to publication and placing it in the context of her tours. I hope that Richard Pankhurst would have liked this book and it is to his memory that it is dedicated.

Sylvia Pankhurst's North American Tours – Timelines

TIMELINE OF THE 1911 TOUR

1910

28 December   Sylvia Pankhurst embarks on the SS *St. Paul* from Southampton, England.

1911

5 January   New York City, New York: Sylvia arrives. She is met by Women's Political Union (WPU) members Lavinia Dock, Eunice Dana Brannan and Beatrice Brown, and press reporters. Taken to WPU headquarters, basement of 46 East 29th Street, where she meets Harriot Stanton Blatch and conducts press interviews. Her photograph is taken at the Hotel Martha Washington, also on 29th Street.

6 January   New York, NY: Speaks at the Carnegie Lyceum, 8 p.m.

8 January   New York, NY: Speaks at WPU meeting at headquarters on 29th Street.

10 January   Boston, Massachusetts: Speaks in Ford Hall. A thousand people attend.

11 January   Cambridge, MA: Speaks in Brattle Hall. Two hundred women and some Harvard students attend.

12 January   New York, NY: Speaks in the evening in the Good Citizenship League, Flushing, Brooklyn. Over 800 attend. Leaves Flushing at 10 p.m. for Manhattan where she takes a train for Pittsburgh.

13 January   Pittsburgh, Pennsylvania: Speaks at 8 p.m. in the Carnegie Lecture Hall on 'My Life in a London Prison'.

14 January   Cleveland, Ohio: Speaks on 'Women in Politics' under the auspices of the College Equal Franchise League. Sometime between 14 January and 16 January visits Cleveland workhouse and speaks with the women prisoners.

17 January	Oberlin, OH: Arrives in the morning and stays overnight.
18 January	Oberlin, OH: Guest lectures in the sociology class at Oberlin College. Travels to Chicago, Illinois, arriving at the Congress Hotel at midnight. Plans to spend the next few days writing and avoiding the press. It is likely that in the following days she makes her first visit to Hull House, the Settlement run by Jane Addams.
21 January	Chicago, IL: Visits Harrison Street's gaol, police court-room and cells with Zelie Emerson and Olive Sullivan.
22 January	Chicago, IL: Article on Harrison Street published in the *Chicago Sunday Tribune*.
25 January	Minneapolis, Minnesota: Arrives from Chicago in the evening and is the guest of Mrs Alexander Hughes.
26 January	Minneapolis, MN: Speaks for nearly two hours at the First Unitarian Church. Is unwell and spends much of the day in bed.
27 January	Minneapolis and St. Paul, MN: Guest of honour at the luncheon of the 1915 Suffrage club at Donaldson's tearooms. Travels to St. Paul in the evening and speaks at the Hotel St. Paul.
28 January	Chicago and Evanston, IL: Guest of honour at the luncheon provided by the Illinois Equal Suffrage Association in the Chicago Woman's Club parlours in the Fine Arts Building. Speaks for three hours on 'Life in a London Prison' at the Music Hall, Fine Arts Building. In the evening speaks at Fisk Hall, Northwestern University, Evanston.
30 January	Kansas City, Kansas: Speaks to around 300 people at the annual State Dinner of the Women's Dining Club.
31 January	Kansas City, KS: Speaks at the Shubert Theatre in the afternoon. In the evening takes the sleeper train.
1 February	Des Moines and Boone, Iowa: Around 8 a.m., arrives in Union Station intending to change trains for Boone but is informed that she is to address the state government in Des Moines. At the Chamberlain Hotel, osteopath Dr Nina Dewey helps restore her lost voice. 12 noon: addresses the state government in joint assembly at the State House, followed by a reception. Travels to Boone

with Rowena Edson Stevens and rests at her house. Evening: speaks for two hours at the Christian Church, Boone.

2 February Boone, IA to Cincinnati, OH: Was expected to arrive in Cincinnati this day, but due to missing a train arrives next morning.

3 February Cincinnati, OH: Arrives 7:43 a.m. Picked up by local suffragists from the Sinton Hotel and taken to the Art Museum and Rookwood Pottery, and a tour of the suburbs. Guest of honour at luncheon, Hotel Alms. 4–6 p.m.: reception at the Sinton Hotel. 8 p.m.: speaks on imprisonment to a full house at the Memorial Hall.

4 February Columbus, OH: Addresses women at the Chamber of Commerce in the afternoon. Speaks in the Memorial Hall, East Broad Street.

Between 4 and 6 February, travels to New York.

7 February New York, NY, to Ottawa, Canada: Train arrives from New York into Ottawa in the afternoon, having been delayed for two hours by a snowstorm. Speaks in the evening for around two hours to an audience of 500 in the Russell Theatre.

8 February Ottawa, Canada: Guest of honour at afternoon reception given by her hostess, Mrs George Clarke Holland. Visits the prison in Ottawa on this or the following day.

9 February Ottawa, Canada: Guest of honour at Mrs Cromwell Cox's luncheon.

10 February Ottawa and Toronto, Canada: Leaves Ottawa in the morning, arrives in Toronto in the evening.

11 February Toronto, Canada: Speaks in the evening in Massey Hall.

12 February Toronto, Canada and Syracuse, NY: Train from Toronto is three hours late, so misses planned lunch with Miss Anne Miller at Lochland, Geneva in New York State. Travels instead from Buffalo to Syracuse where she speaks to an audience of 1,000 at the Grade Theatre.

13 February Rochester, NY: Speaks in the evening under the auspices of the Labour Lyceum at the Second Baptist Church.

14 February Geneva, NY: Guest of honour at luncheon in Anne Miller's home, Lochland, Geneva. Speaks in the Smith Opera House on 'Women in Politics'.

17 February	New York, NY: Speaks about her prison experiences in a lecture at the Hotel Astor.
21 February	Philadelphia, PA: Joint guest of honour with Mrs Rachel Foster Avery, former president of the Woman Suffrage Society of the County of Philadelphia, in the lunch room of the Century Club. Speaks for over an hour at the New Century Drawing Room which is filled to overflowing (capacity 600); hundreds have to be turned away.
22 February	(Washington's birthday) Washington, DC: Arrives at 7 a.m. Speaks at 11 a.m. in the Columbia Theatre on 'The New Struggle for Liberty'. Is joint guest of honour, with Anna Kelton, at a luncheon at Ebbitt House. Taken by car to visit Belle Case La Follette where a reception is held. Brief visit to the Capitol and the Senate gallery before heading to the train for Boston at Union Station.
23 February	Boston, MA: Marches in the front row of the women's suffrage torchlight procession in the early evening from Park Square to the State House. Speaks to crowds outside and to meetings in Ford Hall. Addresses the State House.
24 February	Boston, MA: Speaks at the Massachusetts Woman Suffrage Association meeting in the headquarters of that organisation and of the *Woman's Journal*. Between 25 and 27 February: Travels to Albany, NY, to participate in 'Suffrage Week' campaign. She is advertised as speaking there on 25 and 26 February, though a letter from Sylvia to Keir Hardie on which she wrote 'Boston 26 Feb' casts doubt on whether she was in Boston or Albany on these days.
28 February	Albany, NY: Speaks on 'Prison Experiences of a Young Suffragette' in the Ten Eyck Hotel as part of Suffrage Week.
2 March	Train journey from Albany, NY, to Denver, Colorado: Met by local suffragists when the train stops at Lincoln, Nebraska.
3 March	Denver, CO: Arrives at Denver in the morning and addresses the Colorado Legislature. Speaks in the evening at the Unity Church. She is the guest of the suffragist Sarah Platt-Decker.

6 March	Los Angeles, California: Stays at the Alexandria Hotel and meets the press there. Speaks on 'Women in Politics' at the Temple Auditorium in the evening.
7 March	Venice and Pasadena, CA: Taken by car to Venice and speaks in the auditorium there. Driven to Pasadena where she speaks at Clune's Pasadena Theatre in the evening. She is the guest of her cousin Helen Herendeen (née Pankhurst) and her husband who were spending the winter at Pasadena's Hotel Maryland.
8 March	Los Angeles, CA: Luncheon at the California Club. Visits the country prison and juvenile court. Guest of honour at tea in the home of suffragist Frances Wills which she attends with Mr and Mrs Herendeen. There are around 60–70 guests. In the evening speaks again at the Temple Auditorium, this time on 'Women in Industry'.
9 March	Train journey from Los Angeles to San Francisco, CA.
10 March	San Francisco, CA: Was due to speak in the Christian Science Hall but heavy rains delayed the train and the meeting is postponed until the following day.
11 March	San Francisco and Oakland, CA: Speaks at the Christian Science Hall at 2:30 p.m. Speaks at 8 p.m. at Idora Park Theatre, Oakland, on 'Women in Politics' to an audience of nearly 2,000.
12 March	San Francisco, CA: Boards an evening train for Kansas.
15 March	Arrives in Lawrence, KS.
16 March	Lawrence, KS: Speaks at the State University's chapel in the morning to over 2,000 students. Luncheon held in her honour by Mrs H.H. Fiske, wife of the superintendent at Haskell College. It is likely this day she visits Haskell. Leaves Lawrence on the train that evening.
17 March	St Louis, Missouri: Arrives in the morning into Union Station. Interviewed by a reporter for the *St Louis Post-Dispatch* on car journey to breakfast. Addresses the City Club at midday for 55 minutes. Debates former Assistant Attorney General Isaac H. Lionberger at 3:30 p.m. before an audience of around 800 at Founders' Hall, Mary Institute. Guest of honour at tea and a dinner in the city. Takes a train at 10:10 p.m. for Topeka.

18 March	Topeka, KS: Speaks in the evening at the First Baptist Church.
20 March	Hutchinson, KS: Arrives in the evening from Topeka.
21 March	Hutchinson, KS: Visits the Reformatory. Guest of honour at the Philomath Club reception in the afternoon at the Elks Club house. Lectures in the high school in the evening.
23 March	Indianapolis, Indiana: Arrives at 7 a.m. Guest of honour at breakfast where she meets the novelist Booth Tarkington. Is taken for a drive around the city. Speaks at lunch at the Claypool Hotel provided by the board of directors of the Women's School League. Informal reception in the Odd Fellows building. Speaks in the auditorium there at 3:45 p.m. Leaves on 7 p.m. train.
24 March	Lansing, Michigan: Addresses the joint meeting of the state government.
25 March	*Fire at the Triangle Shirtwaist Factory in New York kills 146 workers.*
	Detroit, MI: Guest of honour at the luncheon held by the Men's League for Woman Suffrage in Michigan at the Elliott-Taylor-Woolfenden Café. Taken by Dr Mary Thompson Stevens to rest until dinner. Speaks for three hours in the evening at the Church of Our Father.
26 March	Detroit, MI: Day of rest at the home of local suffragist Clara Arthur. Is driven around the city and in the afternoon visits Pewabic Pottery makers as a guest of its co-founder Horace Caulkins. Leaves for Baltimore in the evening.
27 March	Baltimore, Maryland: Arrives in the afternoon.
28 March	Baltimore, MD: Speaks at 8 p.m. in the Osler Hall of the Medical and Chirurgical Building, Cathedral Street. Is the guest of Mrs Emma Maddox Funck, the president of the Baltimore Woman Suffrage Club at her home on Eutaw Place.
29 March	Baltimore, MD: Visits the office of the *Baltimore Sun* newspaper. Leaves Baltimore in the evening.
30 March	Concord, New Hampshire: Speaks in the evening.
31 March	Springfield, MA: Lectures in Springfield High School to over 300 people.

1 April	Winchester, MA: Speaks in Winchester Town Hall to a packed audience (capacity 1,000) alongside Helen Frances Garrison Villard at 8 p.m.
2 April	Philadelphia, PA: Met at Broad Street Station by a reception headed by Alice Paul. Stays at the Women's Graduate Club.
3 April	Philadelphia, PA: It is likely that she visits the penitentiary at this time. Speaks on 'English Militant Methods' at 8 p.m. in Witherspoon Hall.
4 April	Train journey from Philadelphia, PA, to New York, NY.
5 April	New York, NY: Attends the funeral procession organised by the International Ladies' Garment Workers' Union for the victims of the Triangle fire.
6 April	New York, NY: Visits Alva Belmont's 14th Assembly District luncheon club.
7 April	New York, NY: Visits Public School No. 62, Hester Street and attends the morning assembly.
8 April	Bedford, NY: Visits the Reformatory for Women at Bedford Hills.
12 April	New York, NY: Departs on the *Majestic* for Southampton, England.

TIMELINE OF THE 1912 TOUR

3 January	Sylvia embarks on the SS *Oceanic* from Southampton, England.
11 January	New York City, NY: Sylvia arrives.
12 January	New York, NY: Speaks alongside Mary Dreier, Elizabeth Gurley Flynn and Margaret Sanger at the Harlem Arcade, 211 East 124th Street, to striking laundry workers.
15 January	St John, New Brunswick, Canada: Arrives in a snowstorm and is taken by sleigh to Warren Franklin Hatheway and Ella Hatheway's home where she is a guest for this and the following night. Speaks at an afternoon reception. Sleeps before speaking for more than two hours at the Opera House.
16 January	St John, Canada: Sleeps until lunch. Speaks to a party of ladies who arrive in the evening.

17 January   Train journey from St John, Canada to New Brunswick, Maine. Taken by sleigh to the train station, boards the 6:45 a.m. train and arrives at 5 p.m.

18 January   Brunswick, ME: Speaks in the Memorial Hall, Bowdoin College.

19 January   Train journey from Brunswick, ME, to Boston, Massachusetts.

20 January   Train journey from Boston, MA, to New York City, NY: Visits her agent, William B. Feakins, and stays with sisters Alice and Irene Lewisohn on 5th Avenue.

21 January   New York, NY: Sees child prodigy Virginia Myers dance. Attends a rehearsal of one of the Lewisohns' productions and speaks at a suffrage 'at home' meeting. Boards a train at 6:30 p.m. for her journey to St. Louis.

22 January   Train journey from New York, NY, to St. Louis, Missouri: Arrives in the evening and stays at the Southern Hotel.

23 January   St. Louis, MO: Gives press interviews in the hotel in the morning and visits the Public Library. Guest of honour at luncheon provided by the Woman's City Club at Scruggs-Vandervoort-Barney tea room. Speaks in the evening on 'Why More Suffragette Methods will be Needed to Win the Vote' at the Wednesday Club auditorium at Westminster Place and Taylor Avenue.

24 January   Train journey from St. Louis, MO, to Chicago, IL: Leaves in the morning and stays in Chicago with the Herendeens.
              In Chicago for the following days, it is likely that she attends dinner at Hull House with her cousin Helen Herendeen on either 25, 26, or 28 January.

27 January   Chicago, IL: Guest of honour at the Chicago Political Equality League banquet in the evening. Also attended by Jane Addams. Catharine Waugh McCulloch is among the speakers.

29 January   Milwaukee, Wisconsin: Arrives in the afternoon and is met by reporters, Mary Swain Wagner of the American Suffragettes and Martha C. Heide who will translate for her with German audiences. Taken to the Aberdeen Hotel, she later visits the Wisconsin Industrial School for

Girls where she gives a short speech. She sends a letter of introduction to the mayor of Milwaukee, Emil Seidel.

30 January   Milwaukee, WI: Visits the House of Correction in the morning. Rosa M. Perdue and Miss Miller drive her to visit the Ideal Laundry on Wells Street and the New Model Laundry on State Street. At 3:30 p.m. visits Mayor Emil Seidel at City Hall. Then visits the National Straw Works on 18th Avenue and Scott Street with Perdue and Miller.

31 January   Milwaukee, WI: Returns to City Hall and visits the Health Department and the Bureau of Efficiency and Economy. At noon she is the guest of Elsie and Wilbur Phillips of the Welfare Commission, and of suffrage campaigner Crystal Eastman. Meets the Inspector of Prisons Martin Mies, who organises a visit to the site for the new prison farm.

1 February   Milwaukee, WI: Posed for photographs and spoke with the press in the morning. In the evening, she is the guest of Miss Isabelle Miller and Mrs George P. Miller at a social reception at their home on Juneau Avenue. Gives an informal talk to Miss Miller's friends.

2 February   Milwaukee, WI: Has a private lunch with local suffragists. At 8 p.m. speaks to an audience of 500 in the Pabst Theatre followed by a public reception in the St. Charles Hotel. Leaves on the midnight train to Fargo.

3 February   Train journey from Milwaukee, WI, to Fargo, North Dakota: Train pipes burst and all passengers are forced to wait at the station in St. Paul, Minnesota, for three hours for a new train. Arrives at Fargo at 11 p.m. rather than 5:30 p.m. as expected. The meeting planned for this night has to be abandoned.

4 February   Fargo, ND: At an informal gathering at the home of Mary Darrow Weible, Sylvia suggests and advises upon the formation of the Votes for Women League of North Dakota. Speaks in the evening at the Grand Theatre.

5 February   Train journey from Fargo, ND, to Madison, WI.

7 February   Madison, WI: Speaks in the evening in the Fuller Opera House on 'The Need for Woman Suffrage'.

8 February	Appleton, WI: Speaks for over an hour on 'Woman's Suffrage and Prisons in England' at the Appleton Theatre with only five people in attendance.
9 February	Appleton, WI: Visits Ormsby Hall at Lawrence University. Speaks on women's suffrage in the chapel at Lawrence.
10 February	Chicago, IL: Intended to return to Milwaukee and may briefly have done so before travelling to Chicago to speak at a meeting chaired by Jane Addams in the Orchestral Hall to replace Ethel Arnold who had been booked to speak but was unable to attend.
13 February	Sleeper train journey from Chicago, IL, to Nashville, Tennessee.
14 February	Nashville, TN: Arrives and is taken to Andrew Jackson's Hermitage in the afternoon. Attends the Eligibles Ball in the evening. Stays at the Hermitage Hotel, 231 6th Avenue North.
15 February	Nashville, TN: Speaks in the Ryman Auditorium at 8:15 p.m. to an audience of 2,000.
16 February	Nashville, TN: Speaks in the chapel of Fisk University. In the evening speaks in the chapel of Belmont College, followed by a reception provided by faculty and students.
17 February	Nashville, TN: Visits factories in the morning. At 2 p.m. speaks to the girls at Ward Seminary where she dines. Attends a tea in the afternoon given by Mrs Guilford Dudley and gives an informal address on women's suffrage.
19 February	Nashville, TN: Tours the factory district.
20 February	Lebanon, TN: Travels from Nashville by train, having been invited to Lebanon by socialist students at Cumberland University. Arrives at noon and is met by students. Takes the bus to West Side Hotel where she has lunch and where she is to stay. Visits a pencil factory and a blanket factory. In the evening speaks at a public meeting organised by students in Caruthers Hall.
21 February	Nashville, TN: Travels back to Nashville in a blizzard and visits the prisons. Takes the sleeper train to Des Moines, Iowa.

22 February   St. Louis, MO: Snow delays the trains; she misses the connecting train and has a 7-hour wait in St. Louis. Walks out and sees the town. Telegrams Dr Nina Wilson Dewey in Des Moines to inform her of changed arrival time.

23 February   Des Moines, IA: Arrives in the morning from St. Louis expecting to speak at the Coliseum to find that there has been a mistake in the bookings. Stays with Dr Nina Wilson Dewey awaiting communication from Feakins and rests. After discovering the booking is for Streator, Illinois, sets out only to abandon the attempt when it becomes clear she will be unable to arrive in time.

24 February   Des Moines, IA: Hosted by local suffragists at 6 p.m. in the Chamberlain Hotel. A reception is held in the hotel parlour to which the public are invited.

25 February   Cincinnati, OH: Lectures in the evening.

26 February   Lima, OH: Arrives at noon and speaks in the evening in the Trinity Methodist Church.

27 February   Detroit, MI: Arrives in the afternoon and stays at the Pontchartrain Hotel where she gives press interviews.

28 February   Jackson, MI: Lectures in the evening.

1 March   *Mass window smashing campaign in London's West End co-ordinated by the Women's Social and Political Union. Emmeline Pankhurst under arrest.*
Detroit, MI: Guest of honour and speaks at lunch at the Newcomb-Endicott tea room provided by the College Equal Suffrage League. Speaks at the rooms of the New Thought Alliance. Leaves in the evening for Ann Arbor.

2 March   Ann Arbor, MI: Provides press interviews and meets society women in Mrs Frederick Waldron's drawing room. Speaks at a meeting.

3 March   Detroit, MI: Speaks for over two hours on 'The Need for Woman Suffrage' in the Garrick Theatre in the afternoon to around 600 people. Leaves for Toronto in the evening.

4 March   Toronto, Canada: Arrives in the morning. Speaks in the evening for two hours in the Association Hall.

6 March   Toledo, OH: Speaks in the evening in the Memorial Hall to around 3,000 people.

	Returns to Toronto, Canada, after this and remains there for a few days.
12 March	New York, NY: Arrives and stays with the Lewisohns on 5th Avenue where she gives press interviews in the library. Remains a guest with the Lewisohns until 15 March.
16 March	Poughkeepsie, NY: Speaks in the evening at the Columbus Institute.
18 March	Salem, MA: Speaks at the YMCA Hall.
19 March	Brockton, MA: Speaks in the YMCA Hall in the evening to around 500 people. Then heads to Boston where, arriving at the end of the Boston Equal Suffrage Association meeting in the Chauncey Building on Boylston Street, she is invited to give an address.
25 March	Gloversville, NY: Speaks at the Darling Theatre at 8 p.m. and tours for the following days with the WPU in their Mohawk Valley campaign in New York State.
27 March	Schenectady, NY: Speaks alongside Rose Schneiderman in Red Men's Hall at 8 p.m.
28 March	Cohoes, NY: Speaks in Manufacturers' Bank Hall at 8 p.m.
29 March	Troy, NY: Speaks alongside Rose Schneiderman in Harmony Hall at 8 p.m. Eunice Dana Brannan chairs the meeting.
30 March	Utica, NY: Speaks alongside Rose Schneiderman in the Auditorium, New Century Club at 8 p.m.
1 April	New York, NY: Farewell address in the Carnegie Lyceum speaking on 'Militant Methods – Why'.
3 April	New York, NY: Holds a midnight reception with suffragists on the SS *Mauretania* in the stateroom. The ship sets sail at 1 a.m. on the morning of 3 April bound for Southampton, England.

Note on the Text

The text here is a reproduction of Sylvia Pankhurst's original text, which exists largely as a typescript, with a few handwritten sections. The original text is in the Estelle Sylvia Pankhurst Papers at the International Institute of Social History, in Amsterdam, and can be viewed online: https://search.socialhistory.org/Record/ARCH01029. In my editorial policy, I have endeavoured to reproduce the text as faithfully as possible – both with regard to the manuscript as a historical document and in appreciation of what would have been the author's likely expectations of publication. Therefore, obvious typos have been corrected, variations in spelling have been standardised and a few archaic spellings have been modernised (for example, 'underweigh' has been transcribed as 'underway'). Underlined text in the original has been italicised. Capitalisation of chapter titles has been standardised throughout the text. Where there are words clearly missing in the text, I have added these in brackets to indicate the editor's hand. In the chapter footnotes, {SP} indicates Pankhurst's footnotes in the original text.

Introduction

Katherine Connelly

Passenger number 12 on the SS *Oceanic* which set sail from Southampton to New York on 3 January 1912 was Estelle Sylvia Pankhurst, 29 years old, female, single. Occupation: artist. Immigration officials asked her if she had been to America before, to which she replied she had previously visited a year earlier, as well as asking whether she was a polygamist and whether she was an anarchist, to which she replied no. Asked if she had been to prison, she said yes and added proudly 'twice as a suffragette' – words that were duly entered on the passenger list.[1]

* * *

In January 1911, Sylvia Pankhurst undertook a lecture tour of North America which lasted just over three months, and she would return for a second tour of similar length in January 1912. In the course of these tours, she travelled thousands of miles undertaking a frenetic schedule of engagements: 'I travelled almost every night, and spoke once, twice or thrice a day.'[2] She did all this to tell audiences about the militant suffragettes' struggle for votes for women in Britain, a struggle in which she was an active participant.

Lecture tours provided opportunities to amplify the suffragettes' own story of the campaign as well as a chance to embarrass and put pressure on the British government by winning over crowds in the wider English-speaking world. In Canada, the suffragettes appealed for solidarity for their cause within the British Empire. America, by contrast, allowed access to a self-consciously modern nation. When Sylvia first arrived in America, women already had the right to vote in Wyoming, Colorado, Utah, Idaho and Washington, DC.

During her first tour, Sylvia was promoting the book she was still hastily finishing – *The Suffragette: The History of the Women's Militant Suffrage Movement, 1905–1910*. By the time of her second tour in 1912, the book had been published in Britain and America, making Sylvia one of the first historians of the suffragette movement. Written at a

time of increasing state repression of the campaign, the book uncritically reproduced the heroic narrative propagated by the leaders of the
militant suffragettes' Women's Social and Political Union (WSPU),
Sylvia's mother Emmeline and older sister Christabel Pankhurst. Sylvia
suppressed any expression of her own misgivings about the growing
elitism of the campaign, its marginalisation of working-class women and
its increasing hostility towards the socialist and labour movements from
which it had sprung. The two voyages to North America removed Sylvia
from the intense political and personal pressures of the British suffragette movement – and it was here that she began to conceive of a very
different book.

In 1911, Sylvia's tour took her from New York, Boston and Philadelphia on the East Coast, through the states of the Midwest as far south as
Kansas, before travelling north to Canada where she spoke in Ottawa
and Toronto, and then through New York State to Washington, DC.
These were followed by more engagements on the East Coast and then
a journey across the country to Colorado and California. After this she
returned to New York, speaking in Kansas, Michigan and Maryland on
the way. Sylvia was feted by some of America's wealthiest suffragists and
her lectures were booked into the largest venues in the towns and cities
she visited. She was put up in grand, modern hotels but she also spent
days travelling on sleeper trains which broke down in the middle of the
night, disrupting carefully planned itineraries.

The 1912 tour was organised around a sparser series of engagements;
the novelty of the first tour could not be replicated and the escalation
of militancy in Britain was alienating some former supporters. This
afforded Sylvia a greater opportunity to determine her own schedule and
to explore beyond the elitist boundaries in which much of the American
suffragist movement was contained. Wanting to 'see a Socialist city',
Sylvia spent a week in Milwaukee, Wisconsin where a socialist mayor
had recently been elected.[3] Since touring British suffragettes had not
yet been to the South, she also decided to go to Tennessee, where she
encountered the legacy of slavery and challenged racial segregation.
This time there were fewer elegant hotels. In her writings and letters, she
described staying in a shabby, provincial hotel in Lebanon, Tennessee, to
speak to a group of socialist students; in Canada's St John, she stayed in
the home of the progressive Hatheway family and in the early morning
was driven to the railway station in a sledge across the snowy landscape;
in Chicago, she stayed with her cousin's family (her father's brother, John

Pankhurst, had emigrated to America in his youth) only to find herself frustrated with the 'empty headed' wife of the household.[4] Significantly, it was the more challenging 1912 tour that provided most of the material for Sylvia's writings on America.

In her later memoirs of this period, published in 1931 as *The Suffragette Movement: An Intimate Account of Persons and Ideals*, Sylvia would record a breathtaking (though selective) list of public speaking engagements and exciting personalities. These features are not, however, present in the manuscript she produced at the time; the reader will search in vain for the names of so many of the pathbreaking reformers and radicals of this era that Sylvia met: Jane Addams, Crystal Eastman, Rose Schneiderman, Lillian Wald, Alice and Irene Lewisohn – none of them are mentioned by name, though their presence lingers just below the textual surface. Sylvia herself endeavours to join these figures in the margins, remaining true to her stated intention in the Preface not to provide 'a chronicle of my travels' but instead to write of 'experiences of people, places and institutions'; she briefly introduces herself as 'a militant suffragette' as a means of explaining her access to such a range of American society (p. 65). She avoided detailing her own extensive itinerary, writing instead about other people, most of them anonymous, who taught her about contemporary America.

Sylvia's lecture tours took place at an exciting time in American history, later termed the 'Progressive Era'. Aggressive, capitalist expansion and innovation saw huge fortunes amassed by a few through the exploitation of the many. The American working class was developing rapidly as women, African Americans, Native Americans and immigrants were increasingly dragged into its ranks. At the same time, this process produced growing resistance to inequality. The ideas of feminists, socialists, trade unionists and reformers provided hope to those embroiled in bitter, desperately fought battles to shape the future.[5] Sylvia was deeply struck by the disparity between what was possible and the reality in modern America. She explored this contrast in her speeches: 'As I have gone through your country, I have been filled with admiration for its ingenuity and its wonderful progress and enterprise. But everywhere I see such poverty, such overcrowding of cities, such wretchedness of many.'[6]

Sylvia echoed these words in the Preface here, contrasting the 'endless possibilities of new growth' in America with its 'cruel waste of precious human energy' (p. 66). The disregard for human life that accompanied the growth of modern capitalism was starkly realised on 25 March 1911 when a fire broke out in the Triangle Shirtwaist Factory in New York City and 146 workers, mostly women from immigrant backgrounds, were killed. Sylvia was in America when this took place and it would impact on her speeches and on this work.

The lecture tours of America provided Sylvia with the opportunity to explicitly situate the demand for women's political emancipation as a part of wider struggles against oppression and disempowerment which sustained capitalist exploitation. This approach is reflected in her man-uscript's concern with the way working-class experience interacts with the oppression of women and with racism. In so doing, Sylvia begins to articulate her view of democracy as an instrument to dismantle inequality by providing all with an equal voice. On her return to Britain, Sylvia sought to apply these ideas to the militant suffragette movement, with profound political and personal consequences. This manuscript, which Sylvia did not complete and which has not previously been published, allows us to hear Sylvia's voice at a crucial moment of her political development. This introduction is about how Sylvia came to write the manuscript, her tours of America and how they impacted on suffrage history.

FROM AMERICA TO EAST LONDON: CHANGING THE COURSE OF SUFFRAGE HISTORY

If things had happened differently, Sylvia Pankhurst would have designed murals to adorn the walls of a chapel in a women's prison in Boston, Massachusetts. The project, worked out with the prison governor whilst Sylvia was engaged with her 1911 lecture tour, appealed to Sylvia's interest in the plight of prisoners and her belief in the emancipatory potential of art – the prisoners themselves would be trained to help in the work. During the 1912 lecture tour, Sylvia began to make plans: if she was offered a studio in Boston, she would stay for the summer, then embark on another series of lectures before returning home.[7] Perhaps she would not return at all; towards the end of her 1911 tour she had told reporters in Philadelphia that she found the United States 'delightful', adding 'I would even like to live here. This desire, I must confess, is largely due to the lack of fog, which is so depressing at home in London.'[8]

She would later recall the way in which America captured her imag-ination: 'Life in the States seemed a whirl, with harsh, rude extremes, rough and unfinished, yet with scope and opportunity for young people and with more receptivity to new ideas than is found in the old countries: I thought that some day I might become an American citizen.'[9]

Thirty years on from those tours, during the Blitz, when Sylvia was living in Woodford, in Essex, 'directly on the Luftwaffe's flight path to London', she reminisced about these years to her teenage son Richard.[10] He later remembered, 'she recalled that had things been otherwise we might then have been American citizens.'[11] Had things been otherwise. But on 1 March 1912, stones flung in London reverberated around the world and changed everything.

Sylvia was in Ann Arbor, Michigan, when she heard the news. In Britain, the Conciliation Bill, which proposed to enfranchise around a million women who were heads of households, was now faced with a rival Reform Bill introduced by the government – with no mention of women's suffrage. The apparent possibility of a more democratic women's suffrage amendment in the Reform Bill served to justify government opposition to the Conciliation Bill. The actual prospect of a women's suffrage amendment was uncertain (and would eventually be ruled out), especially as Prime Minister Herbert Asquith was a well-known opponent. Sensing betrayal, the WSPU leadership announced an escalation of suffragette militancy: 'The argument of the broken pane is the most valuable argument in modern politics', declared Emmeline Pankhurst.[12] Two weeks later, at 4 p.m. on 1 March 1912, women strolling through London's West End pulled out hammers, clubs and stones and smashed the windows of the fashionable department stores. Emmeline Pankhurst threw stones through the windows of 10 Downing Street. An arrest warrant was issued for the WSPU's leaders; Emmeline and Frederick Pethick Lawrence and Emmeline Pankhurst were charged with conspiracy, but the authorities could not find Christabel Pankhurst.

A few weeks later, Sylvia found herself at the centre of the rumours concerning Christabel's whereabouts. Major George William Horsfield of the Essex and Suffolk Royal Artillery was certain he had seen her on the passenger liner bound for New York City. 'No one who has ever seen her aggressive-looking face, with its overhanging black eyebrows, could make a mistake', he told a reporter from the *New York Times*. The newspaper's front page announced 'Miss Pankhurst Is In Hiding Here', and continued that it 'understood' she had held a secret conference with Sylvia in New York, who gave her sister the proceeds from her tour before departing to direct the struggle in London.[13]

In fact, the Major had made a mistake: no such meeting ever took place. The events that led up to Christabel's disappearance, however, convinced Sylvia that she had to return to England. Her mother faced months, perhaps years, of imprisonment and so it was clear that the movement was not on the threshold of victory. Sylvia concluded: 'I neither could nor would now withdraw to another country, nor immerse myself in any large work unconnected with the movement.'[14]

On her return from America, Sylvia travelled in disguise to Paris where she had been informed Christabel was hiding. There she found that Christabel did not envisage handing any organisational control to those she distrusted politically, including Sylvia. Christabel, it seems, would not have minded if Sylvia had stayed in America – indeed, Sylvia later recalled that Christabel's advice at this time was to '[b]ehave as though you were not in the country!'[15] It was advice that Sylvia entirely disregarded. Concerned that an elitist campaign relying upon ever smaller numbers of activists would be inadequate to overcome government opposition and the increasing levels of state repression, Sylvia attempted to transform suffragette agitation into a mass movement. She began by organising a series of huge demonstrations over the summer to support the imprisoned WSPU leaders, and then, more fundamentally, by taking steps to galvanise mass, working-class involvement.[16] She would initiate this latter project in East London where she aimed 'not merely to make some members and establish some branches [of the WSPU], but [at] the larger task of bringing the district as a whole into a mass movement, from which only a minority would stand aside'.[17] In the autumn of 1912, she looked for a suitable headquarters for this East London campaign. She later recalled that: 'I set out with Zelie Emerson down the dingy Bow Road' and found a shop to rent.[18]

What followed is familiar to suffrage historians. Sylvia and the East London suffragettes were expelled from the WSPU in 1914 after Sylvia appeared on a platform supporting the victimised workers of the employers' lockout of trade unionists in Dublin. Forming the East London Federation of Suffragettes (ELFS), they continued to organise a radical campaign which linked women's political emancipation to labour struggles and Irish anti-imperialists. The ELFS's divergence from the WSPU would become most starkly apparent with the outbreak of the First World War, when Emmeline and Christabel announced that the WSPU would suspend campaigning for the vote and support the war effort, while Sylvia and the ELFS established community services to support working-class women facing further hardship in wartime, and eventually adopted an explicitly anti-war stance.

The developments of 1912, then, are understood to have had a profound impact on the history of the suffrage movement in Britain. Less well understood, however, is what prompted Sylvia to take the action she did then, when previously she had kept her political differences with her mother and sister private. Sylvia's lecture tours of America in 1911 and 1912 traverse her dramatic change of approach. Yet few connections have been drawn between the transatlantic change in Sylvia's environment and the change she effected soon after in the suffragette movement.[19] Moreover, with the expanding historiographical interest in the role of friendship networks in feminist campaigns, it is surprising that there has been so little attention afforded to the fact that Sylvia outlined that, from the outset, she was supported in her East London endeavour by Zelie Emerson, a young American woman who she met on tour.[20]

It seems that it was in the midst of creating the East London suffragette campaign that Sylvia was writing her book about America: a reference in Chapter 4 to something happening 'now' was provided with a handwritten footnote reading 'February 1913' (p. 105). Sylvia was particularly busy in February 1913. Early in that month, she and Emerson opened a new suffragette headquarters on East London's Roman Road. On 14 February, the two were arrested and imprisoned for window smashing only to be released after Emmeline Pankhurst had their fines paid (perhaps to keep them from the limelight). On 17 February, Sylvia and Emerson again smashed windows during an East London suffragette protest and were sentenced to prison, this time to two months' hard labour without the option of a fine. In protest at their treatment they undertook hunger and thirst strikes and endured the horrors of forcible feeding. At the end of the first month, Emerson was so tormented by her experience that she had tried to cut through an artery, while Sylvia forced her own release through adopting a rest strike – walking continuously, day and night, up and down the prison cell.

It was in this context that Sylvia was recalling her American experiences. She evidently envisaged speedy publication of the American book: it is full of topical references and up-to-date figures while, as will be discussed, potentially compromising personal details associated with the manuscript's origin were carefully expunged, indicating preparation for public consumption. It was apparently never sent to a publisher, probably because Sylvia did not complete the work. Some of the typescript was evidently lost as it ends mid-sentence, though the planned end to that paragraph can be found in the handwritten copy which concludes with the words 'end of Chapter 8'.[21] Not, presumably, the intended end of the book.

Sylvia did not explain why she abandoned the work which she nevertheless preserved in her papers. The East London campaign certainly placed a huge demand on her time, but Sylvia always managed to sustain extensive written work alongside campaigning and imprisonments. Perhaps, rather, it was that the question Sylvia strove to resolve on paper, about how working-class people might truly articulate their own emancipation, was being answered in practice in the mass movement she was helping to create. The manuscript became part of the preparatory intellectual work for the movement which took priority as it further shaped and developed Sylvia's thinking. Placed in its context, this manuscript provides the link between Sylvia's private criticisms of the WSPU and the public action she would take to change the course of suffrage history.

AMERICAN LETTERS: EARLY DRAFTS

Sylvia's published writings on the suffragette movement, *The Suffragette* (1911) and *The Suffragette Movement* (1931), resemble the great nineteenth-century novels of her youth, with dense, descriptive prose and guiding linear narrative. Sylvia's American book forms a stark contrast when placed alongside them. The style here is experimental and changing, from the lyrical, dream-like evocation of a performance of *Sleeping Beauty* on New York's Lower East Side, to the empirical precision behind her critique of economic inequality, and the haunted tone of the nightmare vision of a prison in Tennessee. This immediate and thematic approach reflects the book's origins in Sylvia's writing during the course of the tour in the spare, quiet hours that she could find in train carriages and hotel rooms.

In a draft of the Preface, Sylvia mused over the title of the manuscript: 'I have called this book American Letters because' she wrote, before abandoning the sentence here and striking a vertical line down the whole page.[22] Whether or not this remained the intended title is unclear as there is no title page to the manuscript, but the explanation for this draft title is to be found in the final Preface: 'The following pages were in the first place written in the form of letters to a friend in England' (p. 65).

Keir Hardie

In the main, the letters were written to the Labour MP and former Labour leader, Keir Hardie. A long-standing friend of her parents, Sylvia grew better acquainted with Hardie after she moved to London as an art student. While her mother and sister initially established the WSPU where they lived in Manchester in 1903, they aspired to create a national campaign with its headquarters in the capital. Before Christabel moved to London in 1906 to take up the role of organising secretary, this task had initially fallen to Sylvia, who regularly sought the advice of Hardie, the WSPU's most steadfast supporter in Parliament. At some point, the relationship became romantic, for which the most decisive evidence remains the letters they exchanged whilst Sylvia was travelling in America. Her letters combined reflections on American politics and her expressions of love, loneliness and longing for Hardie's company. Filled with endearments – Hardie addressing her as 'sweetheart' while she began her letters 'Darling' and concluded with 'love and kisses my sweetheart' – these letters expressed a passion that was concealed from public view.[23] In 1879, Hardie had married Lillie Wilson from whom he was evidently emotionally as well as geographically distant; she lived with their children in Scotland far away from Hardie's Merthyr Tydfil constituency in South Wales and his London lodgings close to Parliament. The relationship was further complicated by developments in the suffragette movement, as Emmeline and Christabel insisted upon the separation of the WSPU from all political parties and expressed increasing hostility towards the Labour Party. Sylvia's letters from America, then, represented a personal and political rejection of WSPU policy. By the summer of 1913, the romantic relationship had become unsupportable for Sylvia, whose loyalties were painfully divided, though their friendship and political co-operation would last until Hardie's death two years later. The relationship between Sylvia and Keir Hardie, which produced the 'first draft' of the text, informed a prominent concern in the manuscript with the relationship between the women's and labour movements.

Hardie, as recipient of the first draft, was perhaps also the inspiration for Sylvia's attempt at writing an impressionistic work from letters. By the time Sylvia first embarked for America, Hardie had already undertaken quite extensive foreign political tours. During two tours of America, in 1895 and 1908 (he would travel there again, after Sylvia, in 1912), and a 'world tour' from July 1907 until April 1908, he wrote letters detailing his experiences for publication in the British socialist press. These foreign travels enabled him to establish contact with socialists in other countries with whom he could discuss politics and share strategies, and it also allowed for him to amplify an internationalist, anti-racist political approach that was not universally held by other leading members of his own party. Departing from Liverpool in 1907, Hardie told the assembled farewell party 'that wherever he went he would refuse to recognise distinctions of colour of skin or of race or creed. He would see in all peoples his fellow-men only.'[24] In his letters from India, he denounced British imperialism and established fraternal contacts with the Congress movement for independence, causing uproar in the British establishment.[25] He published these letters shortly afterwards, in 1909, as a volume entitled *India: Impressions and Suggestions* in which he explained that though there were 'drawbacks' to basing the work on letters, he felt it justified as '[i]mpressions recorded while they are warm are more virile than when laboriously compiled out of stale memories.'[26] It seems likely that Sylvia perceived her own journey abroad in similar terms, as she too sought to establish international connections and use the opportunity to bring wider questions of inequality, particularly regarding workers' exploitation and racist oppression, to bear upon her organisation's narrowing political focus on suffrage. Like Hardie, Sylvia published her impressions in her organisation's press – her article 'Some American Impressions' appeared in the WSPU newspaper *Votes for Women* in April 1911 – and she planned to use her letters as the basis for a book.[27]

Hardie was evidently supportive of the idea that Sylvia adapt her letters for publication. In May 1915, conscious that he was dying, Hardie wrote to Sylvia about the objects he would like her to have, prominent among which were her American letters:

> I have a great many letters of yours, especially those from America, & a good many others. They are well worth preserving and I should like to return these to you. I could let you have the whole of those now at Nevill's Court; [Hardie's London home] & you could use your discretion as to which are worthy of being kept & published, and which should be destroyed.[28]

Much of the material in Chapters 2, 5 and 6 can be seen to draw on surviving letters to Hardie. The February 1913 date on the typescript indicates it was written before Hardie's death, which implies that Sylvia made copies of, or detailed notes from, her letters before she sent them. It may be that considerably more of the book was derived from letters to Hardie that were destroyed or have been lost.

Emmeline Pethick Lawrence

Strictly speaking, there were two friends in England to whom letters from Sylvia formed the basis for her American book – something that has not previously been acknowledged.[29] In March 1911, the *Woman's Journal*, the organ of the National American Woman Suffrage Association, published Sylvia's letter to Emmeline Pethick Lawrence, the WSPU's treasurer and, with her husband Frederick, co-editor of the WSPU newspaper *Votes for Women*. In this letter Sylvia described her address to both houses of Iowa's state government in February. It was a historically important engagement; the only other woman to have been afforded this opportunity was the famous American suffragist leader Susan B. Anthony, who had spoken in favour of a married women's property Bill. When Sylvia spoke there in favour of a women's suffrage Bill, she thereby appeared as one of the leaders of the new generation of the women's movement. Her letter to Emmeline Pethick Lawrence therefore underscored the role of militant suffragettes in furthering the cause internationally: 'I thought of you all in England and held my head high as they all turned to stare at the English suffragette.'[30] This letter was largely incorporated into Chapter 7. Sylvia's decision to write the letter to Emmeline Pethick Lawrence, and not for example to her mother or sister, could be justified on the grounds that Pethick Lawrence's editorial role made her a suitable person to send her 'impressions' for publication. In hindsight, however, the decision appears revealing. By the time Sylvia was typing the manuscript in February 1913, Emmeline and Frederick Pethick Lawrence had been forced out of the WSPU, having disagreed with Emmeline and Christabel's policy of further escalating militancy. In contrast to her older sister, Sylvia remained lifelong friends with Emmeline Pethick Lawrence. When Sylvia's son Richard was born in 1927, she chose Keir Pethick as his middle names in tribute to her profoundly close relationships with Keir Hardie and Emmeline Pethick Lawrence – the same two people she chose to write to from America. The choice of recipients for these American letters, then, indicated Sylvia's growing estrangement from her mother and sister's politics and the emergence of her own dissenting voice.

SYLVIA AS A PROFESSIONAL LECTURER

North American–British lecture tours were a well-established phenomenon by the time Sylvia travelled to America in 1911. From the mid-nineteenth century, these tours became increasingly professionalised and involved a prominent figure lecturing in various locations where they would be hosted and guided around local institutions and points of interest, often providing inspiration for further literary work. Charles Dickens, Oscar Wilde and Matthew Arnold were just three of the British authors who toured America in the nineteenth century, while figures travelling in the other direction included Ralph Waldo Emerson, Mark Twain and Henry James.[31] Campaigning networks developed tours along similar lines, beginning with the American anti-slavery movement. In 1845, Frederick Douglass, having escaped slavery, provided first-hand accounts of its horrors during a hugely successful lecture tour of Britain. Emmeline Pankhurst would proudly recall that her father was on the welcoming committee for the lecture tour of Henry Ward Beecher, the abolitionist campaigner and brother of Harriet Beecher Stowe, author of the popular anti-slavery novel *Uncle Tom's Cabin*.[32] As the labour and socialist movements developed, they too organised lecture tours – in 1886, Eleanor Marx and Edward Aveling undertook a similar route to Sylvia's and later published a book based on their research and experiences titled *The Working Class Movement in America*.[33] Meanwhile, as previously mentioned, Keir Hardie toured and published his impressions on three separate occasions. The women's suffrage movement likewise forged links across the Atlantic Ocean, with members of the British National Union of Women's Suffrage Societies (NUWSS) and National American Woman Suffrage Association (NAWSA) corresponding, reading their counterparts' publications and hosting travelling speakers attending international conferences.[34]

The WSPU's tactical and organisational separateness from the non-militant NUWSS did not facilitate their inclusion into these pre-established networks; when the Pankhursts toured America they relied upon professional lecturing agencies, who promoted their speakers as celebrities, and secured bookings in conjunction with American suffragists sympathetic to militancy. Using professional agencies allowed for the individual lecturer to benefit financially from the tour. Emmeline Pankhurst's first tour of America in late 1909 was in part motivated by her need to raise money for medical treatment for her seriously ill son,

Harry, who died shortly after her return in January 1910. For Sylvia, who strove to maintain her independence by not joining the WSPU payroll, both the 1911 tour, organised by the Civic Lecture Forum Bureau, and the 1912 tour, organised by the successor to and former secretary of the Bureau, William B. Feakins, provided an opportunity to earn a living.

The challenges of a commercial tour

The fund-raising objective informed the nature of the tours. Sylvia had come to America around the time that a number of extremely wealthy individuals were taking an interest in the suffrage cause; their support could ensure much-needed financial assistance for the travelling lecturer as well as for the domestic suffrage movement. Towards the end of her first tour, on 6 April 1911, Sylvia attended the suffrage luncheon club in New York run by Alva Belmont, 'the millionaire Suffragist', who was among the campaign's very richest supporters.[35] Three days later, the *San Francisco Examiner* claimed that 'Mrs Belmont offered to pay Miss Pankhurst's expenses, and these will run up to the many thousands.'[36] In fact, Sylvia's fees were not paid by a sole donor – her expenses were paid by a number of local groups – but whether or not Belmont was among the contributors, Sylvia's tour was nevertheless dependent upon groups or individuals advancing enough money to pay her lecturing fees and with the resources to fund or arrange accommodation. Hosted by wealthy supporters, Sylvia's speeches in large venues were often combined with smaller luncheon and dinner gatherings in which she was the guest of honour. A select group of eminent and powerful individuals would be invited with the intention of using Sylvia's moving account of the British suffrage struggle to win their adherence. Thus, on 14 February 1911, Sylvia spoke at the Smith Opera House under the auspices of the Geneva Political Equality Club in Geneva, New York, and was also the guest of honour at the lunch held by that organisation's leading members, Elizabeth Miller and her daughter Anne. Also invited to the Millers' luncheon at their extensive house and grounds by Seneca Lake were two local attorneys and a former loyal mayor.[37]

Many of the suffrage events emulated the elegant functions that Sylvia's hosts were accustomed to attending in their social lives. When Sylvia spoke at the Columbia Theatre in Washington, DC on the celebrated 'Washington's birthday', on 22 February 1911, the stage was lavishly adorned with potted plants and palms that had been loaned by local wealthy supporter Lucia Blount, who was said to have 'generously sent her gardener early in the morning to arrange them'.[38] Elegant clothes took on considerable importance at such events and, despite her own meagre financial resources, Sylvia evidently experienced some pressure to outwardly conform by acquiring at least one evening dress. She spoke in a yellow satin gown at the Carnegie Lyceum in New York, and in her letter to Emmeline Pethick Lawrence about her speech at the Iowa State House she relayed the pressure exerted on her to change her attire, possibly to the same dress worn at the Lyceum: 'The ladies of Des Moines had insisted that I must not wear ordinary clothes, but must go in my cream coloured silk evening frock with its long trailing skirt. It seemed strange to me, but I did as I was bid.'[39]

Needless to say, this was a wildly impractical imposition on a speaker travelling alone for thousands of miles. After arriving in St John in Canada, where she was to speak to an evening 'party of ladies' and to lecture in the Opera House, Sylvia found 'the dress I had to wear at the meeting was creased, as I was a very bad packer.'[40]

Sylvia clearly became frustrated with the lecture tours' attendant elitist gatherings. She complained to Hardie about a group of suffragists taking her to 'a stupid play', and Chapter 8 records her discomfort at the flirtatious Valentine's Day party she attended in Tennessee.[41] When an interviewer in Kansas asked if she 'ever had time for a girl's fun, parties, for instance', Sylvia responded with a laugh 'Oh, I announced to my mother when I was ten years old that I wasn't going to accept any invitations to parties.'[42] It was reported that at the Women's Dining Club in that city she expressed her opinion that: '"Bridge, balls, dinners – I think the women who give their lives to such things as that ought to be swept off the face of the earth," and Miss Pankhurst's face flushed, and her blue eyes sparkled – and she said: "I would love to be one of those to do the sweeping."'[43]

Sylvia's means of escaping the bridge, balls and dinners brigade was ironically provided by the lecturing agency itself. On arriving for the 1912 tour she was dismayed to discover the lack of bookings, complaining to Hardie that even these were spread so far across the country she worried that 'I shall not do very much more than pay expenses out of this trip.'[44] The fact that Sylvia travelled so much, crisscrossing the country on routes with little geographical coherence, was due to most of the bookings being secured haphazardly after she arrived. Hardie, who was familiar with America from his aforementioned tours, considered the 1911 tour route to be 'clearly impossible', and it was evident to Sylvia that the 1912 tour would be filled with 'long long journeys for a single meeting!'[45] Sylvia blamed Feakins for having 'pressed' her to come so soon after her mother's second lecture tour (Sylvia arrived on 11 January only five days after Emmeline sailed for England), which had diminished interest in Pankhurst bookings – on one of those long train journeys Sylvia passed through Indianapolis, 'where I spoke last year but where this year they have had mother and so don't want me'.[46] One consequence of the threadbare schedule was Sylvia's decision to 'manage things a bit myself', leading her to spend a week in Milwaukee, a city which had a socialist administration.[47] Upon arrival she 'very definitely' informed the local suffragists 'that I was not going to spend any time at theatres or concerts and that as little time as possible would I spend at social functions and that I must have time to study as far as possible the institutions and general conditions of Milwaukee'.[48]

She also decided to go to the South, which took her to Tennessee. Her explanation of her decision to Hardie reveals, amidst a mix of motivations, her interest in radical, social exploration:

> I have determined to go South where no one ever goes much where mother did not go and where above all things there is much much to do. Awful conditions of labour for women and children especially children and everything generally backward moreover it is warm there and the country beautiful I am told.[49]

This book emerges primarily from Sylvia's 1912 tour, in particular the parts she organised herself; there is no mention of a single elegant function from the 1911 tour while the trips to Milwaukee and Tennessee are covered in three of the eight chapters and form some of the most important and extensive material that Sylvia wrote on America.

Despite her more active role in shaping her own tour, Sylvia remained reliant upon sympathetic hosts to guide her around the local institutions, such as prisons, factories and colleges, which she was so eager to explore. Sylvia's hosts frequently chose local institutions with the expectation of winning her approval. It is striking, then, that her opinions were often at variance with those of her hosts. In this text, Sylvia criticises the implementation of the new Taylorist scientific compartmentalisation of workers' jobs, the preparation of Native American students for factory work, and the top-down implementation of reform – all of which had been vaunted by respective guides. Sylvia's estrangement from many of her hosts was politically informed, as she felt that their reforming zeal was limited by their lack of understanding of or empathy with those people whose lives they sought to change. For Sylvia, then, their efforts reproduced the problems of disenfranchisement against which she was seeking the suffrage.

Sylvia disagreed most sharply and openly with her hosts over racial politics. In this period, the dominant forces in the American women's suffrage movement were complicit with racism against black Americans. American suffragists not infrequently utilised racist depictions of black male voters to appeal to racist politicians to grant suffrage to white women, whom they portrayed as racially superior. Black suffragists resisted this trajectory but found themselves subject to discrimination by leading suffragists intent on winning the support of racist lawmakers, particularly those in the South. Thus, in the 1913 women's suffrage parade in Washington, black suffragists were told to march separately at the back and not with the suffrage organisations from their state – a command with which black suffragist Ida B. Wells-Barnett refused to comply.[50] It was in this context that Sylvia was warned by her hosts in

1.   Sylvia Pankhurst in Toronto, Canada standing beside a car adapted to advertise her lecture in the Massey Hall on 11 February 1911. (Toronto Star Archives/Toronto Star; courtesy of Getty Images)

Tennessee not to speak at Fisk University, a college for black students (see the editor's introduction to Chapter 8). Sylvia defiantly went anyway and wrote about this in the last chapter of the typescript. That chapter deals extensively with racism as she observes the legacy of slavery and the racist violence of the prison authorities. Sylvia's actions in Tennessee and her written reflections afterwards reflect her identification of her struggle against women's disenfranchisement with the struggle against racial oppression – challenging the trajectory of the contemporary American suffrage movement. This work therefore testifies to Sylvia's increasingly independent choices and politically distinctive voice.

The challenges of suffragette celebrity

As a member of the Pankhurst family and a suffragette who had experienced imprisonment, Sylvia was well-placed to capitalise on the phenomenon of 'suffragette celebrity'.[51] Moreover, she arrived as an experienced activist and was evidently a very effective public speaker. She had been one of the WSPU's earliest speakers, developing her skills in front of small audiences in halls, parks and on the streets; she had also spoken before the WSPU's largest audience on one of the platforms at the enormous demonstration in Hyde Park in 1908. Her lectures in America were booked for large venues in the middle of town, such as the Carnegie Lyceum in New York, the Ryman Auditorium in Nashville, Tennessee and the Pabst Theatre in Milwaukee. She spoke to audiences of hundreds, often holding their attention for around two hours with speeches that were compelling, funny and tear-jerking; in Detroit, Michigan, it was said she 'moved her audience from enthusiasm to laughter and from laughter to tears'.[52] She succeeded in winning overwhelming press endorsement of her skills as a speaker. Reports from her speech at Ottawa's Russell Theatre, which declared her 'one of the cleverest women speakers ever heard in Ottawa', and described her vivid accounts as 'a series of word pictures', were typical of the press response.[53] Sylvia was a confident, polemical and uncompromising speaker, of whom one listener, with a fondness for mixed metaphors, said: 'She hits straight from the shoulder, and calls a spade a spade. She does not mince matters. I went four miles and a half to hear her, and would go twice as far to hear her again.'[54]

Sylvia's intellectual and rhetorical skills were particularly evident when she was invited to St Louis, Missouri in March 1911. Arriving on the morning train, she gave interviews to the press before going on, at midday, to address the all-male City Club which had 'to suspend tempo-rarily its most stringent rule' to allow Sylvia to speak there.[55] Her speech, lasting 55 minutes, attracted the largest audience in the club's history: 'The club was crowded. Men climbed on chairs and tables to hear the little woman speak, and they applauded her frequently.' By mid-after-noon, Sylvia was debating Isaac H. Lionberger, described by the local press as a 'lawyer, capitalist and one time Assistant Attorney General of the United States', in front of an audience of over 800 at the Mary Institute Hall, a school for local privileged girls, one of whom was Lionberger's daughter.[56] According to all reports, Sylvia was wittier, quicker and cleverer than the prominent lawyer nearly thirty years her senior. When Lionberger tried to justify an exclusively male franchise on the grounds that women were not able to fight for their country, Sylvia told him he did not understand politics – which received applause – and asked 'Do your presidents settle their campaigns for office by prize fights?'[57] 'Worse still', commented an amused reporter, 'a few of the men hissed when Mr Lionberger derided the right of women to vote.'[58] It was said that the first to congratulate Sylvia on her victory was Lionberger's daughter who thanked her for 'taking father down'.[59]

The successes of Sylvia's tours, in which she commanded respect as a speaker, were achieved despite significant challenges which constantly threatened to undermine her. The professional lecturing agencies presented the suffragette lecturer as a novelty attraction which focused attention on her image and thus reproduced many of the barriers that the suffragettes were seeking to overcome. Sylvia was frequently infan-tilised by the press. Although she was 28 years old when she arrived on her first tour, the New York Times asserted: 'The youngest suffragette, as she is called, Miss Pankhurst, is 20, looks younger, and might belong to any group of schoolgirls to be seen in New York.'[60] The Boston Globe, reporting on her meeting in the Ford Hall, stated she looked no older than 20 and had 'a soft, pathetic voice that would be quite in keeping with a girl of 12', which seems implausible alongside the claim that her speech held 1,000 people in 'rapt attention'.[61] In Ottawa, she was reported as being 'a typical English girl of twenty-one' and 'very girlish in appearance', while the Los Angeles Herald stated she was 23 years old, before adding 'she looks no more than 18.'[62] The effect was to undermine Sylvia as a serious political activist and intellect. Under a subtitle declaring her 'Small as a Schoolgirl', the Times described the audience at her first lecture in the Lyceum laughing at her discussion of unequal pay 'as one would laugh at one's own child talking seriously of the differences between husbands and wives and the care of children'.[63] At the same time, the known chronology of Sylvia's life led to the outlandish claim that her first imprisonment in October 1906 must have taken place 'when she was only sixteen'.[64] Sylvia was evidently irritated by the misreporting of her age, as she told a journalist in Detroit: 'No, it's not true that I'm only 20 years of age. I'm a good bit over that, and I don't know what makes them say it unless they're rather fond of telling lies'.[65]

By contrast, Sylvia, the experienced political activist, regarded the press reporters she first met on arrival as rather immature themselves – '[t]hey were exceedingly young, almost like schoolboys, I thought' – and, shocked that none of them were taking notes, ordered notebooks and pencils so that they could quote her more accurately.[66]

Despite Sylvia's efforts to control her representation, her own agent, Feakins, was colluding in her infantilisation. The promotional brochure he produced for her 1912 tour carried quotations from three newspapers, the first of which was from the *New York Times* report of her Lyceum lecture, beginning with the words 'a little rosy-cheeked slip of an English girl', while the second described her 'child face'.[67] It seems likely that Feakins pandered to sexist stereotypes, judging that a girlish suffragette would be a more marketable product than an unmarried, educated woman in her late twenties.

Sylvia found herself a product in high demand with a sensationalist press eager for scoops that promised to reveal what a militant suffragette was really like. Sections of the press assumed Sylvia's total compliance and were prepared to ensure that any objections on her part were met with unpleasant consequences, as she soon found out. Arriving at the Congress Hotel in Chicago at midnight on 18 January 1911, after a journey from Oberlin, Ohio, Sylvia told the assembled reporters that she would 'talk later'. With *The Suffragette* still to complete, she informed them 'I have to do a lot of writing for two days and until I have finished that I will do little talking'.[68] The reporters did not receive this announcement well, as Sylvia later recalled:

> Some battered persistently on my door, others invented the most atrocious interviews, which were published with faked photographs in which I appeared an appalling hooligan. A newspaper containing one such caricature was flung over the head of the chambermaid as she

entered my room. Seeing it, I capitulated immediately, but the Press men and women did not entirely relent.[69]

On 20 January, the *Chicago Daily Tribune* published three cartoons of Sylvia as an angular, flat-chested figure in a variety of attention-seeking poses above a purported interview with 'Miss Emaline Sylvia Pankhurst'. Evidently confusing her first initial (for Estelle) with an erroneous spelling of her mother's name, this surely was a mistake that would have been corrected in the course of a genuine interview. The publica-

2. These mocking caricatures of Sylvia Pankhurst were published in the *Chicago Daily Tribune* on 20 January 1911 after she declined to speak to the press. (Courtesy of the *Chicago Tribune* and newspapers.com)

tion triumphantly announced that though '[f]or seven or eight hours she insisted that she "had more important business than to talk to the newspapers"' she had now relented. Described as 'a sharp contrast' to her vivacious mother, Sylvia was portrayed as a 'willowy' figure who spoke 'in a drawling, languid tone'.[70] The *Tribune*'s insinuation of self-indulgence on Sylvia's part would certainly have horrified her and was perhaps the trigger for her capitulation.

Henceforward, as Sylvia recalled, there was a partial change in tone. On 22 January, the *Chicago Sunday Tribune* published a long interview with Sylvia accompanied with photographs and with a more lifelike and animated caricature. The interview was conducted by Belle Squire, herself a suffragist whose book *The Woman Suffrage Movement in America* was published that year. Sylvia's sympathetic interviewer expressed her own 'admiration and sincere regard' for her subject, whose artistic successes and stories of the campaign she enthusiastically relayed. In the course of the interview, Squire recalled *The Convert*, the popular novel about the British suffragettes by the actress, writer and WSPU member Elizabeth Robins. Published in Britain and America, *The Convert* brought the characters and events of the movement to life and shaped the expectations of American audiences. Squire was anxious to know if Sylvia was 'really the original' of the character Ernestine Blunt, as she had been told.[71] The most charismatic and talented of all the suffragette characters, Blunt was clearly modelled on Christabel. Sylvia denied the parallel, identifying herself instead as the model for the character Cynthia Chisholm, described as 'a gentle-seeming creature, carelessly dressed, grave and simple – [who] faced the mob with evident trepidation, a few notes, to which she never referred, in her shaking hand'.[72] Squire, however, would not be dissuaded: 'looking at Sylvia Pankhurst, I thought it not unlikely that she might play the part of Ernestine Blount [*sic*] with ease.'[73]

The *Tribune* qualified this friendly coverage, however, by printing a more hostile article directly below the interview which recalled comments Sylvia had made towards the beginning of her tour on her first experience of a sleeper train. Travelling from New York to Pittsburgh, Pennsylvania, Sylvia had failed to find the dining car and had enjoyed little sleep because, as she told reporters, she had been shocked to find her berth separated only by a curtain from the other passengers. Gleefully imagining all the indignities Sylvia might have been exposed to, the journalist mocked the contrast between her vaunted suffragette heroism whilst 'to sleep unprotected in an American sleeping car berth,

3. 'I capitulated immediately, but the Press men and women did not entirely relent.' Sylvia Pankhurst gave an extensive interview to the Chicago suffragist Belle Squire, published in the *Tribune* on 22 January 1911. The publication did not entirely forgive her initial attempt to avoid the press: below the interview it printed a hostile column deriding Sylvia's comments on sleeper trains. Both of Sylvia's tours attracted extensive press coverage. (Courtesy of the *Chicago Tribune* and newspapers.com)

with no door to lock against lurking foes or gentlemen who forget their berth numbers – alas, despair, O agony and grief!'[74] The malevolent jest ridiculed the threats a single, female traveller could experience. (In fact, Sylvia did find herself vulnerable on at least one occasion. On board ship to America ahead of the 1912 lecture tour, she attracted the attention of the ship's doctor. In her memoirs, Sylvia claimed that he proposed marriage to 'save' her from the suffragette movement.[75] A letter she wrote shortly afterwards to Hardie suggests she feared being assaulted. Admonishing herself for being 'silly', she told Hardie that she had agreed to go to the doctor's cabin as this was where he saw patients but had not realised 'how very much of a sleeping place a doctor's cabin is and how even a silly old buffer of a doctor may be quite a dangerous person.' She left unnerved but also relieved: 'I was quite lucky that that incident wasn't more unpleasant than it was.'[76])

Much of the time, Sylvia played along with the press – after all, the militants were adept at using press interest to their advantage. She gave numerous interviews and posed for photographs, and even publicly revised her opinion of the sleeper trains. Returning to Philadelphia towards the end of the 1911 tour, she explained to reporters: 'When I first came to the United States … I thought it was a barbarian country. I was not used to riding in sleeping cars where a curtain was the only partition from other sleepers. Now I am used to all the customs, and I think the United States is delightful.'[77]

Sylvia was, however, less tolerant of press interest in her personal life. Asked if she had any romantic admirers, she did not divulge any detail of the complications of her relationship with Hardie; instead she responded that she was 'too busy to get married'.[78] That she visited in 1912, which was a leap year, prompted reporters to ask what she thought of the convention of women asking their beaus to marry them on the extra day in February, which provoked the exasperated response: 'I have other and more important things to think of. You ask me a silly and personal question.'[79]

The personal nature of press interest extended to Sylvia's personal appearance. Unlike Emmeline Pankhurst, who consciously sought to disarm critics by fastidiously conforming to conventionally feminine dress, Sylvia was uninterested in adopting such tactics – indeed, she would later recall her mother's 'frequent complaint that I dressed so poorly'.[80] Despite conceding to wear an evening dress for some lecturing engagements, most of the time she wore more comfortable and practical clothing, drawing remarks in the press on her 'uncorseted figure'.[81] One male interviewer in Kansas invasively commented that 'to the unpractised masculine eye she appeared to be uncircled by a corset.'[82] The American press sought her opinion on clothing, although it was apparent she did not think this particularly important; asked whether the harem skirt was emancipatory for allowing women greater movement Sylvia replied that fashion 'seems a trivial matter to me', adding '[c]ertainly the harem skirt is not a vital factor. Let the women emancipate their heads, and their feet will take care of themselves.'[83]

Lurking behind such enquiries about her romantic life and clothing was the popular caricature of militant suffragettes as frustrated unwomanly women, for whom the fulfilment of their 'natural' desires would displace their misplaced interest in manly politics. Sylvia did not escape such treatment in the newspapers' 'humorous' columns: 'Miss Sylvia Pankhurst, being both young and handsome, will likely fall in love with some live American when she comes to this country. In that case she will marry, perhaps, and really not care a rap whether the women ever vote or not.'[84] Women's campaigns for political representation, and militancy in particular, had destabilised restrictive proscriptions about women's role. Trivialising suffragettes was one means of reasserting those restrictions. Sylvia's vocal resistance to being trivialised was thus intimately bound up with the defence of her cause.

MILITANCY

The appeal of militancy

Sylvia's professional lectures worked in conjunction with local suffrage campaigning organisations that sought to associate themselves with, or attract an audience by, the dynamism of the militant suffragettes. The American suffragist Harriot Stanton Blatch had organised Sylvia's first public engagement in America, a lecture at New York's Carnegie Lyceum, which secured her the necessary welcoming suffrage audience and fanfare for a wider tour. Beside Sylvia on the platform were such prominent figures as Charlotte Perkins Gilman, Dr Anna Shaw and Mrs Katharine Houghton Hepburn, a leading suffragist from Connecticut (her daughter later became a Hollywood actress famous for portraying independent and courageous women). Stanton Blatch had extended invitations to militant suffragettes since 1908, when she organised for Annie

Cobden Sanderson to address a New York audience, followed a year later by Emmeline Pankhurst. In so doing, she was consciously attempting to use the militant suffragettes to effect a change in the American suffrage movement, a process which Sylvia alluded to in her 'impressions' from the 1911 tour:

> All over America the Suffragists declare that they have gained hope and inspiration from our own great British movement. In the early days of our long struggle it was we who drew our inspiration from them. Our movements act and react on each other. We may spur each other on to renewed zeal. We and the world have much to gain from our joint effort.[85]

Sylvia was referring to what one historian has termed 'a transatlantic network of radical suffragists' that had been developed by Stanton Blatch's mother, the leading nineteenth-century American suffrage campaigner Elizabeth Cady Stanton, over seventy years before.[86]

Cady Stanton and Lucretia Mott had organised the first women's rights convention in Seneca Falls, New York State in 1848; they had been prompted, it was said, by their experience at the first anti-slavery conference in London in 1840 where they were excluded from the main audience because of their sex. In London, Cady Stanton had developed a network of friendships with abolitionist and women's rights campaigners to whom her daughter Harriot looked when she lived in England in the 1880s and 1890s. It was through these networks that she came to join the Women's Franchise League, a suffrage organisation in which Richard and Emmeline Pankhurst were involved and with whom she became friends; as children Christabel and Sylvia were sent to Basingstoke, where Stanton Blatch lived, to play with her daughter Nora who was close to them in age. Nora would later be among those seated on the platform of the Lyceum when Sylvia spoke there in 1911.

The Women's Franchise League was founded in 1889 to campaign for votes for women regardless of their marital status at a time when the larger suffrage organisations were prepared to express support for Bills that would only enfranchise unmarried women. League members argued that to support the suffrage on this basis would strengthen the status of coverture, the denial of a married woman's independent legal existence, which many of them had worked hard to overturn – Richard Pankhurst, for example, had drafted the 1882 Married Women's Property Act. At the League's inaugural meeting, Stanton Blatch expressed the dismay she had felt upon finding that the major women's suffrage organisations were 'talking upon such narrow lines'; by contrast, with the formation of the League, 'for the first time in a Suffrage meeting in England I feel at home.'[87] Her comments were supported by another American, William Lloyd Garrison, named after his abolitionist father, who explicitly compared the role of the League to that of the ardent abolitionists in the struggle against slavery:

> Time and time again they [the ardent abolitionists] were implored not to imperil partial Legislation or drive away from the cause friends who were shocked by the naked truth, but their only response was 'immediate and unconditional emancipation.' They knew full well that the moral force of their uncompromising advocacy would mould legislation more powerfully than temporising and wire-pulling to accomplish partial Acts.[88]

The League identified itself as the progressive vanguard of the movement, striving towards general emancipation instead of accepting compromises.[89] The Americans, as Sylvia later observed, were credited with providing a corrective absolutist zeal, with one League member declaring 'I think we could not do better than send Mrs Stanton Blatch round the country to rouse the people in every town in England from their lethargy and sloth on these great social questions.'[90] After moving back to America in 1902, Stanton Blatch now regarded the women's movement there as conservative and making little appeal to the growing constituency of working women. She therefore resolved to revitalise the American suffrage movement through promoting the example of the British militant WSPU, led by her friend from the League days, Emmeline Pankhurst.[91]

Sylvia's invitation came at a crucial moment for Stanton Blatch, coinciding with the transformation of her organisation, the Equality League of Self-Supporting Women, into the Women's Political Union (WPU). Focused upon suffrage and modelled on the WSPU, it even adopted their colours – purple, white and green – instead of the yellow associated with American suffragism.[92] A few weeks before Sylvia's rally in the Lyceum, WPU members had taken to the streets with buckets of paste and posters advertising the event; they proceeded to flypost all across Manhattan attracting press attention and signalling their more

4. Harriot Stanton Blatch (on the right) and other Women's Political Union members flyposting on the streets of New York to advertise Sylvia Pankhurst's first American lecture in the Carnegie Lyceum. (Paul Thompson; courtesy of Getty Images)

extrovert brand of suffragism. The WPU became a driving force in organising street meetings and public demonstrations modelled on the WSPU's spectacular pageants in London. They moved their headquarters to the basement of 46 East 29th Street, a move that Stanton Blatch saw as symbolic of their new approach: 'We had come down to the street level to advertise suffrage.'[93] It was here that Sylvia was taken first upon her arrival in New York in 1911 by WPU members Beatrice Brown, who had bought the paste for flyposting, Lavinia Dock, a nurse serving deprived communities through the Settlement on Manhattan's Henry Street, and Eunice Dana Brannan, the daughter of newspaper editor Charles Dana, who had been a confidante of Abraham Lincoln and had himself fostered radical transatlantic links by publishing articles by Karl Marx in the 1850s. In 1936, Sylvia wrote a piece in tribute to Stanton Blatch on her eightieth birthday, in which she recalled her own nervousness at the Lyceum meeting – 'very much overwhelmed with the great responsibility layed [sic] upon me to interpret our militant Suffragette Movement to the American public' – and her relief at finding a sympathetic audience:

'It had been well educated in the principles of the Women's Movement by able American women advocates, amongst whom Harriot Stanton Blatch has always been a steadfast light, and was already fully informed and keenly appreciative of our militant struggle across the Atlantic.'[94]

Other American advocates included the group called the 'American Suffragettes', also inspired by the WSPU to take their political activism to the streets, under whose auspices Sylvia visited and spoke in Milwaukee in February 1912. Moreover, some American women, most prominently Alice Paul and Lucy Burns, had themselves participated in the British suffragette movement and returned to tell of their experiences. Alice Paul was at the head of a reception committee of omnibuses and taxis decked in suffrage banners to greet Sylvia when she arrived at Philadelphia's Broad Street station in early April 1911.[95] These activists and organisations facilitated Sylvia's participation in the American suffrage movement.

The fact that some American states had granted women's suffrage directed the efforts of suffrage organisations in this period towards winning the vote in individual states and thus to lobbying state governments. In late February, the WPU brought Sylvia to Albany, the capital of New York State, to speak on her prison experiences as part of their 'suffrage week' of campaigning there. Likewise, her visit to Wisconsin in 1912 coincided with suffrage campaigning ahead of a state-wide referendum on women's suffrage.

It was not only the suffrage groups explicitly inspired by militancy that sought Sylvia's contribution. On 23 February 1911, when the State House in Boston, Massachusetts voted on a resolution on women's suffrage, suffragists organised a huge torchlight procession through the city, with music and banners, and Sylvia marching in the front row. She addressed the marchers outside, as well as three overflow meetings and was invited to speak inside the State House to the representatives who would make the decision, despite the fact that she was not a resident of the state or an American citizen: 'The chairman of the committee stated that it was not the custom to allow citizens of foreign countries to speak at such hearings, but they would accord her the privilege. She was received with great applause and listened to with strictest attention.'[96]

In her speech, Sylvia used the example of British militancy to warn against denying women's citizenship, urging: 'Do not drive your women to go the lengths to which we have had to go.'[97] Ida Husted Harper, an American suffragist and historian of the movement, considered that

'Sylvia Pankhurst addressed the committee in a simple and effective way.'[98] It was here that Sylvia met Alice Stone Blackwell, the editor of the *Woman's Journal*, the organ of the National American Woman Suffrage Association. This newspaper was granted the rights to publish Sylvia's *The Suffragette*, which they promoted as their 1911 New Year's Offer, and widely reported on Sylvia's 1911 tour. Sylvia later recalled 'many memories' of meeting Alice Stone Blackwell 'each time I was in America'; in the 1930s, Sylvia replied to a letter from Stone Blackwell telling her that 'the spirit of your letter brings you back to me', and closing with 'kind remembrances'.[99] Likewise, Sylvia's invitations to address the state governments of Colorado, Iowa and Michigan, all discussed in this book, are indications that she was regarded by many as a powerful exponent of their cause.

Defending militancy

The promotion of leading suffragettes was not, however, universally popular in the American suffrage movement. Even Sylvia's first meeting at the Lyceum proved controversial, with some suffrage campaigners complaining that the English suffragettes' lecture fees were depriving the American movement of funds.[100] More fundamentally, American suffragists were divided over militancy, with some arguing that association with English suffragettes would discredit their cause and jeopardise its chances of success. Catharine Waugh McCulloch, the vice-president of the Illinois Equal Suffrage Association and former vice-president of the NAWSA, wrote a furious letter to the organiser of the Wisconsin referendum campaign on the day of Sylvia's arrival there at the behest of the American Suffragettes. Complaining that the suffragettes were 'coining money out of us' because their dramatic stories held appeal – 'people pay hard cash to Miss Pankhurst & want our women to speak for nothing, chiefly because our women have not been in jail' – she went on to object to any association between the referendum campaign and the English militants:

> I am not convinced that the English women who throw stones & go to jail help our cause. They did not reach the goal as fast as did the women in Cal. and Wash. [California and Washington]* and those women did not act like tomboys. Of course they say they understand

* Women won the right to vote in Washington in 1910, in California in 1911.

their own situation & perhaps they do but then we understand our situation best. I really resent their advice about militant tactics & think you and I alone could defeat the Wis. [Wisconsin] measure if we should go out in Milwaukee or Chicago & throw a few stones & get sent to jail.[101]

In many ways, Sylvia's strategy was similar to those adopted by other suffragette speakers in North America as she sought to contextualise militancy.[102] First, she argued that when governments behaved tyrannically by depriving people of a democratic voice then militant, civil disobedience was justified resistance. In front of American audiences, she likened suffragette militancy to the American Revolution: 'We are fighting the battle of human freedom. Americans should be sympatheti[c], for you did not hesitate to plunge your country and ours into war to gain the freedom for which we ask.'[103]

The suffragettes had adopted the American Revolutionary slogan 'Taxation without representation is tyranny', and when Sylvia proclaimed this in Oakland, California in March 1911 she was 'stopped by loud applause'.[104] Further, she argued that militancy was effective, pointing on the one hand to the fifty years' peaceful struggle for women's suffrage in Britain, which had not achieved the franchise, and on the other to 'how the men obtained suffrage'.[105] She then went on to cite examples of acts, far more violent than those undertaken by the WSPU, which had succeeded in expanding the male electorate:

we found that one time after another the men of England had obtained it [the vote] by burning buildings, raiding towns, dragging prominent legislators from their carriages and trampling on them – nay more – by committing murder – that they had verily been forced into this before they got their vote, but that, being forced, they did get their vote.[106]

Militancy was, therefore, not inherently fanatical or female, as its opponents had charged, but a rather more moderate emulation of political protests undertaken by men.

Sylvia also placed suffragette militancy in the context of the much greater, repressive violence they faced. She explained the origins of militancy, graphically describing Christabel Pankhurst and Annie Kenney attending a Liberal rally in 1905 and demanding an answer to their question on women's suffrage only to be roughly ejected, arrested and imprisoned. In words that were repeated in *The Suffragette*, she described Christabel trying to defend her comrade from the stewards: 'her hand where she held them off was torn so and the blood ran down from it on Annie Kenney's white hat and we found it quite stained the next morning.'[107] She drew on her own experiences of imprisonment to vividly describe the humiliation and repressive treatment of suffragettes who were denied the status of political prisoners: 'We were condemned to solitary confinement, made to wear clothes which had been worn by other prisoners and bathe (once a week) in dirty baths.'[108] When women protested against this treatment they were brutally force fed. It was the authorities, not the suffragettes, that were using violence: 'we merely matched spiritual force against violence.'[109]

In a widely reported interview conducted upon her arrival in New York in 1911, Sylvia declared that thousands of English women were prepared to 'rush beneath the hoofs of the mounted police and die as the Christian martyrs of old died in the arena for their faith.'[110] Spoken two years before suffragette Emily Wilding Davison's protest – when she ran onto the racecourse during the Epsom Derby, was knocked down and killed after colliding with the king's horse and commemorated as the first martyr for the cause – these words now read as eerily prescient. Sylvia, however, was referring to the police brutality she had witnessed on suffragette demonstrations in London. Her allusions to martyrdom were by no means abstract, they formed the very substance of militancy and served as an indictment of the violence meted out to suffrage campaigners, violence of which she had painful personal experience. Sylvia's second arrest and imprisonment resulted from a WSPU march on Parliament on 13 February 1907 where

[m]ounted men scattered the marchers; foot police seized them by the back of the neck and rushed them along at arm's length, thumping them in the back, and bumping them with their knees in approved police fashion. Women, by the hundred, returned again and again with painful persistence, enduring this treatment by the hour. Those who took refuge in doorways were dragged down the steps and hurled in front of the horses, then pounced upon by constables and beaten again.[111]

Worse was yet to come. On Friday, 18 November 1910, WSPU demonstrators outside Parliament were sexually assaulted, beaten, kicked, pinched, thrown to the ground, and had their faces rubbed against railings by the police, who also encouraged thugs in the crowd to join in the mistreatment of the women.[112] Sylvia, who was under orders not to get arrested in order to finish her book, *The Suffragette*, watched from a taxi alongside Annie Kenney. When they did join the demonstration they too were subject to abuse:

> Finding it unbearable thus to watch other women knocked about, with a violence more than common on such occasions, we jumped out of the taxi, but soon returned to it, for policemen in uniform and plain clothes struck us in the chest, seized us by the arms and flung us to the ground.[113]

The WSPU responded with a renewed campaign of window smashing which saw more women arrested. Included amongst them was Mary Clarke, Emmeline Pankhurst's sister and the aunt to whom Sylvia had been very close since childhood, both sharing a talent for art. Mary Clarke was imprisoned for a month and released in late December. Sylvia did not spend Christmas Day with her family that year as she was busy writing *The Suffragette* in her West London flat. On Boxing Day, her mother came to tell Sylvia that Mary Clarke had died of a brain haemorrhage the day before. Two days after hearing this news, Sylvia boarded the *St. Paul* at Southampton and sailed for America.

Sylvia's defence of militancy emphasised both women's self-sacrifice for the cause and the effectiveness of their methods. 'They told us we'd put back the cause 20 years by our methods, but instead we're going to have the vote this year', she told a Detroit audience in March 1911.[114] However, when the WSPU launched its mass window-smashing campaign on 1 March 1912, Sylvia found these events affected attitudes towards her in America. The victory suddenly looked as far away as ever and the scale of the destruction to property caused some to regard the women as aggressors and others to distance themselves from militancy. The Mount Morris Church in Harlem cancelled the booking for Sylvia's lecture that had been planned there for 1 April, explaining:

> We are in favour of woman's suffrage as such and we want to hear Miss Pankhurst, but after the English outbreak she indorsed [*sic*] the methods of the militant suffragettes. Just at present we have no desire to indorse militant methods. So the trustees of the church and myself

decided that, in view of all the circumstances, it would be better that she speak on neutral ground.[115]

In response to the British state's seizure of WSPU funds at this time, Sylvia appealed for solidarity donations from Sarah Platt Decker, the suffragist whose guest she had been when she addressed the Colorado state government in 1911. In place of that formerly friendly welcome, Sylvia's telegram was simply forwarded to the Colorado Equal Suffrage Association, who replied: 'Whereas, Colorado numbers less than 300,000 women and our finances are limited, and we have the United States to assist, and whereas we do not approve of the methods of the English Suffragettes, the Colorado Equal Suffrage Association must decline any financial assistance.'[116]

Sylvia's response to the mass window smashing was to focus on the plight of the prisoners, especially her mother, who faced long sentences as a result of an intransigent government. She was not altogether unsuccessful in this endeavour. Two days after the event, she persuaded a meeting in Detroit, Michigan to cable a message of support to the WSPU and another message to Prime Minister Asquith which read 'Detroit mass meeting asks for the enfranchisement for brave British women.'[117] Sylvia would later recall desperately trying to obtain information about what had happened in London, but at the time the press interest in her immediate response caused her to bluff, claiming that 'she had been expecting for several days to hear that such a movement had been started.'[118] It was important to look as though the suffragettes were in control of events and she loyally proclaimed in public that 'today is the beginning of the end.'[119] Privately, however, Sylvia was uneasy about the direction of suffragette militancy. The kind of militancy she would champion on return was one she had begun to advocate for in America.

Applying militancy

Sylvia's historical and political contextualisation of militancy allowed her to tread carefully between appealing for North American support without overtly calling for the same tactics in her host countries. However, as her tours began to include involvement in specific campaigns, she found her advice and direction sought.

The best evidence of Sylvia's intervention in the American suffrage movement comes from Fargo in North Dakota, where she was invited to speak on 4 February 1912 under the auspices of the Grand Free Lecture Course, a cultural organisation sponsored by prosperous members of the local community. The obituary of Mary Darrow Weible, one of the leading sponsors who died in 1965, referred to Sylvia Pankhurst as 'a guest of real significance' for the group and conjured up the atmosphere amongst their social circle around this time as 'at a peak of elegance when entertaining was done in a formal manner in one's home. They were the days of the old opera house when one attended the theatre in evening clothes.'[120] The format would have been familiar to Sylvia who delivered a lecture in Fargo's Grand Theatre, wearing her 'light coloured evening dress', after an informal gathering held in her honour at Darrow Weible's house.[121] It was at this gathering that there began 'an informal discussion of the need for a Suffrage organization in the State', during the course of which, Sylvia later told Hardie, 'I suggested we should form one then and there.'[122] Despite the attendees' privileged backgrounds, Sylvia felt that 'many of them [were] Socialists' and there is evidence that Darrow Weible was attracted by socialist ideas around this time: in 1917, she would shelter Max Eastman from a local mob who, violently objecting to his socialist and anti-war stance, intended to lynch him.[123] Faced with like-minded individuals, Sylvia's suggested guidelines for the new organisation they titled the Votes for Women League of North Dakota are instructive. She advised a non-party stance that operated on the basis of asking electoral candidates for their views on equal suffrage and campaigning against those who were opposed. This, as Sylvia informed Hardie, was 'a very extreme step here. This has only been done in New York as yet and only by one Society who are closely in touch with the English W.S.P.U.'[124] Sylvia was referring to Stanton Blatch's WPU and its importation of militant tactics, although the course that Sylvia herself proposed in Fargo was subtly different from the WSPU's non-party approach, as she advised simply a non-alignment approach which targeted hostile individuals rather than whole political parties. If all candidates were opposed, she recommended organising a campaign: 'send out much literature, organize street meetings, conduct a canvas of voters.'[125]

After leaving Fargo the following day, Sylvia returned to Wisconsin and telegraphed Mary Swain Wagner of the American Suffragettes of her intention to return to Milwaukee where she planned to stay for at least another week to help there with the referendum campaign, as it was reported that Sylvia 'is thoroughly interested in the situation here and believes she can do much good for the cause of equal rights.'[126] She planned to hire a hall in downtown Milwaukee where meetings would be held 'both afternoon and evening during the week' and that '[b]ooks and literature on equal suffrage will be sold.' Concerned that 'the Wisconsin women are not alive to the situation', Sylvia insisted that 'there is a good deal of solid, hard work in front of the agitators if they wish to arouse the women to the present contingency.'[127] Although Sylvia was unable to put this into practice, as she was called away to speak in Chicago, she was consistently advocating a version of militancy which priori-tised street-based campaigning in an effort to win popular support for women's suffrage. She had outlined this as early as March 1911 in Kansas when she commented on how 'English women' would campaign for women's suffrage there:

> We would establish headquarters in your capital, divide the state into districts with sub-headquarters in each and begin a series of demon-strations. We would hold daily meetings, parade the streets, chalk the sidewalks, have torch light processions, hold home meetings much like your weekly house prayer meetings, and resort to every possible means of awakening and holding public interest.[128]

This was precisely the kind of emphasis she tried to achieve within the WSPU when she returned to England two months later, persuading the organisation to call a series of demonstrations 'in all the principal parks and open spaces around London' which 'were worked up by open air speeches, chalking, canvassing and poster parades', and hiring a head-quarters in East London to appeal for popular support in that area.[129] These endeavours were counter to the political trajectory of the WSPU leadership, as Sylvia later recalled:

> There was an outcry in the Union [WSPU] that propaganda meetings were useless, the one thing essential being the destruction of private property to arouse the public, and the terrorizing of Cabinet Ministers. Both in speaking and organizing, I set to work to combat this view, and to secure the extension, not the slackening, of propaganda work.[130]

Sylvia's emphasis on building a popular campaign challenged, above all, the WSPU leadership's approach to the relationship of suffragism to the working class, a theme that would become centrally important in Sylvia's American lectures.

WORKING WOMEN AND THE VOTE

English women workers and the vote

Sylvia was far from being the only women's suffrage campaigner who was articulating a socialist argument for women's political enfranchisement. However, socialist advocates were generally predisposed to support adult suffrage, which demanded an abolition both of the property qualification required for the franchise and the sex disqualification from it. Women's suffrage 'as it is or may be granted to men', which the WSPU campaigned for, implicitly did not challenge the property qualification, though this position did win the support of some socialists on the grounds of expediency, either believing that women's suffrage would be a step towards adult suffrage, or fearing that in practice adult suffrage would see the women's claim jettisoned once again. However, as the WSPU abandoned its roots in the socialist and labour movements, the foremost socialist advocates were increasingly found outside its ranks. Two of the most prominent socialist WSPU members, Charlotte Despard and Dora Montefiore, left the organisation in 1907.

In the summer of 1907, Sylvia had set off from her home in London and travelled northwards, stopping in towns where she would stay with local people. She spent her time painting women in their workplaces and interviewing them about their work, with the intention of producing 'a book dealing with the work of women in a large number of trades', accompanied by her own illustrations.[131] The planned book was never completed, but Sylvia did publish extracts as an article titled 'Women Workers of England' along with her illustrations in *The London Magazine* in 1908. She repeatedly demonstrated that women workers were paid less than their male counterparts. Thus, her painting of the banksworkers pushing the tubs of coal at a Wigan colliery was accompanied by the observation that: 'A bankswoman earns from 1s. 10d. to 2s. 4d., whilst a banksman, doing exactly the same work, gets from 4s. 9d. to 5s. a day.'[132]

Sylvia's decision to explore women's working conditions in 1907 can be seen as an expression of her uneasiness with WSPU policy at this time. She would later recall her dismay at her tour being interrupted by communications from her mother and sister, variously instructing her to suspend her own work to participate in WSPU campaigns during by-elections and justifying their transformation of the WSPU into an autocracy, which latter development prompted Despard's departure and her formation of a new militant suffrage organisation, the Women's Freedom League. Sylvia was in disagreement with the WSPU leadership in both these areas.

The WSPU's policy of campaigning to 'Keep the Liberal Out' in by-elections was presented by the leadership as an effective means of exerting pressure on the governing party. However, it could also be seen to advocate voting for the government's strongest electoral challenger, the Conservative Party. The insistence upon the WSPU's 'non-party', but anti-government, stance marked a break with the labour and socialist movement origins of the organisation. It swiftly developed into explicit hostility towards the Labour Party for the support it gave to progressive measures introduced by the Liberals, particularly around welfare and Home Rule for Ireland, while, conversely, implied praise for the reactionary opposition of the Conservatives to the government's entire programme. Meanwhile, with the dissolution of the WSPU's democratic constitution, the organisation redefined itself as a 'women's army' in which policy was dictated by the leaders, whom the rank and file were encouraged to follow unquestioningly. The mission was redefined as a spiritual crusade that transcended class boundaries, though in practice it represented a capitulation to contemporary social divisions, as middle-class women were cast as saviours acting on behalf of a much greater number of poorer women.[133] Thus, in 1908, leading WSPU member Emmeline Pethick Lawrence appealed 'to the strong to come forward now and take upon their shoulders the burden of the weak. It is not the toiling mother, the sweated worker, the deserted wife, the worsted in life, who can bear the strain and stress of the battle we are fighting for women's deliverance to-day.'[134]

Working-class women were thus reduced to a series of archetypal and helpless victims whose salvation would be delivered through the efforts of middle-class women who were assumed to be the movement's natural leaders. This was evidently the message that the WSPU expected to be articulated before American audiences, as Emmeline Pankhurst's own speeches demonstrated; in her farewell address in New York at the end of her 1909 tour Emmeline proclaimed: 'We have broken down class distinctions' before explaining that it was 'the privileged women, the honoured women ... who have never had to face the struggle for existence' that were undertaking 'the hardest and most unpleasant' work of the suffrage campaign.[135]

Before travelling to North America, Sylvia had refrained from public criticism of WSPU's increasing elitism. However, the character of the independent projects she pursued, in particular her 1907 research into working women's specific grievances, nevertheless expressed an implicit rejection of the WSPU's commandment to its followers: 'if you have any class feeling you must leave that behind when you come into this movement.'[136] For Sylvia, the position of working women linked the socialist and women's movements, underscoring their shared interest in co-operation. Crucially this approach implied that for a women's movement to make reactionary political alliances, or for socialists to dismiss the need for women's representation, would be to forsake above all the needs of working-class women. Sylvia did, therefore, make efforts to relate the 1907 research, which was full of 'class feeling', to the WSPU; her contact with the boot- and shoe-making industry in Leicester was facilitated by the local working-class trade unionist WSPU member Alice Hawkins, and Sylvia later published some extracts from her research in the WSPU newspaper *Votes for Women*.[137]

However, in her North American lecture tours, Sylvia found herself able to situate her independent research firmly within the framework of the WSPU's suffragism in a way that she was unable to do in England. She chose 'Women in Industry' as one of her three lecture titles in 1911 and 'English Industrial Conditions Affecting Women' in 1912, which allowed her to share the results of her research (the other two lectures dealt with the history of the women's movement and the prison experience). Reporting on her first meeting at the Carnegie Lyceum under the headline 'Miss Pankhurst Has Some Jolts in Store', the socialist *New York Call* noted 'the contrast' between Sylvia, who spoke for 'an hour and three-quarters ... on the economic, political and social conditions of Great Britain' and her audience, 'the "parlour suffragettes" of Fifth avenue and [its] vicinity who automobiled to [the] Carnegie Lyceum'.[138] Sylvia reportedly told this audience:

Without exception women in industry are the sweated workers. They are paid lower wages than men, although it has been proved time and again that they are doing the same amount of work. In the shoe trade in England women do the finest and most skilled work. Yet they get about one-fourth of the price which men get for the same, and even for cheaper work, which is less nerve-straining.[139]

According to the *New York Times*, '[s]he told of the difference in pay received by the English working women, those at the mines carrying tubs with the men, the identical work, the men getting four shillings ninepence and five shillings, and the women only one shilling sixpence to two shillings fourpence.'[140]

After speaking in Los Angeles on 7 March 1911 on the subject of 'Woman in Politics', Sylvia arranged for a second meeting to take place 'especially for the benefit of working women' on 'Woman in Industry'.[141] The local press, which described her speech as 'dramatic', reported that '[h]er accounts of the drudgery and labor performed by English women were startling', with women supporting themselves and their families by '[t]he hardest kind of manual labor in coal and tin mines and in stove factories'.[142] Speaking the following year at the Grand Theatre in Fargo, she returned again to the shoe trade and 'told how she had seen in a shoe factory in one of the English cities two women and a man seated side by side working at exactly the same thing and the same number of hours. He received $6 a week, while each of the women received $1.75.'[143]

All these examples were drawn from Sylvia's 1907 research. Above all, her work emphasised the double burden borne by working-class women, showing that their oppression *as women* enabled employers to intensify their exploitation *as workers*. Sylvia's approach challenged those in the socialist and labour movements who argued that focusing on women's suffrage distracted from working-class struggle, since the specific and intensified levels of exploitation experienced by women necessitated their independent representation to remedy this situation. When Sylvia met Emil Seidel, the socialist mayor of Milwaukee, she felt he 'showed no enthusiasm' for votes for women, arguing that male and female members of the capitalist class would be equally predisposed to exploit the working class. Writing to Keir Hardie about the exchange, Sylvia reported that she had agreed but then drawn his attention to the unevenness of exploitation within the working class, with examples from the forges in Cradley Heath and the Staffordshire potteries:

'look at the position of the woman who is employed by a workman. The woman for instance who blows the bellows for the chain maker or the woman who treads the lathe for the turner. What sort of position is she in?' I felt just a shade of indignation at the line he was taking. I felt my cheeks grow hot, and my voice sounded so. He answered in quite a sad changed voice 'She's the slave of a slave' and after that we got on better.[144]

There were, nevertheless, limitations attached to speaking about English working conditions in America, as Sylvia would soon discover. Elite American audiences might concede that regrettable conditions existed in the 'old country', maintaining that these were the problems of backwardness and thus not of modern America. If sweated women's labour was acknowledged, it was dismissed as marginal to American capitalism. As Sylvia complains in this book: 'one is frequently told that over work, under pay, and bad conditions of employment amongst women are confined to the foreign immigrants, and that the American woman does not need to work in a factory, and is always well paid and well cared for' (p. 75). This narrative implicitly threatened arguments for women's suffrage, like those advanced by Sylvia, that women needed political representation as a means of overcoming their vulnerability to greater exploitation. For some commentators in America, such problems would be solved not by women's democratic participation but rather by unimpeded capitalism.

Countering this argument is one of the central themes of Sylvia's book. On arriving in a new town, Sylvia insisted on viewing workplaces where women were employed, making detailed observations of the ratio of male to female workers, the differentiation in their pay and treatment, as well as the ethnic composition of the workforce; she also read reports on women's labour, such as Ruby Stewart's study, *Women's Wages in Milwaukee* (1911). Alongside examples from England, Sylvia began to cite examples from her American research in her lectures, which she would later record in an expanded form in this book. Sylvia's research showed that far from women's low-paid work in factories existing as an aberration, this kind of work was becoming increasingly important as a result of unequal pay which ensured that, as she told her audience in Fargo in 1912, 'the women will force the men out [of employment]' because employers could pay them less for the same work.[145] Unregulated capitalism, then, would result in more not less of women's sweated labour and this was increasingly the case in modern America. At the Women's City Club in Missouri, Sylvia angrily confronted the complacency and, she implied, sense of racial superiority that characterised those who praised American working conditions as she created something of a sensation by telling her hearers that they were no further advanced than the Chinese and the Turks whom they held in contempt. 'You are,' said Miss Pankhurst, 'the most backward nation in the Western world, and here in Missouri you have the most backward State.' She cited cases to prove her statement and showed that the evils resulting from low wages and the unjust economic conditions under which women lived in that city were worse than existed elsewhere.[146]

In March 1911, she told reporters in Detroit: 'Another thing that annoys me terribly is to hear about the wonderfully good conditions existing in this country for women. Why, I never saw anything worse in London than the way the garment workers in Chicago suffered. Women need the vote badly in this country.'[147] The example of the Chicago garment workers is instructive, and points to the turbulent atmosphere in which Sylvia undertook her tours.

The uprising of working women in America

Sylvia arrived in America in 1911 in the midst of a huge wave of working-class militancy that was led by working women. The movement had emerged in November 1909 from strikes of garment workers, most of whom were women from immigrant backgrounds, in two shirtwaist factories in New York City. Frustrated with the passive response from the trade union leadership, they called for a general strike of the city's garment workers which captured the mood in the sweatshops and fundamentally changed the pace of the struggle: the 'uprising of the 20,000', as it became known, had begun. The uprising inspired a new movement, as low-paid women in city after city voted to strike, downed tools and picketed their sweatshops.

The strike wave erupted in the garment factories of Chicago on 23 September 1910, four months before Sylvia arrived in the city, at the Hart, Schaffner and Marx clothing factory after a cut in women workers' piece rates was enforced. It was clear this was a final hardship that caused mounting tension to snap – the women objected to the way they were treated every day in the factory, from 'the petty tyranny' of the foreman who was paid extra if he could drive his workforce to produce over a certain amount; the 'abusive and insulting language ... frequently used by those in authority in the shops', and the punitive system of fines, for such misdemeanours as a 'liberal use of soap in washing hands', which reduced their paltry wages still further.[148] The strikers turned for help to the United Garment Workers Union but found this union uninterested in organising low-paid, immigrant women workers and pessimistic about their prospects of success, and so the women approached and won the support of the Chicago Federation of Labour and the Chicago Women's Trade Union League (WTUL). By the time Sylvia arrived in Chicago, the strike was in its last, bitter stages. The United Garment Workers Union had negotiated over the heads of the strikers themselves for the workers at the Hart, Schaffner and Marx factory to return to work on 14 January, as arbitration had commenced. This, however, left 30,000 garment workers from other shops who had joined the strike and were still picketing. (Two weeks later, the United Garment Workers' leader suddenly called off the strike, leaving these workers without an agreement and subject to victimisation by furious employers.)

5.   Sylvia Pankhurst (left, numbered 7) looks into a prison cell at Harrison Street, Chicago on 21 January 1911. The women beside her are (from left to right) Elizabeth Belmont, the assistant police matron, Olive Sullivan, from the Women's Trade Union League, and Zelie Emerson, a Settlement worker who played a crucial role in the strike of garment workers in the city. Emerson would later help Sylvia construct the East London Federation of Suffragettes. (Courtesy of the Chicago History Museum)

On 21 January 1911, Zelie Emerson and Olive Sullivan, two women from the Chicago WTUL, took Sylvia to visit the Harrison Street Gaol and police courts to convey just how difficult the garment workers' struggle had been.[149] Upton Sinclair's sensational novel *The Jungle*, published five years earlier, had exposed the collusion in Chicago between police, politicians, employers and organised crime, which enabled an elite few to make huge profits out of sweating immigrant labourers. Any resistance to that was met with vicious and organised brutality, as the garment workers soon discovered. Male and female strikers were attacked and beaten on the picket lines by thugs hired by the employers as well as by the police. Pickets were arrested and imprisoned, and two strikers were shot dead by the police in the course of the strike.[150] Harrison Street left Sylvia with an enduring sense of horror (see Chapter 4, pp. 98–99). After seeing where the pickets had been incarcerated, Sylvia wrote an impassioned denunciation of the Harrison Street cells, which was published in the *Chicago Sunday Tribune*:

> I heard of some of the women and girls who had been picketing in the garment workers' strike, as I am told in a perfectly legal way, who had been arrested and thrust either into these police court cells or into the annex, in both of which the risk of contamination at all times is exceedingly great. Happily, their trade union organizations have been able to come to their aid and bail them out within a short time, but it must be remembered that the people being on strike were practically penniless and had no money of their own, and therefore had others not come to their assistance they would have been obliged to continue suffering this terrible form of confinement.[151]

This article was considered significant enough for the Chicago WTUL's official report into the strike to include thanks to Sylvia because her 'telling description of the Harrison Police Station, where many of the young girl strikers were sent when arrested for picketing, was a challenge to the social conscience, as well as an indictment of the industrial conditions of Chicago.'[152]

Sylvia's article acknowledged the support that the striking garment workers received and Zelie Emerson was well-placed to describe the scale of the solidarity efforts. A member of the Chicago WTUL, Emerson had been in charge of a restaurant to feed strikers and their families on Noble Street, she was the 'Chairman' of the Rent Committee and, with another woman, the director of the relief work.[153] As Colette A. Hyman's work has shown, the Relief and Rent Committees were crucial in maintaining the strike and women's participation within it, as families were fed and landlords persuaded to wait for rent.[154] The scale of the task was daunting; at its height there were around 40,000 previously unorganised workers on strike, and the WTUL estimated that the number of strikers and their dependents who would need assistance over the bitterly cold winter months amounted to 100,000 individuals. Four months into the strike, the WTUL reported the 'tramp of thousands of weary feet' in their headquarters, the 'stream of stories of hardship and privation', and 'more than 7,000 tiny toddlers wailing for milk' – 1,250 babies were born during the strike.[155] There was also the challenge of helping the strikers overcome linguistic and cultural barriers to organise together – between them the strikers spoke nine different languages.[156] Instead of dismissing working-class women as weak, or speaking for them, Sylvia and some progressive middle-class women in Chicago, like Emerson, were striving to amplify working women's experience so that they could effect change. It is easy to see why Sylvia and Emerson struck up a friendship; Emerson, originally from Michigan, was from a wealthy background, but was said to have 'abandoned "society" for sociological investigation', and took jobs as a hotel kitchen worker, scrub woman and salesgirl in a department store to study working conditions.[157]

Democracy from below

Gaining an insight into what working people themselves wanted to change, by speaking with them and experiencing their working conditions, was precisely what Sylvia had aimed to do in her 1907 tour. The value of first-hand experience was also what attracted Sylvia to the Settlement Houses which embedded themselves in deprived communities and sought to use their experience of the neighbourhood to deliver services that people needed. Women were often in the forefront of the Settlement movement and Sylvia was soon in contact with many of the most radical adherents; Emerson, for example, worked at the Northwestern University Settlement. Sylvia met Jane Addams, the founder of the Hull House Settlement in Chicago, during her visit there in 1911 and described her as 'the greatest American I have met so far in my travels through this country'.[158] Sylvia was also invited to dinner at Hull House during her 1912 tour.[159] In New York, Sylvia met Lillian Wald, a nurse who established the Henry Street Settlement on the Lower East Side. Also working there, producing innovative theatrical productions with local young people, were Alice and Irene Lewisohn, two wealthy and philanthropic sisters whose combination of social commitment with artistic endeavour particularly appealed to Sylvia (see the editor's introduction to Chapter 3). She became warmly attached to them and stayed at their home when she was in New York in 1912.[160] Some of the Settlements actively assisted striking workers, Hull House and Henry Street having particularly close relationships with their local WTUL.[161] Daily life in the Settlement proved that capitalism was not solving its own problems and caused many Settlement workers to call for reform. As Jane Addams observed, 'their neighbourhood experiences had made them only too conscious of the dire need for protective legislation.'[162] Women who worked in the Settlements could therefore use their experience to comment authoritatively upon pressing social problems. Moreover, women's expertise in these areas further supported their claims for inclusion in the franchise.

Prioritising experience 'from below' began to inform Sylvia's conception of socialism. As Les Garner has argued, Sylvia's reflections on Milwaukee indicate that Sylvia 'was beginning to show her distaste for reformism or socialism imposed by managers and benevolent individuals', as well as 'her growing belief in socialism from below, created by, and in the interests of, working men and women'.[163] As Sylvia discusses in Chapter 5, she found herself disappointed that the administration's emphasis was upon efficient management, with permanent advisers who lacked 'special knowledge of social conditions or of working lives', excepting, she judged, the representative from the Settlement House (p. 113). It was in relation to what she saw in Milwaukee that she articulated her view here that

> all forms of labour must receive due representation, one may look forward to the time when the garbage collectors, the scrub women, and the other city employees, will be powerfully represented by those who will be able to speak for them with direct knowledge of their lives and work, when plans for the reconstruction of the departments employing them are underway. (p. 121)

This emphasis on class implicitly rejected the view that elite, propertied women could represent working-class women either in the struggle for the vote or the employment of the vote. Instead, Sylvia articulates here her view of democracy as a mechanism for the representation of class feeling.

Capital and labour

Towards the end of her lecture tour in 1912, Sylvia joined up again with the WPU which had first welcomed her to New York the year before. The WPU were running a campaign in New York State's Mohawk Valley to galvanise popular support for a state vote on women's suffrage and Sylvia participated in their lecture circuit. Her speeches now reflected upon the accumulation of experiences and research that she had gained in the course of her tours. America, she concluded, was afflicted by 'graft and commercialism'.[164] 'Graft' – Sylvia chose the American term – referred to the corruption of politics which she had witnessed, a theme she returned to on multiple occasions during her 1912 tour. Arriving in Milwaukee at the end of January 1912, she complained of its pervasiveness in American politics: 'While riding in a train in New York I overheard a candidate for the legislature say that when he failed to win his hearers by a speech he took them into a saloon and gave them beer. The law would not permit anyone to talk like that at home.'[165]

Although she did not deny corruption in British politics, she felt that it was far more openly accepted as a facet of political life in America. Moreover, she saw this as a threat to winning popular support for women's suffrage since 'the average American has much less regard for government, a lower ideal of it, than the Englishman.'[166] It was not therefore that modern American capitalism had made women's suffrage obsolete, in fact the capitalist belief in the supremacy of wealth was undermining what existed of democratic political life and thus its triumph over women's suffrage would signal women's further subordination and exploitation.

Sylvia also objected to 'commercialism ... going ahead of that great other side – conservation of human life'.[167] The most grotesque example of this was the fire at the Triangle Shirtwaist Factory on New York's Lower East Side on 25 March 1911. The factory occupied the top floors of the building, too high for the fire department's ladders. The fire escape was wholly inadequate and swiftly became blocked and then collapsed when the desperate workers tried to use it for escape. One of the doors on the factory floor was locked; though against regulations, the company owners did it anyway – they did not want their employees stealing from them. The fire spread quickly through the garment factory and 146 workers, most of them women, and most from immigrant backgrounds, were killed. Some were burnt to death in the factory, others in desperation leapt from the windows and were killed on impact with the pavement below.[168] In the Preface to this book, Sylvia recalls her attendance at the huge funeral for the victims in New York. In the Mohawk Valley, towards the end of her 1912 tour, Sylvia found herself speaking on the same platforms as Rose Schneiderman, a trade union organiser and garment worker herself who, in the aftermath of the fire, delivered a powerful speech denouncing the priorities of modern America where '[t]he life of men and women is so cheap and property is so sacred.'[169] Undoubtedly, Schneiderman and Sylvia would have discussed the fire which they both highlighted in their speeches as demonstrating the need for working women's political emancipation. What happened at the Triangle factory was not because there were no safety regulations, but because women lacked power. As Sylvia explained: 'Laws have been passed affecting working conditions and supposedly for the safeguarding of the employed, but they are not enforced. The Triangle fire in New York was but one sad example.'[170]

Eighteen months before the fire, the strike of workers at the Triangle and another nearby garment factory had begun the uprising of the 20,000. The Triangle bosses had been among the most intransigent of all; their strikers returned to work with small wage rises but without the closed shop union policy they wanted. The balance of power at the Triangle remained, essentially, the same as before. Sylvia argued that what was needed was for 'that great other side', the protection of humanity, to be reasserted and that women needed this as men did: 'When we think of capital and labour ... we think of armies of workingmen. It does not strike us that women, too, are working.'[171] Moreover, like men, women needed more than trade unionism: they needed protective legislation to be enforced, which meant employing female factory inspectors, who could 'get the confidence' of women workers, and granting women political power.

This, she concluded, was needed as much in America as it was in England. According to one report, Sylvia explained: 'She was beginning to learn that England was not the only place where things were not just as they ought to be. She had been told that America was the land of freedom and the place where men put women on a pedestal and worshipped them.'[172]

Yet, she went on, she had landed in New York during the laundry workers' strike, and through investigating their conditions, '[a]nother fallacy that was soon exploded was the matter of enormous wages paid women here' and she quoted figures from the fifteen factories she had investigated.[173] She went on to describe the conditions in prison, highlighting Tennessee where inmates were terrorised into false confessions. The structure of this speech, starting with the laundry strike, examining wages and conditions of women workers, and ending in the darkness of the Tennessee prison follows the structure of this book.

Sylvia had arrived with a book that was loyal to the WSPU leadership. It was, however, in the process of promoting this book that she became involved in a process of research and political discussion which challenged and developed her as a thinker, political activist and writer. She speedily recorded her impressions and their impact on her ideas in her speeches and in her letters. The result would be a typescript that distilled those experiences, pitting modern capitalism against 'the great other side': humanity.

THE IMPACT OF THE TOURS ON SUFFRAGE HISTORY

On the night of 2 April 1912, fifteen women wearing yellow suffrage sashes and carrying banners came down to the New York harbourside to say goodbye to Sylvia Pankhurst. Sylvia held a midnight reception in the stateroom of the SS *Mauretania*, and the women distributed their suffrage literature to the other passengers. At 1 a.m., the ship set sail.[174] Sylvia never returned to North America.

The effects of her lecture tours, however, remained profound and enduring. After her return to Britain, she appealed to her American contacts to exert pressure on the government. A Bill proposing Home Rule for Ireland was before Parliament which made no inclusion for women's suffrage, despite widespread Irish Nationalist support, and which would prevent any chance to amend this for three years. Christabel, who was closer to the Unionists than the Nationalists, called for Parliament to avenge the women by voting down the Bill. Sylvia later expressed her view that any hope of influencing the Irish Nationalists to make women's suffrage a decisive issue in the Bill's progress 'could only be by the efforts of Irish women' and that the WSPU should 'leave the Irish question to them'.[175]

At the time, however, Sylvia took a more active stance on this question than her memoirs indicated. Instead of calling for the Bill to be voted down, she tried to garner American support for a women's suffrage amendment to it. She wrote to Lillian Wald and Jane Addams, her friends in the Settlements, asking them to seek American messages of support for a women's suffrage amendment to the Bill.[176] Wald received a favourable response from Oswald Garrison Villard, the editor of the *New York Evening Post*. Villard's mother, Helen Frances Garrison Villard, had spoken alongside Sylvia at a suffrage meeting in Winchester, Massachusetts, in April 1911, and his maternal grandfather was the William Lloyd Garrison who had spoken of the uncompromising reformers in Britain and America at the founding meeting of the Women's Franchise League in 1889. Wald also received a favourable response from Henry Moskowitz, involved in investigating factory conditions in the wake of the Triangle fire, who wrote to Sylvia stating his view that Irish Home Rule and women's suffrage were 'expressions of the same movement' and therefore 'there is no logic in answering the democratic demands of the Irish People by an undemocratic home rule bill.'[177] However, not all of those Wald contacted were so favourably disposed; George Foster Peabody, president of the Men's League for Woman Suffrage in America, objected on the grounds that he opposed militancy and believed that Emmeline Pankhurst was 'at heart a Tory' whose reactionary politics would ensure 'that the effect of such letters as Miss Silvia [*sic*] Pankhurst wishes written respecting the Government of Ireland would only tend to defeat the giving of Home Rule to Ireland.'[178]

Beyond seeking political support, Sylvia's communications with her American contacts reveal the warm friendships she constructed in America and their importance to her. Sylvia ended her letter to Addams 'With very kind regards and remembrances to all friends at Hull House'.[179] She wrote to Lillian Wald: 'I think of you very often and all the dear people at the Settlement, and hope that I shall see you again before very long', closing her letter 'Yours with affectionate remembrances'.[180] Wald's letter to Sylvia asked her to send 'my deep love' to Emmeline and indicates that Sylvia was writing regularly, only a month after leaving America, to Alice and Irene Lewisohn: 'I know that Alice and Irene have kept you informed from time to time of our movements here and our concern about the affairs in England, particularly those affecting your family. They have permitted me to read your interesting letters, and we have all wanted to be posted on the situation.'[181]

Shortly after Sylvia's return to England, imprisoned suffragettes, once again denied the status of political prisoners, began hunger striking and were forcibly fed. Sylvia wrote a letter of protest, pointing out the dangers of force feeding, which was brought to the Home Secretary's notice by Sir Charles Henry. Sir Henry was 'a virulent anti-Suffragist' but he was also the brother-in-law of Alice and Irene Lewisohn.[182] Alice Lewisohn's memoir of her work in theatre, published in 1959, departs briefly from her theme to recall her visit to England in the summer of 1914 in which she was profoundly struck by the contrast of Sylvia's campaign in East London and the complacency of the English upper class:

> A scuffle with the police, then Sylvia Pankhurst shoved back into prison, threatening a hunger strike which might end in death. Meanwhile, suave and decorous Parliament lords and ladies, cabinet ministers, politicians, sipping tea on the terrace, with an air of 'all's well with the world.' Delegations, marches and bands, festivities and trooping of the colours for his Majesty's birthday, turbulent meetings of non-enfranchised women labourers.[183]

Sylvia's work to create an East London campaign was undertaken alongside Emerson, who had moved to London to participate in the British suffragette movement. Emerson, with her immense experience of organising amongst working-class women in the Chicago garment workers' strike, played an important role in East London and was appointed honorary organiser 'to keep all the others going'.[184] After their expulsion from the WSPU, Emerson suggested that the now independent ELFS establish a newspaper of their own, launched in March 1914 as the *Woman's Dreadnought*.[185] In the quest to fund this project, Sylvia turned to America's millionaire suffragist, Alva Belmont. However, Belmont, who had formed a close friendship with Emmeline and Christabel, turned down Sylvia's request, leaving her to politely retreat, conceding that she could 'quite understand your great need for funds in America'.[186]

Sylvia herself was able to survive on the money she had made in the 1912 tour, despite her fears at the time that it would prove unprofitable. She later tried to support herself by offering articles to the American press. She was not always successful in her endeavours – the article she offered to the *Century Magazine* on Norway did not appear, while a second article was sent twice to the *New York Times* to no avail.[187] However, in July 1913, the *New York Times* published Sylvia's account of her work in East London, for which she was paid $72.90.[188] The following month, *McClure's Magazine* published her harrowing account of forcible feeding.[189] Twenty years later, Sylvia would re-use much of this material written for the American public in *The Suffragette Movement*.

Meanwhile, Sylvia and Emerson expanded the ELFS, eventually renting a house and hall on the Old Ford Road to be the centre for their organisation and to provide wider services: 'to organize a lending library, a choir, lectures, concerts, a "Junior Suffragettes' Club," and so on'.[190] Sylvia and Emerson seemed to be applying the model of the Settlement, based in the community, to political agitation. This was certainly the impression of Lavinia Dock, the nurse at the Henry Street Settlement who had been among the first three women to greet Sylvia upon her arrival in New York in 1911. Dock was in London in the spring of 1914 and wrote to an American friend about calling on Sylvia and Emerson where she said, applying a New Yorker's geography to the city, she observed their 'work among the toilers on the East Side':

> Sylvia has the settlement idea in her mind. She was deeply impressed with our settlement, especially, and she is planning a settlement life down there for herself ... Then, after the vote is won, she looks forward to settlement life, a return to her art, but always keeping a political centre as a main purpose. She is a wonderful and inspired girl.[191]

Sylvia would never return to her art, but the ELFS would become increasingly like a Settlement, especially when the impoverishment occasioned by the First World War saw them establish cost-price restaurants, a nursery, a toy-making workshop and medical services. Emerson left the day after the Women's Hall on the Old Ford Road was opened, sailing for America (though she would later return to help the ELFS during the war). She had suffered immensely from force feeding in prison and had been a target of police brutality: a blow to the head had fractured her skull. Sylvia had persuaded her to leave for her own sake: 'I had the greatest difficulty to induce her to go, and suffered many a painful hour of distressful heart-searching on her account. I was grieved to lose her.'[192] An undated letter from Emerson to Sylvia, which was probably written on the occasion of their second parting during the First World War and which was preserved by Sylvia in her papers, conveys how Emerson felt about being asked to step back from the campaign, seemingly for the second time. Clearly distressed, Emerson asked, 'what was the cause of you not wanting me to speak for us any more.' She thanked Sylvia for giving her a lock of her hair, wrote her a poem recalling old times and stated 'you know that nothing that has happened or may happen between us can ever alter my feeling toward you.'[193] On the basis of this letter, some biographers have speculated that Sylvia and Emerson's relationship had been a romantic one.[194] The Settlements themselves provided a way for women to live together and this may have been what one or both of them envisaged at some point. Whether or not the relationship was romantic, it was inseparable from their shared political endeavour. It has been little appreciated since how much the ELFS owed both to Emerson's political experience and Sylvia's American tours.

POSTSCRIPTS

The outbreak of the First World War highlighted the divergence of the WSPU and the ELFS. While the ELFS adopted welfare schemes that emulated the work of the Settlements, the WSPU suspended its militant campaign for the vote and backed the war effort. In America, however, that country's entry into the war would see militancy, previously on the fringes of the suffrage movement, propelled to centre stage. Departing from the previous emphasis on winning the vote in individual states, Alice Paul, the American campaigner who had participated in the British suffragette movement, began to focus on attaining a women's suffrage amendment to the Constitution. In 1917 she initiated 'silent sentinels': women pickets who resolved to stand silently outside the White House with banners demanding their political emancipation until President Wilson capitulated. Like the early militant suffragettes, they directly confronted the government with street-based protests. Unlike the WSPU, they continued this action when their state was at war (the United States joined the war in April 1917). The activists involved were met with a brutal response by the authorities which the suffragettes would have recognised. They were arrested and imprisoned, many of them in the Occoquan Workhouse. Some of the women hunger struck in protest and were force fed. Alice Paul, who had previously endured force feeding in an English prison, was locked up in a psychiatric institution – a threat the British authorities had once held over hunger striking suffragettes. On 14 November 1917, her comrades in the workhouse were subject to what became known as the 'night of terror', when the male guards rushed in armed with clubs and savagely beat the women.[195] Sylvia would have known many of the imprisoned pickets. Alice Paul had arranged the flamboyant greeting for Sylvia in Pennsylvania in April 1911; Lucy Burns had participated in the British suffragette movement; Eunice Dana Brannan had met Sylvia at the dock when she arrived in New York for the first time in January 1911; Doris Stevens had heard Sylvia lecture in Oberlin in January 1911, and Sylvia had been joint guest of honour at a luncheon in Washington in February 1911 alongside Anna Kelton, then celebrating her engagement to Dr Harvey Washington Wiley, a chemist whose work led to the passing of the Pure Food and Drugs Act. In November 1917, Mrs Kelton Wiley was smuggling workhouse food out to her husband to expose the unsanitary food to which the prisoners were subjected.[196]

* * *

In 1918, women in Britain won the right to vote at 30 years of age – though men could vote from the age of 21. Women won votes on the same terms as men in 1928. In America, the 19th Amendment was ratified in 1920, giving the vote to women nationwide. In Canada, most women were granted the vote in 1918, but Asian people were disenfranchised until the 1940s, and indigenous Canadians until the 1960s.

* * *

Sylvia Pankhurst dedicated the rest of her life to political activism. She supported the Bolshevik Revolution in Russia and was inspired by the more direct democracy of the workers' and soldiers' soviets (councils). She participated in international communist debates into the 1920s and campaigned to stop British military intervention in Russia. As a consequence of her communist activism, she was imprisoned one last time in 1921. She remained resolutely opposed to imperialism and racism. She was the first newspaper editor in Britain to employ a black journalist. Sylvia was among the earliest British campaigners to identify the dangers of the rise of fascism from Mussolini's rise to power in Italy in 1922. The triumph of fascism represented the destruction of democracy, of workers' and women's rights, and the propagation of racial hatred resulting in the attempted annihilation of Jewish people. Fascism also aspired to imperialist expansion. When Italy invaded Ethiopia in 1935, Sylvia made campaigning for that country's freedom and, later, the rebuilding of the country the last great causes of her life. Understanding that fascism represented an existential threat to all the progressive movements to which she had dedicated her life, Sylvia turned to her old comrades, including those friendships forged in the American tours. In the 1930s, she corresponded with Alice Stone Blackwell, the former editor of the *Woman's Journal*, to enlist her support in anti-fascist activities.[197] In 1936, Sylvia's birthday message to Harriot Stanton Blatch, her parents' old friend who invited her to America in 1911, concluded by warning '[w]e are faced with a new reaction ... Fascism is a real menace to humanity.' She recalled the memory of their past shared struggles:

> When we were facing ignominy to win our citizenship, we were spurred on always by the thought that women had a great part to play in sweeping away the evils of war and poverty, and soulless greed and competition. Now we must forge ahead to achieve the Brotherhood and Sisterhood of mankind, the Golden Age of plenty for all by mutual aid.[198]

Sylvia never forgot the experiences of the American tours and the stances that she took. In the 1940s and 1950s, Sylvia's campaigning in solidarity with Ethiopia led to her correspondence with the American W.E.B. Du Bois, a leading Pan-Africanist intellectual, and staunch supporter of women's suffrage. In a letter from 1946, discussing means of facilitating African American support for Ethiopia, Sylvia recalled challenging racism in Tennessee over thirty years before: 'I have always had sympathy for the American Negro and had some lively experiences when I was in the United States on that account.'[199] For Sylvia, her American experiences were not a cause for nostalgia. Instead, her experiences, changing ideas and friendships forged in those intense months in 1911 and 1912, recorded so vividly here, inspired her lifelong campaigning efforts against oppression and for democracy.

NOTES

1. New York Passenger lists, Roll T715, 1895-1957, 1001-2000, Roll 1795, access via Ancestry.co.uk. The form wrongly records her age as 28.
2. E. Sylvia Pankhurst, *The Suffragette Movement: An Intimate Account of Persons and Ideals* (London: Virago Limited, 1977), p. 347.

3. E. Sylvia Pankhurst to J. Keir Hardie, undated letter [late January 1912], Estelle Sylvia Pankhurst Papers, 9, International Institute of Social History, Amsterdam [henceforward ESP Papers].
4. Ibid.
5. Howard Zinn, *A People's History of the United States* (New York: Harper Perennial, 2015), pp. 321–357.
6. *Des Moines Register*, 2 February 1911, p. 5.
7. On plans towards this project see Pankhurst to Hardie, 22 January [1912], ESP Papers, 9; Pankhurst, *The Suffragette Movement*, p. 382.
8. *Philadelphia Inquirer*, 3 April 1911, p. 16.
9. Pankhurst, *The Suffragette Movement*, p. 350.
10. Richard and Rita Pankhurst, *Ethiopian Reminiscences: Early Days* (Los Angeles, CA: Tsehai Publishers, 2013), p. 23.
11. Richard Pankhurst, *Sylvia Pankhurst: Artist and Crusader* (New York and London: Paddington Press Ltd, 1979), p. 140.
12. Quoted in Pankhurst, *The Suffragette Movement*, p. 372.
13. *New York Times*, 5 April 1912, p. 1.
14. Pankhurst, *The Suffragette Movement*, p. 383.
15. Ibid., p. 384.
16. On this process see Katherine Connelly, *Sylvia Pankhurst: Suffragette, Socialist and Scourge of Empire* (London: Pluto Press, 2013), pp. 46–48.
17. Pankhurst, *The Suffragette Movement*, p. 416.
18. Ibid., p. 417.
19. Kathryn Dodd identifies a link between Sylvia's American tours and her East London work but tantalisingly does not develop this: 'Her tour of the US seems to mark a turning-point in Pankhurst's political development; she began to carve out a place within the Union for her long-held belief in the need to develop a socialist-feminist mass movement; and by 1913 she had established the East London Federation, a working-class base for the WSPU': Kathryn Dodd (ed.), *A Sylvia Pankhurst Reader* (Manchester and New York: Manchester University Press, 1993), p. 32. I suggested some links in Connelly, *Sylvia Pankhurst*, pp. 44–49.
20. For a pioneering and influential study that integrated friendship networks into the writing of suffrage history, see Liz Stanley and Ann Morley, *The Life and Death of Emily Wilding Davison: A Biographical Detective Story* (London: The Women's Press, 1988).
21. [Notebook re. journey to United States: n.d.], ESP Papers, 29.
22. Ibid. Whether or not 'American Letters' remained Sylvia's intended title, it would obviously have been misleading to have published the manuscript under this title today. Since Sylvia did not supply a title page, the title of this book was chosen by myself.
23. Hardie to Pankhurst, 10.3.11, and Pankhurst to Hardie undated letter [late January 1912], ESP Papers, 9.
24. *Labour Leader*, 19 July 1907, p. 49.
25. Kenneth O. Morgan, *Keir Hardie: Radical and Socialist* (London: Weidenfeld & Nicolson, 1975), pp. 190–198.

26. J. Keir Hardie, *India: Impressions and Suggestions* (London: Independent Labour Party, 1909), p. xi.
27. E. Sylvia Pankhurst, 'Some American Impressions', *Votes for Women*, 28 April 1911, p. 495.
28. Hardie to Pankhurst, 27 May 1915, ESP Papers, 9.
29. Hardie's importance as audience is so predominant that the letter to Emmeline Pethick Lawrence has not previously been acknowledged as a source. The International Institute of Social History, Amsterdam has titled the folder containing the typescript 'Chronicle of two visits to Canada and the United States, based on letters to J. Keir Hardie'.
30. *Woman's Journal*, 4 March 1911, p. 66.
31. Amanda Adams, *Performing Authorship in the Nineteenth-Century Transatlantic Lecture Tour* (London and New York: Routledge, 2014), pp. 1–21.
32. Emmeline Pankhurst, *My Own Story* (London: Virago Limited, 1979), p. 2.
33. Thanks to Rachel Holmes for pointing out the similarities with the Marx-Aveling tour to me; on this tour, see Rachel Holmes, *Eleanor Marx: A Life* (London: Bloomsbury, 2014), pp. 268–289; Yvonne Kapp, *Eleanor Marx: Volume II: The Crowded Years (1884–1898)* (London: Lawrence and Wishart, 1976), pp. 135–170.
34. Patricia Greenwood Harrison, *Connecting Links: the British and American Women Suffrage Movements, 1900–1914* (Westport, CT and London: Greenwood, 2000).
35. Pankhurst, *The Suffragette Movement*, p. 493; *New York Times*, 7 April 1911, p. 8.
36. *San Francisco Examiner*, 9 April 1911, p. 66.
37. Robert A. Huff, 'Anne Miller and the Geneva Political Equality Club, 1897–1912', *New York History*, October 1984, Vol. 65, No. 4, p. 341; see Sylvia's place card for the luncheon in the Miller NAWSA Suffrage Scrapbooks, 1897–1911; Scrapbook 9 (1910–1911), *Sylvia Pankhurst, Lochland*. Geneva, New York, 14-Feb-11. Photograph. Retrieved from the Library of Congress, <www.loc.gov/item/rbcmiller002643/>.
38. *Woman's Journal*, 11 March 1911, p. 77.
39. Quoted in *Woman's Journal*, 4 March 1911, p. 66; on her gown at the Lyceum, see *New York Times*, 7 January 1911, p. 3.
40. Pankhurst to Hardie 'train from Brunswick Maine to Boston', ESP Papers, 9.
41. Pankhurst to Hardie, 22 January [1912], ESP Papers, 9.
42. *Hutchinson Gazette*, 21 March 1911, p. 8.
43. *Guthrie Daily Leader*, 2 February 1911, p. 1.
44. Pankhurst to Hardie, 22 January [1912], ESP Papers, 9.
45. Hardie to Pankhurst, 10 March 1911; Pankhurst to Hardie, 22 January [1912], ESP Papers, 9.
46. Pankhurst to Hardie, 'train from Brunswick Maine to Boston', and Pankhurst to Hardie 22 January [1912], ESP Papers, 9.
47. Pankhurst to Hardie undated [late January 1912], ESP Papers, 9.
48. Pankhurst to Hardie, 5 February 1912, ESP Papers, 9.

49. Pankhurst to Hardie undated [late January 1912], ESP Papers, 9.
50. See Angela Y. Davis, *Women, Race & Class* (New York: Vintage Books, 1983), pp. 145–146.
51. See Barbara Green 'Suffragette Celebrity at Home from Abroad: Feminist Periodicals and Transatlantic Circulation' in Leslie Eckel and Clare Elliott (eds), *The Edinburgh Companion to Atlantic Literary Studies* (Edinburgh: Edinburgh University Press, 2016). Although Green employs the term with regard to Sylvia's tours to refer to her enhanced profile in Britain, her notion of suffragette celebrity as popular interest and media attention in the personalities of the campaign, is adopted here.
52. Quoted in *Woman's Journal*, 8 April 1911, p. 107.
53. *Ottawa Journal*, 8 February 1911, p. 10.
54. Quoted in *Woman's Journal*, 22 April 1911, p. 126.
55. *St Louis Star and Times*, 13 March 1911, p. 9.
56. *St Louis Star and Times*, 18 March 1911, p. 1.
57. *St Louis Post-Dispatch*, 18 March 1911, p. 4.
58. *St Louis Star and Times*, 18 March 1911, p. 1.
59. *Woman's Journal*, 22 April 1911, p. 126; see also *St Louis Star and Times*, 18 March 1911, p. 1.
60. *New York Times*, 7 January 1911, p. 3.
61. *Boston Globe*, 11 January 1911, p. 5.
62. *Ottawa Citizen*, 8 February 1911, p. 10; *Ottawa Citizen*, 2 February 1911, p. 12; *Los Angeles Herald*, 4 March 1911, p. 12.
63. *New York Times*, 7 January 1911, p. 3.
64. *Pittston Gazette*, 6 January 1911, p. 4, one of a number of newspapers that ran with this version.
65. *Detroit Free Press* quoted in *Woman's Journal*, 8 April 1911, p. 107.
66. Pankhurst, *The Suffragette Movement*, p. 347.
67. 'Miss Sylvia Pankhurst' promotional brochure, Pankhurst, E. Sylvia, Subject File, 1851–1953, Reel 49, National American Woman Suffrage Association Records, Manuscript Division, Library of Congress, Washington, DC.
68. *Chicago Daily Tribune*, 19 January 1911, p. 1.
69. Pankhurst, *The Suffragette Movement*, p. 347.
70. *Chicago Daily Tribune*, 20 January 1911, p. 3.
71. *Chicago Sunday Tribune* 22 January 1911, p. 59.
72. Elizabeth Robins, *The Convert* (London: The Women's Press Limited; New York: The Feminist Press, 1980), p. 101.
73. *Chicago Sunday Tribune*, 22 January 1911, p. 59.
74. Ibid.
75. Pankhurst, *The Suffragette Movement*, p. 346.
76. Pankhurst to Hardie, 28 January 1912, ESP Papers, 9.
77. *Philadelphia Inquirer*, 3 April 1911, p. 16.
78. *Des Moines Register*, 10 February 1911, p. 6.
79. *Buffalo Courier*, 12 January 1912, p. 3.
80. Pankhurst, *The Suffragette Movement*, p. 219.
81. *Muskogee Times-Democrat*, 16 January 1911, p. 5.

82. *Lawrence Daily Journal-World*, 15 March 1911, p. 1.

83. *St. Louis Post-Dispatch*, 19 March 1911, p. 1.

84. *Los Angeles Times*, 21 January 1911, p. 16.

85. Pankhurst, 'Some American Impressions', *Votes for Women*, 28 April 1911, p. 495.

86. Sandra Stanley Holton '"To Educate Women into Rebellion": Elizabeth Cady Stanton and the Creation of a Transatlantic Network of Radical Suffragists', *American Historical Review*, Vol. 99, No. 4 (October 1994), pp. 1112–1136.

87. Women's Franchise League, *Report of Proceedings at the Inaugural Meeting* (London: 1889), p. 22.

88. Ibid., pp. 25–26.

89. On the League's adoption of a Garrisonian approach to reform see Holton, '"To Educate Women into Rebellion"', pp. 1129–1130; Holton 'Now You See It, Now You Don't: The Women's Franchise League and its Place in Contending Narratives of the Women's Suffrage Movement', in Maroula Joannou and June Purvis (eds), *The Women's Suffrage Movement: New Feminist Perspectives* (Manchester and New York: Manchester University Press, 1998), pp. 17–27. The League's efforts to achieve an amendment to 1894 Local Government Act, which allowed married and unmarried women to vote in local government elections, succeeded in demolishing coverture and its divisive role in the suffrage movement.

90. Women's Franchise League, *Report of Proceedings*, p. 27.

91. Ellen Carol DuBois, *Harriot Stanton Blatch and the Winning of Woman Suffrage* (New Haven, CT and London: Yale University Press, 1997), pp. 98–106; Ellen Carol DuBois, 'Working Women, Class Relations, and Suffrage Militance: Harriot Stanton Blatch and the New York Woman Suffrage Movement, 1894–1909', *Journal of American History*, Vol. 74, No. 1 (June, 1987), pp. 52–53; Sandra Adickes, 'Sisters, Not Demons: The Influence of British Suffragists on the American Suffrage Movement', *Women's History Review*, Vol. 11, No. 4 (2002), pp. 675–677.

92. Harriot Stanton Blatch and Alma Lutz, *Challenging Years: The Memoirs of Harriot Stanton Blatch* (New York: G.P. Putnam's Sons, 1940), p. 136.

93. Ibid.

94. [Harriet [*sic*] Stanton Blatch], unpublished typescript, pp.4, 5, ESP Papers, 128.

95. *Philadelphia Inquirer*, 3 April 1911, p. 16.

96. *Woman's Journal*, 18 March 1911, p. 86.

97. Ibid., 4 March 1911, p. 71.

98. Ida Husted Harper, *History of Woman Suffrage*, Vol. 6 1900–1920 (New York: Arno & The New York Times, 1969), p. 295.

99. Pankhurst to Mrs Wood Park, 14 April 1950 and Pankhurst to Stone Blackwell, n.d. [mid-1930s], General Correspondence, Box 23, National American Woman Suffrage Association Records, Manuscript Division, Library of Congress, Washington, DC.

100. Blatch and Lutz, *Challenging Years*, pp. 137–138; *New York Times*, 29 November 1910, p. 10.
101. Catharine W. McCulloch to Ada Lois James, 29 January 1912, Ada Lois James Papers, Wisconsin Historical Society Library and Archives.
102. For a useful examination of Emmeline Pankhurst's militant narrative which touches on similar themes, see Katja Thieme, 'Uptake and Genre: The Canadian Reception of Suffrage Militancy', *Women's Studies International Forum*, Vol. 29 (2006), pp. 279–288.
103. *New York Times*, 7 January 1911, p. 3.
104. *Oakland Tribune*, 12 March 1911, p. 33.
105. *Los Angeles Herald*, 7 March 1911, p. 12.
106. Ibid. These examples were drawn from a letter to the press in July 1906 by T.D. Benson of the Independent Labour Party which Sylvia quoted in E. Sylvia Pankhurst, *The Suffragette: The History of the Women's Militant Suffrage Movement, 1905–1910* (Boston, MA: The Woman's Journal, 1911), p. 90.
107. *New York Times*, 7 January 1911, p. 3; cf. Pankhurst, *The Suffragette*, pp. 28–29.
108. *Los Angeles Herald*, 7 March 1911, p. 12.
109. Ibid.
110. Quoted, for example, in *Chicago Daily Tribune*, 6 January 1911, p. 5.
111. Pankhurst, *The Suffragette Movement*, p. 253.
112. Dr Jessie Murray and (Henry Noel) Brailsford, *The Treatment of the Women's Deputations by the Metropolitan Police* (London: Woman's Press, 1911).
113. Pankhurst, *The Suffragette Movement*, pp. 342–343.
114. *Detroit Free Press*, quoted in *The Woman's Journal*, 8 April 1911, p. 107.
115. *Times-Democrat*, 2 April 1912, p. 16.
116. Quoted in *Woman's Journal*, 30 March 1912, p. 98.
117. *New York Times*, 4 March 1912, p. 1.
118. Pankhurst, *The Suffragette Movement*, p. 382; *New York Times*, 2 March 1912, p. 2.
119. *New York Times*, 3 March 1912, p. 5.
120. *Fargo Forum, Daily Republican & Moorhead News*, 5 March 1965, p. 5, press cutting in Biography – Misc. File S-2, North Dakota State University archives.
121. *Fargo Daily Courier-News*, 5 February 1912, p. 1.
122. Votes for Women League of North Dakota Minute Book, 4 February 1912, Votes for Women League of North Dakota, Fargo Chapter, Mss 49, Box 1, Folder 3, North Dakota Institute for Regional Studies; Pankhurst to Hardie, 5 February 1912, ESP Papers, 9.
123. Max Eastman, *Love and Revolution: My Journey through an Epoch* (New York: Random House, 1964), pp. 53–56. Darrow Weible would later renounce her belief in 'centralization and socialism' as 'not the solution' in a 1948 interview included in her obituary. See *Fargo Forum*, 5 March 1965, p. 5.

124. Pankhurst to Hardie, 5 February 1912, ESP Papers, 9.
125. Votes for Women League of North Dakota Minute Book, 4 February 1912, North Dakota Institute for Regional Studies.
126. *Milwaukee Leader*, 10 February 1912, p. 1.
127. Ibid., 12 February 1912, p. 1.
128. *Lawrence Daily Journal-World*, 15 March 1911, p. 1.
129. Pankhurst, *The Suffragette Movement*, p. 393.
130. Ibid., p. 385.
131. *Votes for Women*, 26 August 1910, p. 776.
132. Sylvia Pankhurst, 'Women Workers of England', *London Magazine*, 1908, p. 306.
133. On this process see Connelly, *Sylvia Pankhurst*, pp. 26–30.
134. *Votes for Women*, 9 July 1908, p. 296.
135. Quoted in DuBois, *Harriot Stanton Blatch*, p. 115; see also Sandra Adickes, 'Sisters, Not Demons', p. 677.
136. *Votes for Women*, October 1907, p. 6.
137. Richard Whitmore, *Alice Hawkins and the Suffragette Movement in Edwardian Leicester* (Derby: Breedon Books, 2007), pp. 57–60; Sylvia's research was published as Sylvia Pankhurst, 'The Potato-Pickers', *Votes for Women*, 28 January 1909, p. 294; 'Pit Brow Women', *Votes for Women*, 11 August 1911, p. 730; 'Women Farm Labourers in the Border Counties', *Votes for Women*, 26 August 1910, pp. 776–777.
138. *New York Call*, 7 January 1911, p. 3.
139. Ibid.
140. *New York Times*, 7 January 1911, p. 3.
141. *Los Angeles Herald*, 8 March 1911, p. 7.
142. Ibid., 9 March 1911, p. 5.
143. *Fargo Daily Courier-News*, 5 February 1912, p. 6.
144. Pankhurst to Hardie, 5 February 1912, pp. 26–27, ESP Papers, 9.
145. *Fargo Daily Courier-News*, 5 February 1912.
146. *Votes for Women*, 16 February 1912, p. 305.
147. *Detroit Free Press*, quoted in *Woman's Journal*, 8 April 1911, p. 107.
148. Women's Trade Union League of Chicago, *Official Report of the Strike Committee: Chicago Garment Workers' Strike, Oct 29–February 18 1911* (Chicago, IL: The League, 1911), p. 8.
149. *Inter Ocean*, 22 January 1911, p. 7.
150. Philip S. Foner, *Women and the American Labor Movement: From Colonial Times to the Eve of World War I* (New York: Free Press, 1979), p. 353.
151. *Chicago Sunday Tribune*, 22 January 1911, p. 7.
152. *Official Report of the Strike Committee*, p. 30.
153. Ibid., p. 20.
154. Colette A. Hyman, 'Labor Organizing and Female-institution Building: The Chicago Women's Trade Union League, 1904-24', in Ruth Milkman (ed.), *Women, Work and Protest: A Century of US Women's Labor History* (Boston, MA and London: Routledge & Kegan Paul, 1985), pp. 26–27.

155. *Life and Labor*, January 1911, pp. 9, 4; *Official Report of the Strike Committee*, p. 35.

156. *Life and Labor*, January 1911, p. 4.

157. *Woman's Journal*, quoted in Harrison, *Connecting Links*, p. 178.

158. *Chicago Sunday Tribune*, 29 January 1911, p. 7.

159. Pankhurst to Hardie, undated letter [late January 1912], ESP Papers, 9.

160. Pankhurst, *The Suffragette Movement*, p. 349.

161. Hyman, 'Labour Organizing', pp. 24–25.

162. Jane Addams, *Twenty Years at Hull-House* (Urbana and Chicago, IL: University of Illinois Press, 1990), p. 135.

163. Les Garner, 'Suffragism and Socialism: Sylvia Pankhurst 1903–1914', in Ian Bullock and Richard Pankhurst (eds), *Sylvia Pankhurst: From Artist to Anti-Fascist* (Basingstoke: Macmillan, 1992), p. 71.

164. *Troy Standard Press*, 29 March 1912, press cutting in Harriot Stanton Blatch scrapbook, Vol. III, Reel 1, Harriot Stanton Blatch Papers, Manuscript Division, Library of Congress, Washington, DC.

165. *Milwaukee Journal*, 29 January 1912, p. 1.

166. *Evening Wisconsin*, 29 January 1912, p. 1.

167. *Troy Standard Press*, 29 March 1912, press cutting in Harriot Stanton Blatch scrapbook, Vol. III, Reel 1, Library of Congress.

168. For a detailed account, see David von Drehle, *Triangle: The Fire That Changed America* (New York: Grove Press, 2003).

169. Quoted in Annelise Orleck, *Common Sense and a Little Fire: Women and Working-Class Politics in the United States, 1900–1965* (Chapel Hill, NC and London: University of North Carolina Press, 1995), p. 131.

170. *Troy Standard Press*, 29 March 1912, press cutting in Harriot Stanton Blatch scrapbook, Vol. III, Reel 1, Library of Congress.

171. *Troy Record*, 30 March 1912, press cutting in Harriot Stanton Blatch scrapbook, Vol. III, Reel 1, Library of Congress.

172. *Utica Sunday Tribune*, 31 March 1912, press cutting in Harriot Stanton Blatch scrapbook, Vol. III, Reel 1, Library of Congress.

173. Ibid.

174. *Boston Globe*, 3 April 1912, p. 8; *New York Times*, 3 April 1912, p. 8; *New-York Tribune*, 3 April 1912, p. 7.

175. Pankhurst, *The Suffragette Movement*, p. 403.

176. Pankhurst to Wald, 30 April 1912, Lillian D. Wald Papers, New York Public Library [henceforward NYPL]; Pankhurst to Addams published in *Woman's Journal*, 25 May 1912, p. 161.

177. Moskowitz to Pankhurst, 17 May 1912, Lillian D. Wald Papers, NYPL.

178. Peabody to Wald, 14 May 1912, Lillian D. Wald Papers, NYPL.

179. *Woman's Journal*, 25 May 1912, p. 161.

180. Pankhurst to Wald, 30 April 1912, Lillian D. Wald Papers, NYPL.

181. Wald to Pankhurst, 14 June 1912, Lillian D. Wald Papers, NYPL.

182. Pankhurst, *The Suffragette Movement*, p. 385.

183. Alice Lewisohn Crowley, *The Neighborhood Playhouse: Leaves from a Theatre Scrapbook* (New York: Theatre Arts Books, 1959), p. 38.

184. Pankhurst, *The Suffragette Movement*, p. 439.
185. Pankhurst, *The Suffragette Movement*, pp. 524–525.
186. Pankhurst to Belmont, 1 May 1914, Papers of, and relating to, Sylvia Pankhurst and other family members, 7ESP/6, Women's Library, LSE; see also Harrison, *Connecting Links*, pp. 200–202.
187. Pankhurst to The Editor, Century Company Records, Manuscripts and Archives Division, General Correspondence, Pankhurst, Estelle Sylvia, *New York Public Library Digital Collections*, 1881-1917. http://digitalcollections. nypl.org/items/8def30b0-c1b5-0135-65e5-215293e09ed1; Marshall to Smyth, 14 August 1913 and Marshall to Pankhurst, 18 August 1913, ESP Papers, 226.
188. *New York Times*, 28 July 1913, p. 2; on payment, see Marshall to Smyth, 14 August 1913, ESP Papers, 226.
189. E. Sylvia Pankhurst 'Forcibly Fed: The Story of My Four Weeks in Holloway Gaol', *McClure's Magazine*, August 1913, pp. 87–93.
190. Ibid., p. 542.
191. Letter quoted in *Democrat and Chronicle* (Rochester, NY), 17 April 1914, p. 24.
192. Pankhurst, *The Suffragette Movement*, p. 543.
193. Emerson to Pankhurst, n.d., ESP Papers, 183.
194. Barbara Winslow, *Sylvia Pankhurst: Sexual Politics and Political Activism* (London: UCL Press Limited, 1996), p. 34; Shirley Harrison, *Sylvia Pankhurst: A Crusading Life, 1882–1960* (London: Aurum Press, 2003), pp. 161–162.
195. See Katherine H. Adams and Michael L. Keene, *Alice Paul and the American Suffrage Campaign* (Urbana, IL: University of Illinois Press, 2008), Chapters 7 and 8.
196. Ibid., p. 199.
197. Pankhurst to Stone Blackwell letters dated 5 September 1932, 25 November 1932, 2 March 1936, General Correspondence, 1839–1961, Box 23, National American Woman Suffrage Association Records, Library of Congress.
198. [Harriet [*sic*] Stanton Blatch], unpublished typescript, p. 4, p. 5, ESP Papers, 128.
199. E. Sylvia Pankhurst to W.E.B. Du Bois, 11 October 1946, W.E.B. Du Bois Papers (MS 312). Special Collections and University Archives, University of Massachusetts Amherst Libraries. Accessed at: http://credo.library. umass.edu/view/full/mums312-b111-i470.

SYLVIA PANKHURST'S TEXT
AND EDITOR'S INTRODUCTIONS

Preface

The following pages were in the first place written in the form of letters to a friend* in England during the course of two journeys through the United States and Canada. They were intended neither to give a general review of my impressions of America as a whole, nor a chronicle of my travels there, but to deal with certain particular experiences of people, places and institutions which interested me so much that I felt impelled to write of them.

In reaching any foreign country, one is immediately conscious of an all-pervading atmosphere that is markedly different to that of one's own land, but this characteristic atmosphere is largely indefinable, and one's appreciation of it is continually affected by the circumstances of one's contact with it.

The fact that I was a militant suffragette prompted people, wherever I went in America, to show me over prisons and reformative institutions and to take me to places where women worked.

The same fact brought me many other experiences. The morning of my first reaching New York, January 5th, 1911, was terribly cold, and owing to the congested state of the harbour many hours passed before we could land. Suddenly the Press swooped down upon me, all eager for copy, and insisted on my standing to be photographed right in the teeth of a bitter wind such as in England we do not know, whilst all the other passengers stood round to watch.

That first day New York seemed to me a grey dreary city, with its huge buildings, heavy, gloomy and intensely ugly, wrapped in a withering sullen cold without, and all breathless heat and glaring jarring lights and noise within. How changed it was when, still in the frozen winter, I saw it translated by the brilliant sun, everything a-sparkle, everywhere crowding vivacious life. Seen in far vistas, its great buildings then seemed to me like Venetian palaces, which, in proportion, tower as hugely over the narrow *calli* and *canalli* as do those great flats and warehouses over the

---

* James Keir Hardie (1856–1915), the former leader of the Labour Party and Labour MP for Merthyr Tydfil and, for Chapter 7, Emmeline Pethick Lawrence (1867–1954). See Introduction, pp. 9–11.

broad streets. I have often wondered that with their love of splendour and their frequent journeyings in Italy, the New Yorkers, instead of arranging the windows of their vast houses as mechanically as a chessboard, do not group them and enclose them with richly sculptured arches and columns, and inlays of precious marble, as the Venetians did.*

But even as it is to-day, how wonderful is New York from some high place at twilight, when the lofty buildings of commerce are fading into obscurity, and one sees, not their great walls, faint and shadowy, but their thousand thousand windows like jewels of fire. Their golden patterning and the blue fading light cast a compelling glamour over this city of sub-stantial and materialistic trade. It becomes ethereal as a city of dreams, beautiful and calm as the home of supermen.

Seeing the city thus, it is strange to remember it on a sad day of mourning, when rain poured from a grey sky, and a long procession of saddened workgirls marched in their poor black garments, to show honour and respect to their comrades burnt to death in an awful fire – a fire that was fatal because ordinary means of exit were inadequate, fire escapes were too short to reach the factory's monstrous height, and when the girls sprang from the roof, their tender bodies came hurtling down with an impelling force, that tore the sheets held out for them to shreds.[†]

As one travels over that vast continent of America, teeming with wondrous natural resources, with endless possibilities of new growth, one sees, as in our older and more crowded land, everywhere the cruel waste of precious human energy, and the crushing out of fragile tender things. One sees, perhaps more clearly than in any other country, new ideals of civilization striving with the old. The sharp impersonal pitiless commercial enterprise, that everywhere crushes out the slothful inex-actitudes and rough spasmodic kindlinesses and brutalities of the past,

---

* In 1902, Sylvia, then a 20-year-old art student, was awarded the Proctor Travelling Studentship, the top prize at Manchester School of Art, and chose to stay in Venice. Like New York, Venice had a profound effect upon Sylvia. Compare her description of New York in this text – 'a city of dreams' – in the changing light, with her recollections of Venice: 'first seen in the soft, iridescent gold of the sinking sun; a wondrous city of fairest carving, reflected in gleaming waters swirled to new patterning by every passing gondola. Venice in the brief, violet twilight; Venice in the mournful loveliness of pale marble palaces, rising in the velvet darkness of the night … Venice, O city of dreaming magic!': Pankhurst, *The Suffragette Movement*, p. 160.

† A reference to the fire that broke out on 25 March 1911 at the Triangle Shirtwaist Company factory, killing 146 workers. See Introduction, pp. 46–47.

and would in its turn make the human beings that it uses ever more machine-like, one now sees faced with the new up-springing of public thought and action, that shall place higher than all else the happiness and development of human lives.

It is because the things with which they deal are symptomatic of growth from the waste and hardship of the old ill-regulated past to the splendid hopes and promises of the future, that these chapters have been written.

E. SYLVIA PANKHURST

6.   Around 300,000 people lined the streets of New York and a further 100,000 marched in the funeral procession on 5 April 1911 to pay tribute to the 146 workers killed in the fire at the Triangle Shirtwaist Factory. Sylvia Pankhurst was among those present and her Preface recalls the day 'when rain poured from a grey sky, and a long procession of saddened workgirls marched in their poor black garments, to show honour and respect to their comrades burnt to death in an awful fire'. (Courtesy of the Kheel Center for Labor-Management Documentation & Archives, Cornell University)

1. A Strike of Laundry Workers in New York

EDITOR'S INTRODUCTION

Sylvia Pankhurst's second visit to North America began on 11 January 1912 when the SS *Oceanic* docked in New York. By the very next day, Sylvia had made contact and publicly identified herself with the citywide laundry workers' strike, a decision that reflected her increasing determination to connect the suffrage struggle with the women's labour movement.

The strike, which had started on 1 January, was conducted by a largely female workforce who fought a vibrant campaign, picketing outside the laundries against the efforts of hundreds of organised strike breakers, the constant threat of arrest and the bitterly cold winter conditions that Sylvia recalls here. They attracted the support of the Women's Trade Union League, who established a headquarters at the Harlem Arcade, described by Sylvia as a 'dirty and dingy' dancehall.

On 12 January the League organised a parade of automobiles to drive through the laundry districts adorned with pink and black banners proclaiming: '200 Laundries Organized', 'We Are Striking for More Pay and a Shorter Day', and 'Don't be a Scab'.[1] That afternoon, at a meeting in the Harlem Arcade attended by around two hundred women strikers, Sylvia spoke alongside leading industrial organiser Elizabeth Gurley Flynn, Mary Dreier, the president of the New York Women's Trade Union League, and Margaret Sanger, at that time the secretary of the New York Women's Socialist Committee. Flynn later recalled the 'laundry workers' strike meeting, with her [Sanger] and with Sylvia Pankhurst, the British suffragist' during which Flynn called upon the strikers to stand together and to try and persuade the engineers to strike to strengthen the struggle.[2] Sylvia, meanwhile, 'urged them not only to stand for their industrial rights but for political equality as well. She told them of a recent strike in England and how the strikers there had won success through holding together.'[3] Therefore, whilst Sylvia formally adhered to the WSPU doctrine of urging the importance of political rights, she avoided the WSPU leadership's assertion of the primacy of the political struggle and often dismissive approach towards labour struggles by referring to a successful example of women's industrial action in Britain. This was almost certainly the strike of women working in the packing factories around Bermondsey in August 1911. At the time, Sylvia demonstrated her interest in the details of women's exploitation and their forms of resistance by interviewing three hundred of the strikers about their pay.[4]

Sylvia adopts the same interest in diligently listening to and recording the experiences of working women in this chapter; in fact, she does not even mention her own role as the speaker at the strikers' meeting. Sylvia's combination of empirical and observational detail recalls her 'working women of England' project of 1907, in which text and painting recorded the women's shared experiences of pay, conditions and labour, alongside their individual appearances, characters and relationships. In this chapter, Sylvia's description of an 18-year-old laundry worker is characteristic of her approach. 'She might have been anybody's daughter': Sylvia asserts the laundry worker's individual humanity and, with her artist's eye, captures in vivid detail the colours and textures of her hair, skin and clothes, before reciting the deadening timetable of work to which she is subjected. In the very fabric of Sylvia's writing, the realisation of individuality is integral to the revolt against collectivised exploitation, collapsing, at least in textual form, the WSPU's dichotomy of individual political rights and collective economic struggle.

At the meeting on 12 January, Sylvia told the strikers that 'she knew the conditions which brought about the strike and that it was justified', and this chapter certainly bears out her claim.[5] She evidently listened intently to the laundry workers, her enumeration of the excessive hours worked closely correlates with the contemporary report of the strike provided by Mary Dreier.[6] Using the laundry workers' testimony, Sylvia provides a graphic description of overheated, steam-filled workplaces, the lack of changing rooms and the abusive language foremen and employers used towards their workers.[7]

Sylvia's concern with racism as a mechanism for sowing divisions in the workforce and intensifying exploitation is expressed frequently in the chapter. Her insistence upon the large component of American women in the laundries echoes the speech she delivered at the strikers' meeting in which she stated that '[i]t was a common argument ... that low wages were due to the competition of foreign labor. But in the case of the laundries this did not hold.'[8] As Sylvia states in the chapter, the widespread presence of native-born workers undermined the racist and sexist myth that 'the American woman does not need to work in a factory, and is always well paid and well cared for.' Sylvia's approach blamed employers, and not foreign-born workers, for poor pay and conditions. She reinforces this point by recording the evidence of a (presumably American-born) laundry worker – that two Italian women are paid less than she is for the same work. The solution to these divisions is suggested towards the end of the chapter which describes a white American, a black American and an Italian-born worker united across racial boundaries in a collective struggle against the laundry bosses.

In the end, despite the State Board of Mediation and Arbitration's recommendation that the employers grant the strikers' demands on hours, pay, safety measures and union recognition, the strike was defeated on 31 January 1912. Only six laundries had recognised the union and conceded wage increases; the rest replaced the workers who had the audacity to strike with strikebreaking labour.[9] Sylvia only records a moment in this month-long struggle before it was defeated, and it testifies to the courage of the strikers, and Sylvia's determination that their voices be heard.

A STRIKE OF LAUNDRY WORKERS IN NEW YORK

We went in from the frozen snow of the street, and a hot foetid breath met us. The dingy entrance passage was without furnishings, its walls were scarred, and its carpetless boards were darkened by long worn dirt. A group of poorly-clad men and women stood at the foot of the stairs, and around a door opening from the passage. We passed through them, and into a large room as dirty and dreary as the entrance. At either end was a drinking bar, and the smell of stale spirits filled the air. Cheap bent-wood chairs and small tables were huddled aimlessly together. Various red white and blue posters were hung up to announce forthcoming dances, for this was a New York 'Casino', or 'dance hall', which had been hired for the time being as the headquarters of the laundry workers, who were on strike.

Some twenty or thirty of the strikers were sitting here together. We asked one of them, a girl of 18, to tell us about the work.

She might have been anybody's daughter. Social distinctions had no place beside her. I saw, as I looked at her, a child in an English country lane with her hands full of primroses. The texture of her fair clear skin was as flawless as the imagined flowers. Her abundant hair, coloured like straw, was put back as simply as it should be with those rounded cheeks, delicately arched eyebrows, and quiet wide blue eyes. She was tall and slender, and wore a plain black dress, a white knitted woollen jacket, hanging unbuttoned, and a soft black scarf that fell loosely about her lovely throat. She sat inclining gently towards us, and with a calm sweet gravity, and low, well articulated accents told her tale.

She used to be a 'sales lady' at a 'store' in Albany, and earned 6 dollars a week (24 shillings.) – a wage not worth nearly so much as it would be in this country, owing to the higher cost of living in America.* On coming with her people to New York recently, she was obliged, through lack of other openings, to go into Langfelder's Laundry. Work there was supposed to start on Mondays at 1 p.m., and to continue until eleven o'clock at night. The timetable for the week was as follows: –

Monday 1 p.m. to 11 p.m.
Tuesday 7 a.m. to 8 p.m.
Wednesday 7 a.m. to 8 p.m.
Thursday 7 a.m. to 8 p.m.
Friday 7 a.m. to 8 .p.m.
Saturday 7 a.m. to 3 p.m.

This would mean a 70 hour week, but these hours were often indefinitely prolonged, and nothing was paid for overtime. Half an hour was allowed for the mid-day meal, and this was the only interval permitted during the day, even when the work was carried on until the small hours of the next morning. The women of all ages who were paid a fixed wage in this laundry, got from 4 dollars (16/-) to 6 ½ dollars (26 shillings) a week. This girl, who was engaged in damping collars, got 5 dollars (£1). The piece workers, starchers and others earned more.

Another girl, who was employed at Preuss's Laundry as a 'taker off' at the mangle told us that she was paid 6 dollars a week. She said that two Italian girls who worked beside her only got 4 dollars. She supposed they did not know they could get more. She herself had been offered 4 dollars, but had refused to take less than six. She worked from 7.30 a.m. til 9 or 10 p.m. every day, except Saturday, when work stopped at 3 or 4 p.m. She said that she had been at work in the laundry when a procession of strikers went past. She had stopped work at once, but the doors were

---

* {SP} See appendix to Chapter 2.

locked, and she was told that she could not go. She had then picked up an iron bar, and declared that she would fight her way out. On thus showing her determination, she had been released.

Two women employed as starchers at the Brunswick Laundry, one of whom had worked there 25 years, told us that they began work at 1 p.m. on Monday and went on until 1 a.m. the next morning. On Tuesday they started at 7.30 (6 ½ hours after they had left off), and continued once more till the following 1 a.m. The same thing happened on Wednesday. Thursday they occasionally started at 9 a.m., but more often at 7.30 as before, and finished at 10 or 11 p.m.. This was their weekly timetable: –

Monday 1 p.m. to 1 a.m. (Tuesday).
Tuesday 7.30 a.m. to 1 a.m. (Wednesday)
Wednesday 7.30 a.m. to 1 a.m. (Thursday)
Thursday 7.30 a.m. or occasionally 9 a.m. to 10 or 11 p.m.
Friday 9 a.m. to 6 p.m. or 8 p.m.
Saturday 7.30 a.m. or 9 a.m. to about 4 p.m.*

The week's total therefore varied from 71 to 75 hours per week, with only 3 hours per week deducted for meals, for as, in the other laundries the half hour for luncheon was the only interval allowed each day! A few years of this horribly excessive labour in the heat and steam of the laundry must break down the strongest constitution. These women starchers were paid by the piece, 7 cents a dozen for shirts and 1 ¼ cents a dozen for collars. Some could make 16 to 18 dollars a week, some only

---

* This information correlates with that cited by the Women's Trade Union League. The journal *Life and Labour* quoted Sarah Smith, who had worked in laundries for 25 years: 'This is the way we worked: On Monday we began at one o'clock, and we worked until one o'clock that night. Sometimes the boss gave us supper money and sometimes not. It was oftener not. Then Tuesday morning we began at half-past seven. There was just time enough to tumble into bed and out again. That day we worked until one o'clock at night. It was the same on Wednesday, but on Thursday, maybe, we would get a rest – Thursday, maybe, we stopped at 10:30 at night. Friday we generally had an hour's rest in the morning. Saturday was a real easy day, and we'd get off at three in the afternoon': Mary E. Dreier, 'To Wash or Not to Wash: Ay, There's the Rub: The New York Laundry Strike', *Life and Labour*, March 1912, p. 69. Compare also with the Union's information on collar starchers' piece work at 'Laundry C':
'Mondays, 1 P.M. to 12:30 or 1 A.M.
Tuesdays and Wednesdays, 7:30 A.M. to 12:30 A.M. or 1 A.M.
Thursday, 7:30 A.M. to 10 P.M.
Friday, 9 to 11 A.M. and 3 to 4 P.M.': *New York Times*, 13 January 1912, p. 7.

9 dollars. Then there were various deductions. Any work that was spoilt, perhaps through its being dropped on the floor, or in any other way, had to be done over again for nothing. Then there was what was called the 'overcount'. Each woman counted her neighbour's work in order to find out how much she had earned, but before she was paid the work was again counted, and she frequently found that one dollar, two dollars, three dollars, or even more was deducted from the sum to which she believed she was entitled. The women claimed that if a recount were necessary, it should be made in their presence, in order that they might be satisfied that it was correct.

A woman employed in another laundry, who had been a widow for eight years and had two children of school age, said that she earned 7 dollars a week, and gave as her working timetable: – Monday, 2 p.m. to 6.30 p.m.; Tuesday, 7.30 a.m. to 7 p.m.; Wednesday, 7.30 a.m. to 7 or 7.30 p.m.; Thursday, 7.30 a.m. to 9 or 9.30 p.m.; Friday, 7.30 a.m. to 9 or 9.30 p.m.; Saturday, 7.30 a.m. to 6 or 7. These times, she said, were frequently exceeded. Here, again, one half hour at lunch time was the only interval, and this appeared to be the general rule in the laundries. Many further enquiries elicited but slight variations in the specimen timetables for the week that I have already given. There was general complaint in regard to the sanitary arrangements of the laundries. Few supplied any room where the women could change or keep extra clothing, though this was really a necessity in New York, owing to the fact that the cold outside was very much more intense than anything that we have in England, whilst the heat inside the laundries was, of course, exceedingly great. Many women complained of the bad language used by the 'bosses' and foremen.

When the strike began on New Year's Day 1911,* the laundry workers, two-thirds of whom were said to be women and girls, and one-third men, were quite unorganised, but a Trade Union was quickly formed, and the workers joined in large numbers. Miss Dreier† and other energetic

---

* This is an error; it should read 1912. The laundry workers' strike in New York began on 1 January 1912.

† Mary Dreier (1875–1963) was, at the time Sylvia met her, president of the New York Women's Trade Union League. Sylvia and Dreier spoke together on 12 January 1912 at the Union's headquarters, 211 East 124th Street in New York in support of the laundry workers' strike. See *New York Times* which reported 'Miss Pankhurst and Miss Dreier Exhort Laundry Workers' (13 January 1912, p. 7).

members of the Women's Trade Union League took an important part in this work.

The demands which were being put forward on behalf of the strikers include a 10 hour day for all workers, the raising of some of the time and piece work rates, and the provision of better sanitary and cloak room accommodation.

Whilst we had been talking to the women adjoining, a meeting had begun in the dance hall proper, where there was a stage at one end and some tawdry decorations upon the walls. Looking down upon the crowd of faces, we were again struck by the refinement of the women, both in dress and general bearing. A large proportion of them were certainly American, and it was interesting to notice this, because one is frequently told that over work, under pay, and bad conditions of employment amongst women are confined to the foreign immigrants, and that the American woman does not need to work in a factory, and is always well paid and well cared for. Of the men in this meeting, a larger proportion appeared to be foreign, and their dress and physique seemed, on the whole, to be poorer, though it is very difficult of course, to generalise in such matters.

As we entered the meeting, a bouquet of flowers was just being presented to a woman, an American citizen, just released from prison – one of the strike pickets who was to be tried for obstruction, and who had been arrested and kept in prison for two days before bail could be procured. She replied in a short speech, which was received with great cheering, and immediately afterwards an enthusiastic welcome was given to a negro man strike picket, who also was released from prison that day. Then an Italian, speaking with impassioned eloquence in his native tongue, as a stimulus and encouragement to all present, called upon them to remember the hundreds of British women who have suffered violence and imprisonment in the cause of their Enfranchisement.

It was clear that the laundry strikers would need to bring tremendous courage and determination to their struggle, for American police methods are harsh and cruel and picketing from six o'clock in the morning [in] that bitter weather, must truly have been an awful thing.

2. Laundries from the Inside

EDITOR'S INTRODUCTION

Sylvia continues her exploration of laundries in this chapter, shifting her focus from New York City to Milwaukee in Wisconsin. Eighteen days after embarking at New York, Sylvia arrived in Milwaukee from Chicago on Monday, 29 January to participate in the women's suffrage referendum campaign (see Introduction, p. 29) and was greeted at the railway station by Mary Swain Wagner, from the American Suffragettes who had organised the visit, Martha C. Heide, who was to assist with translation for German speakers, and a group of reporters anxious to scoop a first interview with the English suffragette. Sylvia told the *Evening Wisconsin* that she was 'going to make study of industrial conditions in Milwaukee during her four days here'.[1] Whether or not she already had her American book in mind, this at least reflects her determination to spend her time observing conditions in a city with a socialist council, as she told Keir Hardie: 'From the moment I knew that I was going to Milwaukee I became desperately anxious to know what the Socialist administration was doing and what these fortunate people who had this wonderful opportunity given them were like.'[2]

Consequently, Sylvia was taken to the House of Correction on the next morning, which is discussed in Chapter 5, and to two laundries in the early afternoon, the subject of this chapter. Although Sylvia does not write explicitly on the suffrage campaign in Milwaukee, her discussion of the laundries was trialled in her suffrage speech there and was inextricably linked to her understanding of the interconnection of women's economic and political disadvantages.

Sylvia was taken to the laundries in a car driven by a Miss Miller, whom Sylvia regarded as somewhat naïve and does not mention in the chapter, and Rosa M. Perdue, an editorial writer for the anti-socialist *Milwaukee Journal* whom Sylvia recalls as an unwelcome companion.[3] Together, they visited the Ideal Laundry on Wells Street, which Perdue regarded as an exemplary institution, and the New Model Laundry on State Street, presented as its unwholesome contrast. Sylvia, however, was impressed by neither and her disagreement with Perdue reveals divergent priorities amongst contemporary feminists.[4] Perdue, herself a former factory inspector who had also worked for Addams's Hull House, approved of the efficiency achieved by the Ideal Laundry – revealingly, her report in the *Journal* of her day with Sylvia would disparage a sewing hall they went to see later where 'the girls are not driven, for one sat in her place in front of her machine reading a book of fiction.'[5] By contrast, Sylvia objected to the monotony and inhumanity of the Taylorist scientific management regime imposed by the Ideal on their workers. Sylvia's determination to hear from the women workers themselves is evident in this chapter and even in Perdue's report which acknowledged 'Miss Pankhurst asked innumerable questions, and apparently made a genuine effort to get the point of view of the employes [*sic*] wherever we went.'[6] However, Perdue's article, titled 'Conditions Please Miss Pankhurst', entirely suppressed Sylvia's unease; her claim that Sylvia 'was evidently surprised to find such good conditions [at the Ideal], and girls so healthy, happy and contented', contrasts starkly with every word of this chapter.

In her speech at the Pabst Theatre on her last evening in Milwaukee, Sylvia recalled the unsanitary conditions at the New Model Laundry in words almost identical to those in this chapter: 'The women were ironing over irons from which the noxious gases poured up into their faces. There were pools of water underneath the feet of some of the workers.'[7] One solution was to afford women greater supervisory power: 'The laws you have aren't complied with, and that is because you have not enough women factory inspectors.'[8] Sylvia placed far greater emphasis, however, on empowering the working women themselves, by insisting upon equal pay for equal work. Her outline of the current situation implied that women's low pay was a hindrance to any socialist administration since it served to increase inequality: 'When you underpay your women workers, the community has to step in and make up the difference in charity gifts, while the employers grow rich and the rents go up.'[9] To demonstrate the importance of remedying this situation, Sylvia had to confront the assumptions either that women's wages were not relied upon as a main source of income or that the worst examples of exploitation were aberrations, confined only to recently arrived immigrant workers. Sylvia furnished her speech with examples to prove neither assumption was true, recalling the poor conditions of the laundry workers in New York and citing figures from Ruby Stewart's recently published report *Women's Wages in Milwaukee*; the findings of the latter are examined in Appendix A of this chapter, supported by Keir Hardie's comparative study of the cost of living in America and Britain for the benefit of British readers.[10] Stewart's study of 1,189 women factory workers, Sylvia told the audience at the Pabst Theatre, showed that women's wages were far from peripheral: 'Only six out of the 1,189 work for pin money, and of the others most are supporting either children or other relatives.'[11] Moreover, women's low pay was actually exacerbating households' reliance on their wages, since employers were replacing male workers 'because women do the same work cheaply'.[12] Sylvia (erroneously) claimed that equal pay laws had already been enacted in Australia and New Zealand, two countries where women had the vote, to support her argument that 'votes for women would be a prerequisite to getting equal pay for equal work of men and women.'[13]

This chapter elaborates on the themes Sylvia discussed in the Pabst Theatre in which she sought to prove her argument to Mayor Seidel (see Introduction, p. 39) that women 'need the power to work out our own salvation' by demonstrating women's suffrage was not a marginal concern, but rather a means of tackling widening social inequality.

LAUNDRIES FROM THE INSIDE

It was called 'The Ideal' and was supposed to be a model laundry. Miss Perdue – an ex-factory Inspector – told me that it was the best in Milwaukee. No doubt, as laundries go, it was well managed, but it made me feel sick at heart. The air was hot and the work horribly mechanical and sub-divided to the smallest detail. The workers were absolutely silent, they moved as though they were a part of the machinery.

There were many more women than men in the laundry and the men were only employed in the more highly paid operations.

The women's wages ranged from four dollars (16/ shillings -) to eight and a half dollars (34/ shillings) a week of fifty five hours.*

I was allowed to speak to the women and I asked them about their work. Most of them *said* that they liked it and did not find it hard; but

---

* {SP} The purchasing power of this sum is of course very much lower in America than in England. See Appendix B at [the] end of [the] chapter.

they all looked weary, they spoke in dull expressionless tones and I knew that they were just saying what they thought was wise.

One girl about twenty years of age, was standing at a machine and was constantly feeding it with collars of a certain size and shape. She simply handed the collars to it and they were sucked in and then fell out on the other side smooth and glossy. 'Are you not tired of doing that one thing all day long?' I asked her, 'I should just think I am!' she answered eagerly, when my words were still only half said. She told me that she earned five dollars (£1) a week, and that she had difficulty in living on this small sum, as her husband was out of work. They had been married a short time only and he had lost his employment almost immediately afterwards. That was why she had come to work in the laundry.

Miss Perdue, the ex-Inspector, pointed out to me that the law in regard to lavatory accommodation was complied with. She thought the arrangement here exceptionally good. It consisted of two closets, placed side by side and opening straight from the main room of the laundry, where the men and women were working. On one door was the word 'Gentlemen' and on the other 'Women'. I wondered whether the difference of title was in any way indicative of the relative positions of the men and women employees.

* * *

The 'New Method' laundry was kept by two brothers.* Miss Perdue told me that they were growing rich. She said that one of the brothers had a very bad temper and that if he chanced to be in when we called, we should not be allowed to see the laundry.

The other brother, a dirty, half-dressed, unsavoury-looking individual, met us at the door.

'Have you come to take me for a drive?' he asked, grinning and leering at us. When he heard that we wanted to see the laundry he said indifferently: 'Oh yes, you can go in'.

We passed through the shop into a long low room behind. It was very hot and the smell of gas seemed almost overpowering. The gas irons were all leaking terribly and the fumes were pouring up into the faces of the women who used them.

---

*   Sylvia has evidently misremembered the name of the laundry, which was New Model rather than New Method.

All the machines were old and stiff and hard to work. In using those with a treadle, the worker was obliged to press with all her force and give also several shakes and pushes to the machine, to make it perform a single downward movement. To prevent their fingers being caught in some of the machines the women had to practise constant vigilance.

There appeared to be no young girls in this laundry. The women's wages ranged from five to seven dollars a week. All the women were very poorly dressed, and that fact proved their poverty, even more than it would in England. They all looked ill and jaded and bitterly complained of the heat and the escaping gas.

Downstairs in the basement, where the washing and starching was done, the conditions were, perhaps, even worse. The ceiling was very low and ventilation was only possible at the extreme end of the long narrow room. Dense clouds of steam enveloped everything, almost hiding some of the workers from view, and great jets of it were discharging themselves from pipes into the room. On the uneven floor were pools of water. Two dilapidated and neglected water closets, the unlabelled doors of which were without fastenings, added the final evidence that all factory laws and regulations were being impudently defied.

APPENDIX A TO CHAPTER 2

Notes on Wages

When I first landed in America I was told by numbers of people that women were not sweated there and that practically all the women factory workers were foreigners. Anyone who makes even a superficial investigation must soon learn, as I did, that such statements are quite untrue.

The report prepared by Miss Ruby Stewart for the consumer's League of Wisconsin and published by the Milwaukee Socialist City Council gives a very useful analysis of the wages earned by 1189 girls [and] women in fifteen different factories and shows the nationalities to which these workers belonged. These women and girls, worked in sweet, shoe, paperbox, glove, envelope and clothing factories and shops. 837, or 70 per cent of them were born in the United States and the majority in Milwaukee. 65 per cent of the American born girls were German Americans. The total population of Milwaukee is of course largely German American. Amongst the following population, though many nationalities were represented, the Germans, numbering 147 and the Poles numbering 142, were in the majority. Not more than a dozen out of the 1189 women and girls were unable to speak English.

The wages varied from two dollars to eleven dollars a week, except in three cases, the first of which earned twelve, the second fifteen, and the third eighteen dollars a week. 153 workers, or thirteen per cent of the whole, received more than eight dollars a week, but 236, or nineteen per cent, received less than four dollars a week. There was no great difference between the wages of girls and women. Thirty one per cent of the forty four women over thirty years of age earned less than eight dollars a week and 27 of these women were supporting their entire household. One of them had to keep herself and six children on seven dollars, another had to maintain five children on five dollars. 875 of the total 1189 contributed the whole of their earnings to the family income, and only six were working merely for pocket money. One girl of fifteen was the sole support of a paralyzed father, a half blind mother, and several little brothers and sisters. Miss Stewart says that a work girl living alone *can* exist in Milwaukee on four and a half dollars a week, but only under the most miserable circumstances.

An investigation was also made into the conditions of 230 families engaged in home work. 81 of these workers were born in America and 149 were born elsewhere. 173 of the women were married, twenty five were widows, four were deserted or divorced, and twenty eight were unmarried. Most of them had children, aged parents, or invalid relatives to support, or were themselves in delicate health. At least 90 per cent of the women worked to maintain others.

In the 230 families there were 340 children of school age, 51 of whom were found at home during school hours, working at their mothers' trade.

In 27 cases in which the entire family was working, the aggregate earnings amounted to less than five dollars a week. One of these families consisted of eleven, another of twelve persons.

Fifty-nine of the women 230 families [*sic*] had got into debt or had been obliged to obtain poor law relief or private charity to enable them to live. Thirty-five of them had a deficit over their income of from fifty to one hundred and fifty dollars.

An American cent being worth an English half penny, the following table, taken from Miss Stewart's report, points to some cases of sweating which appear at least as bad as those to be found in England, even without making allowance for the higher cost of living in America.*

Persons	cents per hour
2	1 ½
9	2
11	2 ½
14	3
13	3 ½
26	4
20	4 ½
32	5
5	5 ½
15	6
16	6 ½
12	7
6	7 ½
11	8
1	8 ½
1	9 ½
6	9 ½
18	10
5	12
2	13
2	14
2	16
2	no report

APPENDIX B TO CHAPTER 2

Mr. Keir Hardie, in an article in the *Labour Leader* on the 'Cost of Living,' in the United States, quoted some figures prepared for arbitration purposes by Mr. W. D. Mahon of the Street and Railway Employees Union of America. According to Mr. Mahon an income of £235. 16. 0 a year is necessary in Chicago to keep a family of five persons 'in a respectable environment that should surround every American home.' This sum does not include tobacco or any other luxury of amusement and makes no provision for illness.

---

* {SP} See Appendix B.

The following table shows some of the prices which Mr. Mahon gives to make up his total with the predominant range of prices in Great Britain given in a British Board of Trade Report on 'Working Class Rents, Housing and Retail Prices' published in 1908.

	Mr. Mahon's budget for workmen in Chicago	England & Wales	Scotland	Ireland	London
Cheese	10d per lb	7d to 8d per lb	7d to 8d per lb	7½d to 8½d per lb	6d to 8d per lb
Butter	1/2 per lb	1/- to 1/2	1/- to 1/2 per lb	1/2 per lb	1/- to 1/2 per lb
Coal	34/- a ton	9½ to 1/- per cwt	9½ to 1/0 ½ per cwt	1/- per cwt	1/1 to 1/4 per cwt
Rent	Accommodation for wife and 3 children £3-12-0 a month I.C. 13/- a week	2 rooms 3/- to 3/6 a week 3 rooms 3/9 to 4/6 a week 4 rooms 4/6 to 5/6 a week 5 rooms 5/6 to 6/6 a week 6 rooms 6/6 to 7/9 a week	1 room 2/- to 2/6 a week 2 rooms 3/10 to 4/3 a week 3 rooms 5/- to 5/6 a week	1 room 1/6 to 2/6 a week 2 rooms 2/6 to 3/6 a week 3 rooms 4/- to 5/- a week 4 rooms 4/6 to 6/9 a week	2 rooms 4/6 to 7/6 a week 3 rooms 6/- to 9/- a week 4 rooms 7/6 to 10/6 a week 5 rooms 9/- to 13/- a week 6 rooms 10/6 to 15/6 a week

Mr. Mahon gives the amount of coal to be burnt by the Chicago workman as six tons a year. The intense cold in the United States would necessitate more firing than in England.

Clothes in the United States are very expensive. Mr. Mahon gives the cost of a moderately priced suit for his workman as £5. In Britain suits of men's clothes are to be had at 30/- or even less.

Mr. Keir Hardie also quotes Mr. Ettore Vram of Trieste who compares the cost of living in Britain and America as follows: –

	Rent %	Food %	All costs %	Wages %
Britain	100	100	100	100
United States	207	138	152	230

3. A Festival

This is the most lyrical and also the most cryptic of all the chapters in the book. Following Chapter 2, with tables itemising wages and the cost of living, this juxtaposition demonstrates Sylvia's intention to experiment stylistically in this book, perhaps as a reflection on the diversity of her American experiences. This chapter is filled with colours and sensations; although it occasionally lapses into racial stereotypes (as in the depiction of Cora), the dominant impression is one of disorientation.

Is this a dream? Who are the two 'maiden' sisters who entice her on a journey across New York City? Where do they go? Why is she taken to an apparently Jewish supper – with unleavened bread – and who are the loud American women there? And what of the enchanting performance of *Sleeping Beauty* in a gymnasium by children who live in tenements? Following the clues reveals an important artistic and political encounter.

The chapter begins with Sylvia looking through the proofs of her book. Although this might suggest the period before the 1911 publication of Sylvia's *The Suffragette*, that book was republished in New York in 1912 which appears the more likely year of these events. Sylvia did stay with two sisters, Alice and Irene Lewisohn, in their home in New York City on 20 January 1912, stopping over on her way from Boston to Indianapolis, returning there in mid-March 1912 and then again at the beginning of April before she sailed for England on the 3rd of that month.[1] Twenty years after writing this chapter, in which two New York sisters are portrayed as captivatingly beautiful, Sylvia recalled the romantic admiration she felt for Alice and Irene: 'I lost my heart to the lovely Lewisohn sisters, expending their wealth and talents for the creation of a school of dance and drama for the young people of New York's East Side at Henry Street Settlement.'[2] The daughters of a copper magnate, Alice and Irene Lewisohn were orphaned in their teens and later became famous for creating the avant-garde Neighbourhood Playhouse on the East Side's Grand Street. The Playhouse originated as one of the Lewisohns' contributions to the Henry Street Settlement,

7.   A children's dance class, sometime between 1902 and 1915, in the gymnasium of the Henry Street Settlement which is almost certainly where Sylvia Pankhurst saw the children's performance of *Sleeping Beauty* described in Chapter Three. (Courtesy of Henry Street Settlement)

which initially involved local children, and in the period in which Sylvia was in New York, they were staging their performances in the settlement's gymnasium.

One of the pieces performed in the gymnasium was *Sleeping Beauty*. The performance notes, carefully preserved by the Lewisohns, confirm that this was the production that Sylvia witnessed. Sylvia believed that she had missed the Prologue, although her description of 'a series of figures [who] danced singly across the stage', one with cymbals, suggests she caught the very end of it wherein 'Seven Fairies pass before curtain, one by one', of whom one carries 'cymbals or harp'.[3] This is followed by Scene One in which the 'Sprites of the Earth and Trees ... call upon the spirits of woods and seas and air to dance' before singing in chorus a refrain that ends

Now with elfin pipe and song
Dance yet merrily and long.[4]

This must be those Sylvia surmised were 'the spirits of the trees' and the group with 'flowery garlands ... playing on reedy pipes and set to dancing'. Sylvia observed the snowflakes at the point the performance notes record the entrance of 'Snow Spirits'. She wondered if the entrance and dance of 'a sombre woman' followed by another 'radiant figure' were the 'spirits of night and daybreak, sleep and waking, winter and spring'. This seems to correspond to the dances of the Fairy of Mortality and then of Immortality, which were accompanied by a song that in one version of the programme notes is titled 'Night and Winter, Morn and Spring', and in another is 'Asleep and Awake'. The Lewisohns' performance notes end with the direction '[t]hey all dance the glory of the Spring', just as Sylvia recalled that the play ended with the cast dancing to celebrate 'the spring had come'.[5]

A study of the Neighbourhood Playhouse, however, records that *Sleeping Beauty* was performed in the settlement gymnasium on 28 and 29 December 1911, two weeks before Sylvia arrived back in America.[6] Moreover, the subtitle to the play was 'a midwinter myth', far more appropriate to a performance in late December than to any of the dates Sylvia stayed with the Lewisohns. However, a newspaper feature on the Lewisohns written in 1914, noted that *Sleeping Beauty* 'had to be revived' on a second occasion and, as has been noted, the Neighbourhood Playhouse archive contains two slightly different programmes for *Sleeping Beauty*, which also suggests that it was performed on another occasion with a few alterations.[7] Sylvia was attending cultural events during her first stay with the Lewisohns; she told Keir Hardie that on 21 January she 'went to see a wonderful child who dances. The Lewisohns and other people think she is perhaps the greatest dancer alive.'[8] This was evidently the dancing child star Virginia Myers, admired by the Lewisohns, to whose mother a Mabel Pollen wrote asking if she might visit with Sylvia: 'an artist besides being an ardent suffragette, but she is a very dear child besides everything else – and she has heard of Virginia's dancing and is very anxious to see her.'[9] That afternoon, Sylvia 'went to a rehearsal of a play the Lewisohns are doing' but this is probably not *Sleeping Beauty*, since her description of the latter takes place in the evening and does not accord with the experience of a rehearsal.[10] The rehearsal on 21 January was probably for the *Russian Recital* due to open six days later.[11]

Sylvia's reference to the supper that she attended before the performance, with the unleavened bread, the only part of the meal she felt important to mention, points to a possible explanation. Unleavened bread is central to the Jewish festival of Passover, which began in 1912 on the evening of 1 April. On the evening of 1 April, Sylvia was speaking at the Carnegie Lyceum; however, on the evening of the first full day of Passover Sylvia appears not to have been publicly engaged since the press speculated that she had secretly met with Christabel that night.[12] This timing would also help explain why there were so many 'hostile questions' to the 'British Suffragette', as the recent window-smashing campaign had further polarised public opinion – indeed, the meeting in the Lyceum was hastily arranged after the Mount Morris Church in Harlem, where Sylvia was due to speak, cancelled 'after the English outbreak [of militancy]'.[13]

For Lillian Wald, who founded and lived at the Henry Street Settlement, Passover provided an important opportunity to develop neighbourly relationships with the local community she sought to assist, of which a considerable proportion were Eastern European Jewish immigrants, as she later wrote: 'Hospitality is a tradition in our neighbourhood. One of the invitations most prized at Henry Street is that which bids us welcome to a Passover service.'[14] Alice Lewisohn remembered the inclusivity embodied in the very objects in the Henry Street dining room: 'The brasses and coppers on the mantels, or the Russian bowl on the table, provided the link between the colonial decorum and the foreign homelands of the neighbours.'[15] Sylvia visited Henry Street (see the Introduction, p. 49) and may well have been invited for a Passover meal.[16] Her description of a 'gracious lady mother of the house' likely refers to Wald herself, while the confident political women around the table, the multiculturalism of the event and the 'well-polished brass and copper' brings the dining room at Henry Street to mind – where polished menorahs and Russian samovars still proudly sit today.

It was in the same spirit of assisting and welcoming immigrant communities that the Lewisohns established the Playhouse. They were concerned that children living in overcrowded tenements were deprived of the natural world and its role in the cultural traditions of their communities, and therefore they began to organise a series of festivals. A typescript in the Playhouse archives explains:

> it was because of an intense desire to dignify the the [sic] cultural background of our own club [Settlement] children that the cycle of Hebrew festivals was presented. These festivals were an attempt to

interpret through universal symbols, through the forces of nature, the eternal mystery of life, which we find described in all religeons [*sic*], and through this racial bond, to set forth an ideal of Universal Brotherhood. It was this story that we repeated over and over again, either through the Hebrew festivals or the legendary lore of the Red Men, or Greek or Hindoo myths, or through folk or fairy tale.[17]

Festivals at Passover celebrated the coming of spring, which is certainly a theme of their *Sleeping Beauty* and one more explicitly underlined in the programme in which the song 'Asleep and Awake' is exchanged for 'Night and Winter, Morn and Spring'. It is entirely plausible that the *Sleeping Beauty* performed in December was revived around Passover and that the Lewisohns would have taken their guest, Sylvia Pankhurst, to enjoy a Passover meal with Lillian Wald while they went off to the gymnasium to prepare for the performance at which, knowing Sylvia's artistic interests, they would have encouraged Sylvia to join them later.

Why, then, does Sylvia shroud this journey in mystery in her account? For Sylvia, the mysticism and romance of the play becomes inextricably associated with the Lewisohns themselves; they are described as if characters in their own performance: an 'elfin maiden', a 'Fay' with eyes that recall 'the deep woods at night'. When Sylvia arrived, the performance had already started and so she sat, enchanted, absorbing every detail trying to piece together the story – perhaps her writing of this chapter intended to afford the reader a similar experience.

A FESTIVAL

The little flat was like a tiny piece of England transplanted to New York. The pictures on the plain white walls, the big chesterfield couch, the broad brass bed with its quilt of varied eider plumage, a delight for childish eyes, all had come from London. The house had been built before the advent of steam radiators and there were big open fireplaces, with beautifully carved white marble mantle pieces, such as are not made nowadays. Though it was hard, not soft coal, that was burning, the bright fire helped to make an English traveller think of home. I had told Cora, the dusky maidservant with gleaming teeth, that I could see no one, for my book was going through the press and I was busy cutting it down and correcting it for impatient publishers.

I was sitting on the big chesterfield, with bundles of typewritten manuscript and long strips of proof piled all around me, when suddenly an elfin maiden appeared in the room. She was dressed in black and dark grey, with masses of faint brown hair. Her face, on its slender neck, was delicate as a flower, pale and wan and sadder than a heart should be, yet strangely lit with joy. Her eyes were a soft grey green brown and she had a gift, all her own, of raising her eyelids, so that one saw a glimpse of the white above the iris, as though she would see more keenly into hidden things. Work was forgotten whilst she stayed with me.

Two days later she came again, bringing a sister Fay, an etherialized Rossetti maiden, with brooding gaze and hair and eyes dark as the deep woods at night.

We set out together. I was deceived by the warmth of the house and meeting the bitter outside air, I shivered and held my coat more closely round me; but my companions, with their slender throats uncovered, did not seem even to know the wind was cold. They hurried me along through the streets of immense buildings with huge glaring advertisements of moving lights, that showed Boadicea with chariot wheels revolving, a kitten ever catching its tail and innumerable verbal signs in red green and yellow letters that winked jerkily out and in. They hastened across the wide thoroughfares, until gradually the surroundings grew dingier and more squalid. Now the ways were thronged with dark and swarthy foreigners, and the shops bore Yiddish signs. At last, we turned into a darkened street of houses and at the door of one of these, with hurried introductions they left me and sped away.

* * *

The doorway, reached by high steps, is old fashioned, straight and narrow. Inside is a blaze of light and a bewildering number of kindly women. One of these, with gentle face and silver hair, takes the visitor through quiet rooms to lay aside wraps and then down to where the gracious lady mother of the house receives her guests and leads them into the great dining room, with its well-polished brass and copper and its two dark polished tables, laid, with little white mats and shining glass and silver, for the evening meal.

Except for the big crackling wafers of unleavened bread, it does not matter of what the meal consists. The watchful eyes at the head of the table notice that every one is served, and all who are attuned to it, feel their owner's wholesome spirit of broad mellow tolerance, and wise affection.

This evening there are some unwonted presences. There is a loud discussion at the table. Some of the tallest and most powerfully voiced women that America can produce are besetting with hostile questions one small British Suffragette, without giving her, in their eagerness, a silent instant to reply. Finally a kindly whimsical little old lady, who has written erudite tomes on medical and social matters, rescues the victim, telling her not to mind 'the foghorns'.

* * *

It was late when I entered the crowded gymnasium. I had missed the prologue that explained the festival. The dark curtains of the proscenium were closed. Before them a series of figures danced singly across the stage, passing so quickly that, to me, all were vague and shadowy, save one with yellow garments and radiant and upturned face, clashing her cymbals.

Then the curtains parted and showed a group of tall girl figures, draped in dull greens reds and browns and holding up green boughs. I thought they were the spirits of the trees. I heard playing and singing but the words escaped me. Presently a band of little figures, short skirted and with flowery garlands round their waists, came flocking in, playing on reedy pipes, and set to dancing, as though they had stepped from a Grecian vase, their firm bare legs and sandaled feet prancing most vigorously.

After a time I saw that sitting upon a rocky couch nearby, was a little girl, a fairy tale princess, with long yellow hair falling to her knees, blue eyes and a delicate flawless little face. The dancing stopped and the tall tree spirits and the tiny pipers visited the little girl in turn, each offering some gift. One gave her a long string of pearls. Amongst them came an old woman with a spindle in her hand. This seemed to fill the little girl with delight. She darted forward to seize it, but, as she drew out a thread of the flax, she fell back into the arms of those who stood around her and I knew that this was the old story of the Sleeping Beauty.

When I saw her next, she was lying asleep upon the rocky couch, with little soft grey and white figures hovering around her. I thought that they were evening shadows and flakes of snow. They floated off at the coming of a sombre woman. Her clinging garments were of mournful grey, with shades of dull purple and green. Her hair was dark and mysterious as the trees at night. She held her head as though brooding of sorrow, and danced as though in pain. Slowly, and oftentimes retreating, she approached the sleeper, with sadness and with longing, and at last sank down, with arms outstretched across the child.

As she crouched there, there came dancing a radiant figure with yellow garments and face wrapped in an ecstasy of joy. This bright one bent and placed her hand, upon her sad grey sister and by her pressure, seemed slightly to raise them both. Then gradually, gradually she drew back from the couch, seeming to draw the sad one with her, by the motion of her hands. What were they – spirits of night and daybreak, sleep and waking, winter and spring? A silent contest of strange graceful passes was waged between them. Sometimes as though drawn towards her, sometimes impulsively, the sad grey spirit approached the radiant one, but always retreated before they touched, invisibly repelled. Then the bright figure would steal around behind the couch and touch the sleeper, bringing, it seemed, a thrill of life, but the grey one would creep nearer and the struggle of influences would be renewed. At last the grey sad one caught her bright sister about the waist and for an instant, the radiant figure sank back exhausted, only to triumph, for as in turn, she laid her hands upon her, the mourner drifted from the stage. The radiant spirit then bent over the couch, as though to whisper in the sleeper's ear.

She left, and again we took up the story of the Sleeping Beauty. A little dark haired maiden, dressed as the prince, in dull red hunting suit, with a hunting horn in her belt came shyly in. She found the Sleeping Beauty and waked her with a kiss and the two walked off together with their arms about each other.

Whilst these things had passed, the spirits of the trees had stood there silent, but now the little pipers, bounded in and kneeling before them, offered each one a branch of almond blossom, to tell them that the spring had come. With that spring came dancing the radiant spirit, hand in hand with her darker sister, who had cast off her look of mourning and had wound about her dull grey robe a scarf of many colours.

And so the sisters and their joyous troupe, the piper children and the maiden spirits of the trees, danced on together, with the little story lovers standing by.

As I watched them, it seemed to me that this festival, wrought with love and joy, could tell us of more than the old fairy story of the pricked finger and the long sleep ended by a kiss, more than the vanquishing of the winter by the spring and the fleeting of the darkness from the day.

As they danced on, it seemed to me that we were all whelmed by a flood of love and joy and radiance, and that cleansed of pain and sin, and throwing off social wrongs and false standards of life, we might begin to be brothers and sisters from that hour.

So life appeared to me, till the cold hard world outside dimmed the brightness and warmth glowing in my heart, and seemed to bolster up anew the barriers I had thought so easy to surmount. Just a year afterwards I learnt that the little Sleeping Beauty had died of a lingering illness, which began shortly after the Festival – the one great joyous event of her short life. For months before she died, she had been unable to go out into the fresh air, for the tenement in which her family lived was up so many flights of steps, and she so weak.

4. Prisoners

EDITOR'S INTRODUCTION

Beginning with the written words of a prisoner, this chapter opens with another stark change in tone. Titled 'Prisoners', it addresses a subject that became of considerable interest and importance to many militant suffragettes as their own experiences of imprisonment confronted them, first-hand and often for the first time, with the plight of incarcerated women. Speaking to other prisoners, suffragettes discovered women who had been convicted by all-male juries and sentenced by a male judge for crimes, such as infanticide, that were frequently resorted to by women who suffered desperate poverty, rape and sexual exploitation. Meanwhile, the men responsible for the exploitation of and violence against these women frequently went unsanctioned. The treatment of women in prison reinforced the view that they were morally at fault and individually responsible for the circumstances in which they found themselves. The experience of prison furnished militant suffrage campaigners with further arguments for women's suffrage: firstly, that enfranchised women would reform legislation that discriminated against women and would instead punish sexual abuse, and secondly, that women would instigate prison reform. After her own imprisonment, Sylvia became profoundly committed to this approach. She used her experiences to advocate for prison reform, publishing an article with her own illustrations in the *Pall Mall Magazine* in which she compared Holloway with a prison in Milan that she had visited after her release whilst on a recuperative holiday with Emmeline Pethick Lawrence. The Penal Reform League (which later merged with the Howard Association to form the Howard League for Penal Reform) was formed at the celebratory breakfast to welcome Sylvia and fellow suffragette Charlotte Despard on their release from prison.[1]

Choosing 'Life in a London prison' as one of the three titles for her North American lectures enabled Sylvia to contextualise militancy by exposing the Liberal government's repressive nature and make the case for women's citizenship based on the efforts of militant suffragettes; in her first speech at the Carnegie Lyceum she 'told of the prison reform they

8.   Sylvia Pankhurst wearing the portcullis and prison arrow
brooch she designed which was awarded to all suffragettes
who had experienced imprisonment. This signed photograph
was preserved in the scrapbook of Elizabeth Smith Miller
and her daughter Anne Fitzhugh Miller, leading suffragists
in Geneva, New York whom Sylvia visited in February 1911.
(Miller NAWSA Suffrage Scrapbooks, Scrapbook 9 [1910–1911],
Courtesy of the Library of Congress)

had worked'.[2] As with the question of women's sweated labour, however,
Sylvia found herself under pressure to flatter her hosts for their superior
conditions, to which she responded by undertaking her own research
during her tour. She told one reporter: 'Having served two terms in jail
I have taken every convenient chance to visit the jails in different cities.'[3]
Although she visited prisons in her second tour, all four of the prisons
described here date from visits made during her 1911 tour.

Harrison Street Jail in Chicago, the second prison to be discussed here, was the first of the four that Sylvia visited alongside Zelie Emerson in the last days of the garment workers strike (see Introduction, p. 43). The description contained here is a much shorter version of the article Sylvia wrote for the *Chicago Tribune* in which she stated that the unsanitary conditions she witnessed at Harrison Street undermined claims of 'new world' superiority in this area:

> Whilst I have been in America I have constantly been told that had the suffragets [*sic*] been fighting for 'votes for women' in this country, they never would have been subjected to the treatment which they have received in England, but some of the facts I learned this morning have led me to feel that reformers all over the world have an almost equally hard fight before them.[4]

So profound was Sylvia's sense of horror at Harrison Street Jail that it became the example by which she measured the other prisons she visited. Commenting on the prison in Ottawa, which she visited in early February and which is discussed briefly in this chapter, Sylvia decried the lack of activity and reading material for the inmates but was able to provide an equivocal assessment – 'in many respects better than those visited elsewhere' – because of the example of Harrison Street: 'The worst jail I have visited on this continent was one at Chicago where men and women are kept in darkened cells, serving 30 day terms in a building without any civilized sanitary equipment, the drain being actually an open sewer.'[5]

Sylvia visited the first prison described here, Philadelphia's Eastern State Penitentiary, in early April 1911. Opened in 1829 by reformers who advocated the principles of combining total solitary confinement with hard labour, it would be condemned by Charles Dickens, who visited in the 1840s, for reducing the prisoner to 'a man buried alive'.[6] The system of solitary confinement was breaking down when Sylvia visited; indeed, she noted the cells were overcrowded and whilst she expressed her disapproval at this, she was pleased to see that the prisoners were allowed to develop their artistic talents. The local press were thus able to report: 'It is quite a pleasure to know that the eastern penitentiary meets the approval of Miss Sylvia Pankhurst, the English suffragist ... She found some things to criticize, of course, but her impressions were generally cheerful.'[7]

Weighing the relative advantages of prisons, however, rather precluded a systemic critique of the prison system. This was further indicated by her attempts to employ incarceration figures as evidence of women's moral superiority; the press reported that she said of the penitentiary in Philadelphia, 'there are 1,400 men prisoners there and only 28 women. Now, isn't that another good argument for woman's suffrage?'[8] Moreover, she made this point on more than one occasion; in Milwaukee the following year she observed: 'We hear much about the inability of women to vote rightly. At least they seem to be able to keep out of the house of correction about twenty times and a fraction as well as men.'[9]

It was an argument that could easily be appropriated by elitists, evidenced by WSPU propaganda that upheld women's claim for citizenship by contrasting examples of civic-minded women with male types cast as *unfit* for citizenship. Sylvia's closer approximation to an elitist approach on the issue of prisons is further revealed by comparison with her approach to women at work. Whereas Sylvia's research in this period and experience of working women's collective action developed into a conviction that working women required representation to work out their own salvation, she did not see a way in which imprisoned women could achieve this and looked instead to reforming middle-class women.

The implications of this approach are demonstrated here by Sylvia's glowing description of the reformatory for women at Bedford Hills in New York State. Under the direction of Katherine Bement Davis, it rejected a punitive model of imprisonment. Seeking instead to understand the reasons that women were incarcerated, it aimed to treat, rehabilitate and train prisoners so that they might be able to more successfully integrate into society. In its focus on bettering the individual, the Bedford Hills regime provided a stark contrast with the inhuman and degrading treatment of women prisoners at Holloway and Sylvia responded warmly to this model. In this chapter, Sylvia demonstrates considerable knowledge about the new scheme that Davis was embarked upon to psychologically, and therefore 'scientifically', categorise inmates with a view to separating those deemed to suffer from 'congenital' defects. John D. Rockefeller Jr., then heading an investigation into prostitution, invested in this scheme which could see women judged by class and gendered prejudices, subjected to lifelong custodial sentences and sterilised.[10] Although it is unlikely Sylvia was aware of the full implications of the scheme, she uncritically accepted Davis's justification of complete institutional dominance over the inmates as a benevolent and scientific innovation. The skilful critique she was developing of the 'scientific' control of workers through Taylorism and efficiency is notably absent here.

PRISONERS

'Does it pay to be polite?

B 4059, 2, 10,3,10.

'Yes sir: It pays to be polite, person with polish manners are honored from every body. I try to be as polite as I could, but for some reasons I'm not polite as I like to be; and this is the bigest reason because I cannot use it the English language in the proper way. Among my own people 'Lithuanians' I have a name as delicate boy, but Americans generally making fun of me because I cannot place it the words correctly, for that reason I'm not polite as I mean to be. But in this place polite are not in use, bigest half of the inmates do not know what the polite is. I have been with meny cell mates that as more I try to be polite to them they more cursed me and call me all kinds of names, but if I curse, talking about big Robberyes and other evil things then I be all right.

I have nothing against the rules or officers but companions cell mates that makes my time miserable.

I often thought and thought no body paid attention at us forst timemers, that we are mixed up with hard criminals, that nothing else but school for robberyes sodomiss and others worst crimes that can be commitit.

'Now I am going to stop writing i hope dear Teacher you understand my expressions.

Faithfully Yours.

B 4509'.*

The above is a composition exercise written by an inmate of the Eastern Penitentiary, Philadelphia, Pennsylvania. In this prison there were 29

---

* All spelling mistakes here are in Sylvia's original transcription. The number 10,3,10 likely relates to the date of the composition; if the numbering follows the standard American format (month-day-year), that would indicate the piece was written six months before Sylvia's visit.

women and 1395 men, the average number of men varying as a rule from 1,400 to 1,500. 314 of the men were negroes. A school for illiterate inmates was held from 9 to 2 every day. Those whose education was defective, but who were able to read and write, attended school once a week and could study through a corresponding school after five o'clock each evening. There were 14,000 books in the library and each prisoner was allowed two volumes a week.

The cell accommodation was very restricted, from two to five men occupying the same cell at night and, in the majority of the cases, during the greater part of the day also. The prisoners all worked at some trade or other, being taught by their cell mates if they knew nothing on their arrival. Stocking knitting by machine, cigar making, chair caning and shoe making were all carried on by the men in their cells. The women made lace and did embroidery and very fine drawn linen work. The prisoners made by their work about 20 cents (ten pence) a day and were allowed either to save their earnings, or to spend them at the prison store in buying extras for themselves, such as soap, tooth brushes and powder and tobacco.

The Governor of the Prison told us that most of the inmates learnt exceedingly quickly anything to which they applied themselves. One man, a miner from Wales, who was serving a life sentence for having shot and killed two men in a quarrel, had taught himself to play five musical instruments and had painted large pictures of his home and the scenes he remembered on the walls of his own and the neighbouring cells. All his earnings were spent in paints and brushes. He had never tried either to paint or play before coming into prison. His pictures were not artistic but they were much better than those of the average pavement artist.

One of the women prisoners had been given a harmonium which she was learning to play.

There was a good brass band in the prison which practised twice a week.

HARRISON STREET GAOL, CHICAGO

A foul, foul stench that reaches out into the street, grows stronger as one enters, and catches the breath as one goes down the stone steps. Below, the light is dim. The heat and smell are almost suffocating. Each cell has a black stone floor and its back and side are black also. Its front is a barred gate and its only light comes through the dim corridor. It contains nothing but a wooden bench fixed to the wall. The sole sanitary convenience for the inmates is a narrow gutter in the floor at the back of each cell, along which there is water running: one hears it running always. If the excrement be solid, the matron, or the warder, must come and poke it down a small hole with a stick. Sometimes as many as four or five human beings are crowded into one of these loathsome dens together.

Both men and women are to be found in this gaol. Some are merely awaiting trial – they may be innocent. Others have been found guilty and are serving gaol sentences. The matrons and warders too, are here for long long hours. They suffer much from rheumatism and tuberculosis.

A CANADIAN PRISON AT OTTAWA

A long corridor on one side of which are barred windows and on the other narrow cells with barred fronts. Under the windows are long wooden benches and upon these sit a number of women and girls with idle hands.

One woman, with her head all bandaged round, is sobbing. She speaks half French, half English; she sobs too much to tell her tale: 'It was he – he – but the policeman hit me – they always blame the woman'.

'You would not understand – he always left me – I was so lonely –' another says.

They sit together and in low voices tell what they have done. One alone stands thinking, silent and apart. The winter's afternoon is fading, but no lights will come. When it is dark, the matron locks them in the cells.

BEDFORD REFORMATORY PRISON, NEW YORK STATE

A windy hillside, brown in early spring, dotted with delicate budding saplings. The sky a rain-washed blue, great heaped up driving clouds and brilliant sun. A colony of detached red brick buildings, nestling on the slopes, and broad white concrete paths, with flights of steps here and there, reaching from one building to another. Seen through the veil of little trees, a group of laughing, shouting girls, digging upon the opposite rise. Another band of them upon the path below, their cheeks glowing and hair and skirts blowing in the wind.

This, though there are no walls around it, is a prison too. Dr Kate Davis the principal, a little woman with grey hair round kindly face and the bluest of blue eyes, to whom the institution owes its being, kindly agreed to take us round.

We visited the school first, a fine airy building with spacious classrooms, white painted walls, and polished floors. In each room devoted to academic study was a little table of specimens of the pupils' work. We learned both from these and Dr Davis's explanations, that as far as possible – for these students are not children and their interest must be caught and held – all lessons are made to have a direct application to the affairs of daily life. Therefore, arithmetical calculations frequently deal with such problems as the number of potatoes or onions used in preparing a dinner for the whole Institution, for each home and for every inmate; or with the amount of meat, or butter, used to keep the inmates for a year, or a term of years. Stout paper quart and pint measures, neatly cut and sewn, with ruled divisions for smaller quantities, are made here for actual use in the cookery classes and provide not merely a simple lesson in fractions but an exercise also in manual dexterity.

In the written exercises there was a wide field of difference and one saw, step by step, the remarkably speedy progress, ranging from the first big uncertain roundhand of the illiterate to regular, well-formed characters, that might well arouse many of us to envy. The compositions that were shown to us dealt with innumerable subjects – a lecture given by some visitor to the Institution, a Christmas Entertainment, some historical episode, a walk through the fields. There were botany exercises, and drawings of flowers, simply executed in coloured chalks, and Christmas greeting cards designed by the pupils.

In one of the rooms was a loom, on which the women weave the rugs which one [sic] we saw lying about the Institution and here we learned the secret of the wonderfully polished floors. For the last half hour on Saturday morning some of the inmates, with rags wound round their feet and with a sliding gait, walk in a row, to and fro across the floors. Here we were also shown specimens of the first three months' sewing course, including wonderfully fine hemming, backstitching, herring-boning, buttonholing, darning, and patching in which the pattern was perfectly matched and one would hardly see the join. The preliminary sewing course completed, the women pass on to take part in the making of all the garments and household linen used in the Reformatory. One marvelled, in seeing these things, how quickly people learn in prison.

A large room, with cupboards lining the walls and a long table in the centre, is devoted to cookery classes, and adjoining this is the room where model meals are served. Just then a table was set for lunch, its polished top left bare, with a dainty mat for each plate, as well as for the central vase of flowers. The side board cupboards are kept well furnished with finger bowls, cocktail glasses, and all that the up-to-date American housewife needs. Classes are held in this department for the teachers, as well as for the pupils, in order that a uniform system of domestic economy may be adhered to. Dr Davis has little trouble, in spite of past records, in finding situations for the cooks and waitresses she has trained.

From the school we made our way to the steam laundry, and treading by terraced concrete paths and steps, we regarded with amazement their regular, eminently professional aspect, as Dr Davis told us that her women made them. Our admiration grew when she casually explained that she herself 'just went to watch some men doing it', and then came back and showed her pupils how. Under her guidance, the women of the Reformatory also built a concrete pig pen and the day it was finished, Miss Davis carried thither her best china and gave them all afternoon tea there, before the pigs came in.

Physical training plays an important part in the life of the Institution. There is a fine gymnasium, where every inmate receives an hour's instruction every day. A visiting teacher holds dancing classes twice a week and everyone must take a walk in the open air each day. Each summer the inmates give an entertainment in the grounds, to which visitors are invited. On one occasion they acted *As You Like It* and on another Ibsen's *Pillars of Society*.

Only one of the houses in which the women live contains anything approaching ordinary prison cells and this house was the one building erected before Dr Davis came. She told us that she would not use it at all, if she had room to abandon it, and that at present it was reserved for those who were serving the first three months of their sentence. The cells were of course only tenanted at night time and there was a large room in this house for work and recreation.

The other houses vary, some having one, others two stories. Their rooms have fresh white walls, painted by the women, and wide airy windows, protected on the outside by a thin and scarcely seen, but strong, iron wire lattice, which is securely locked at night. Each house has its own kitchen and laundry, in order that simple domestic cooking and washing may be learnt, and every inmate works directly under the house cook for a time. Each of the homes has a large day room where the inmates may sit together after the day's work is done. The white cloth had been laid for the mid day meal – as we passed through. In every house the day room was gay with flowers and plants, and in one case a common Boston fern had been so carefully cherished, that its broad fronds had grown ten feet long and it was placed up on a high white stand, that they might hang their whole splendid length, without touching the floor.

There is a separate little white walled bedroom for every inmate with window and door of ordinary type, bedstead, dressing-table, looking glass and all that one might expect to find in a girls' boarding school. Each inmate may decorate her room as she pleases with photographs, ornaments and keepsakes from her friends.

Those who are serving the last part of their three years' sentence live in the 'Honour House', unless, which is seldom the case, they have forfeited their right to do so by some act of misconduct. In this house there is one room larger than the rest which is called the 'Honour Room'. For it the girls have made the window curtains and the chair covers and have upholstered the window seat, all in blue and white chintz, and they themselves elect the girl who is to occupy this room. There is self-government in the 'Honour House', the women electing a secretary and other managing officials and making their own rules. There are two day rooms in this house, and in the smaller, a group of twelve women were sitting together doing a little fancy work for themselves, whilst they waited for dinner to be served. They all looked exceedingly neat and fresh in their blue and white print dresses. No two were dressed exactly alike. Some had stiff stand-up collars and cuffs, others wore embroidered linen or lace at the throat. 'They can have their hair and necks as they please', said Dr Davis when questioned on this point, and she explained that as a rule, the women either make their own collars, or have them given to them by their friends.

There was a little stir of excitement in the homes just then, over the dressing of dolls for a bazaar. One of the New York Hospitals keeps a bed always ready for the Bedford inmates and so the inmates were doing what they could to help the hospital in this way.

As we left the house, Dr Davis spoke to one of the girls who met us. 'The silk for your doll's petticoat has come' she said, stopping to admire the tiny muslin dress that the girl had made. We realised in a flash how close and intimate was her knowledge of everyone of these three hundred and fifty souls that she was drawing up from the underworld.

We went next to the disciplinary building where those who become unmanageable are sent. It contains the matron's room and three or four little cells with wooden floors, well warmed and brightly lighted from the roof, but absolutely bare. Not often is this building tenanted and pitiful indeed are the reasons that bring its occasional prisoners there. As a rule, the trouble begins with a misunderstanding between two friends, for these unfortunate ones crave passionately and jealously for affection. That very day one such case had occurred – a girl had tried to choke herself because her favourite companion had exchanged hair ribbons with another. She had been brought away here that she might not alarm and disturb her companions. Now after a violent fit of weeping her sobs were but just hushed. The matron, whose kindly wrinkled face was full of sympathy and concern, told us that the patient had declared that she would 'be good' and was begging to go 'home', by which she meant the prison cottage where she lived. The matron had promised her that she should go back there as soon as she was quite calm.

In the baby house the children had just waked from their nap and were being dressed in warm red coats, caps, and gaiters to go in the sun. The mothers may keep their little ones with them in this home till they are two years old. Then, if possible, the mother is paroled with the child. If this cannot be, a home is found for the baby, either in a private family or in some children's institute.

One baby girl, who had no mother to nurse her, was the matron's special care. The young mother had been brought out from England by her elder sister, a trusted upper servant in an American family. The girl also went into service and was seduced under promise of marriage. When the man refused to fulfil his promise, she shot him dead and tried to drown herself. She was rescued, but contracted inflammation of the lungs. On her recovery she was sent to Bedford Reformatory, where, after the child's birth, it was found that she had developed tuberculosis. It was necessary that she should be removed to a Sanatorium and on leaving the prison, she begged Miss Davis to keep the child and not to send her to 'an institution'.

She realised that, prison though it is, Bedford is in very truth a real reformatory, a place where bodies are built up, where minds are strengthened and developed, and souls germinate and expand. Dr Davis tells her prisoners that, if they will have it so, Bedford shall be for them an industrial boarding school, and looking at those who have just come in and those who are nearing the end of their term, one sees, almost with awe, the change that this little woman has wrought.

Dr Davis also told us of other schemes that she was hoping soon to develop. She felt the need of greater opportunities for classifying, according to their needs and capabilities, the women and girls placed in her charge. Some of those who were in the prison had come into conflict with the law under stress of great misfortune or temptation; some had failed to be law abiding and successful for want of training and opportunity to earn a living. Some had had no education; some had not had the right kind of education; but there were others who suffered from congenital defects. The Institution as then organised, could give an excellent all round education in the management of a home and the general academic and other knowledge necessary for ordinary life, as well as teaching a good many things that the average person does not know. It could provide technical training for expert laundresses, cooks, waitresses and seamstresses. But some of the inmates were not suited to earn a living in any of these ways. Some could not withstand the difficulties and temptations of domestic service, (when shall we learn that this form of employment is more fraught with temptation than any other?). Some of those whose brains were perhaps too slow for the rushing speed and precision and the heat of a steam laundry, too dull, perhaps, for the neatness and accuracy required for household service, had yet strong limbs and sinews fitted for the hard toil of farming and might have their dormant faculties quickened by the broad and simple things of agriculture and the life in the open air.

Bedford Reformatory itself was built on land unsuited to cultivation but just next to it was a farm for sale which had good fertile soil. On that land could be grown the food that the reformatory consumes and Dr Davis believed that the farm, could, in time, be made self supporting. Even more important, it would serve as a training ground for those of the women who would benefit by and are suited to farm life. In England one might hesitate as to whether there would always be openings for large numbers of women trained in dairying, poultry keeping and such things, but in America with its vast farming territories there can be no such doubts.

Since I was at Bedford the farm of which Dr Davis spoke and which consists of eighty-eight acres of land has been bought and added to the Institution and last summer from twenty-five to one hundred girls and women were set to do temporary work there with excellent results. Eighteen women living with their officers in a cottage on the farm are now* engaged in the regular work of dairying and caring for the calves, the chickens and so on. Two other cottages, each to accommodate twenty-two inmates, are shortly to be built.

Much is being done also in the direction of scientific study. When I was at Bedford Dr Davis had recently obtained a grant from New York State for a resident woman pathologist, who would make careful tests and records, with the object of discovering the physical causes that have led the unfortunates to fall below the normal, and the means by which they may be raised up and made whole and strong. For some time, careful careful [sic] card catalogue records had already been kept, to report the progress of each inmate.

Since then on land adjoining the original Institution and the new farm the building of a scientific department has begun. This is to consist of a reception house to accommodate fifty women where all new comers will stay for a time under careful observation. There will also be a laboratory and a residence house for the staff who will work from the psychological, medical and sociological points of view.

I wonder how long it will be before such a work as that of Dr Davis, a practical genius of whom her country may be proud, is begun in Great Britain and before our British Parliament decides to give such an opportunity for usefulness to a British Woman!

---

* {SP} February 1913.

5. A Socialist Administration
The Milwaukee City Council

EDITOR'S INTRODUCTION

On 5 February 1912, after helping to establish the Votes for Women League of North Dakota in Fargo, Sylvia boarded a train for Minneapolis where she would change for another train to Madison, Wisconsin. It was late afternoon, 'the prettiest part of the day', and Sylvia, with an artist's palette in mind, watched the changing colour of the sky from 'pure and limpid blue pale grey and palest palest gold with the bright sun sinking lower and lower' to 'soft greenish blue with faint dull purple clouds closer to the horizon'. The shadows, 'far bluer than the sky', turned 'pale lilac' as the sun began to set upon a blanket of snow 'tinged with pinkish gold'. Woodland obscured the last rays as 'the bleakness of the night' descended and turned the trees 'all dead black'. It was only after the sunset, and once she had changed trains, that Sylvia was able to return to the main subject of her letter to Keir Hardie though 'not for long', she informed him, as she would arrive in Madison at 3 o'clock in the morning.[1] She ended up writing over fifty pages more about her visit to Milwaukee, where she had left three days earlier, most of which would form the basis of this chapter, with the section on laundries being used in Chapter 2.

In 1910, the socialist Social Democratic Party triumphed in the elections to Milwaukee city and county offices, with Emil Seidel becoming the first socialist mayor of a major city in America. A committed socialist herself, Sylvia was interested in how a socialist administration operated in practice and in the course of sharing her observations with Keir Hardie – 'because I think you will be interested to hear what I thought about it and why' – she elaborated upon her own conception of socialism.[2] This chapter, which further develops the insights of her letter, constitute Sylvia's most extensive writing on socialism prior to her expulsion from the WSPU.

Sylvia first met Mayor Emil Seidel at Milwaukee's City Hall on 30 January immediately after the visit to the Milwaukee laundries with Miss Perdue and Miss Miller described in Chapter 2. Sylvia complained to

Keir Hardie that she felt inhibited by the presence of these two women in her interview with Seidel to whom she wanted to articulate her views on women's suffrage and socialism without allowing for 'a sensational story for the reporter lady [Perdue]'.[3] She was evidently acutely aware of the political sensitivities around her visit to Milwaukee as a representative of and participant in the women's suffrage movement, which organised women across political parties. Moreover, although Sylvia's sympathies were with the socialists, she felt Seidel's approach to the question of women's suffrage was lukewarm whilst among his rivals, who had united to challenge the socialists at the upcoming election, was Robert La Follette, who had declared his support for women's suffrage and whose wife Belle and daughter Fola were active suffragists. Sylvia, however, felt that La Follette's participation in the alliance against the socialists ran counter to his progressive political stance, observing to Hardie: 'It appears to me that the present Socialist Council ought to be considered ideal from the La Follette point of view.'[4] By contrast, Sylvia's own criticisms of the socialist administration sought after greater co-operation with and understanding between the suffragists and the socialists.

A friendly but critical tone informs Sylvia's treatment of the Milwaukee socialist administration in this chapter. She returned to City Hall the morning after her first visit, this time, she told Hardie, 'in company with two socialist ladies' – probably a reference to Crystal Eastman, then helping to organise the Wisconsin suffrage campaign, and Elsie Cole Phillips, from the Milwaukee Child Welfare Commission, as Sylvia was recorded as their guest at noon on the same day.[5] Her experiences here form the main part of this chapter, as she describes her encounters with the various departments in City Hall and the Bureau of Efficiency and Economy established by the socialists. Sylvia was impressed by the rigour displayed by the Bureau, telling one interviewer that '[t]he charts and exhibits [at the Bureau] showed the reduction of city governing to an exact science' – a statement that nevertheless also indicates the misgivings she expresses in this chapter.[6] Throughout her study of Milwaukee's administration, from her visit to the site of the House of Correction farm to her diligent reading of the Bureau's bulletins cited extensively in this chapter, Sylvia outlines three major concerns. Firstly, she argues that the emphasis on efficiency was a 'top down' approach that failed to encompass working people as participants in the socialist project. Secondly, she observes that women's needs were often overlooked. Thirdly, she notes that necessary, long-term radical solutions were being compromised by a short-term focus on electoral success. Sylvia would grapple with these problems herself over the coming years, leading to her championing revolutionary direct democracy, on the model of soviets, after the Bolshevik Revolution in 1917. Writing here, seemingly in early 1913, she articulates her view that 'the very basis of representative government' is the 'interplay of minds and wills, variously reflecting the interests of every section of the community' and therefore its 'more perfect application' would be realised in a time 'when the garbage collectors, the scrub women, and other city employees, will be powerfully represented by those who will be able to speak for them with direct knowledge of their lives and work'. It was to be Sylvia's growing insistence that working people, and particularly working women, must be the authors of their own emancipation that would lead to her expulsion from the WSPU in January 1914 by Christabel, who argued instead that socially privileged women should campaign on behalf of working women. Sylvia's response was contained in the first issue of the East London Federation of Suffragettes' newspaper:

> It is necessary for women to fight for the Vote because, by means of the Vote, if we combine in sufficient numbers to use it for definite ends, we can win reforms for ourselves by making it plain to Governments that they must either give us the things we want, or make way for those that will. Working women – sweated women, wage slaves, overworked mother [sic] toiling in little homes – these, of all created beings, stand in the greatest need of this, the power to help themselves.[7]

Sylvia's conception of democracy in 1914 recalled her response to the administration of Milwaukee, wherein she proposed a democratic socialism, controlled 'from below', that would necessarily ensure radical change and empower women.

A SOCIALIST ADMINISTRATION
THE MILWAUKEE CITY COUNCIL

My first impression of the Milwaukee Socialist administrators was of their eager zest for their work and their great readiness to take the world into their confidence and to explain all that they were doing. To me, a stranger, as to anyone desirous of ameliorating social conditions, to any seeker after administrative knowledge, they gladly extended a cordial welcome to the City Hall, and an invitation to inspect all its activities.

Mayor Seidel   Emil Seidel,* the Mayor, I found to be a gentle, kindly man, small in stature, with grey hair, a pale face, lined a little wearily, but with an expression singularly hopeful and serene, and dark bright eyes – an idealist, but that rare and priceless treasure, an idealist with a head full of practical details.

One realizes in talking to him that he is one of those people who are quick to understand what is going on in the minds of others, and that he meets them with a broad tolerant sympathy. On whatever subject presents itself he takes instinctively the wise human point of view. Speaking of the reorganisation of the police force, he said that he wanted to make it the duty of the policeman to report as to whether the streets upon his beat were kept free from refuse and the garbage cans emptied in due time. 'I want the policeman to have some useful work to do beside marching round with a truncheon,' he said, raising his hand for an instant, as though shouldering the weapon, with a wry little smile and a comical air of pretended pomposity. 'Doing nothing but that is bad for any man, it tends to make him the tyrant of the street.'

He spoke with evident hope and pleasure of the work that was being accomplished by the 'Dependent Children's Home', of the farm that was to take the place of the dismal 'House of Correction',† and other plans; but he added wistfully that most of the work which the administration had wished to initiate was as yet hardly begun. Every Municipal Department had been in such a bad state when they had taken office, so much 'graft'‡ and corruption had had to be uprooted, so many muddles had had to be put straight, that a large part of the eighteen months that had passed had been spent in this way. Moreover the City Charters gave the Council but limited powers of action, and whilst injunctions were several times procured to restrain the Socialist administrators from going beyond

---

*   Emil Seidel (1864–1947), socialist mayor of Milwaukee 1910–1912. Born in Pennsylvania the son of German immigrants, he grew up in Milwaukee and became a socialist whilst studying woodcarving in Germany. In the 1912 presidential election the Socialist Party chose Eugene V. Debs and Seidel as their candidates for the presidency and vice-presidency respectively; they won nearly a million votes.

†   {SP} The equivalent of an English 'Local Prison'.

‡   'Graft': the misuse of funds for political gain.

these powers, Bills to extend them were defeated by the Wisconsin State Legislature. Amongst other things, the Milwaukee Councillors were debarred from Municipal trading and were unable to municipalize the trams, gas, electric light, and other public utilities, which have become so fruitful a source of revenue to our English City Councils and which help to pay for costly social reforms.

Economy and Efficiency. The Mayor's first and last words to me were of warning. 'You will find that we have been able to do very little yet, the time has been so short for all that there was to overcome.' Yet he spoke with glowing enthusiasm of the future and of the great world-wide Socialist Movement, of which the Milwaukee Administrators were a part.

As Mayor Seidel had explained, the first work of the Socialist administration had been to make order out of chaos, to grapple with corruption, waste and mismanagement. They had found, though the fact seems barely credible, that hitherto there had been no systematic keeping of Municipal accounts and that consequently the City's financial business was in a state of terrible confusion. The comptroller's office was therefore entirely reorganized, a businesslike system of accounting to cover all Municipal departments was instituted, and every possible legal precaution was taken to prevent future administrations overthrowing this system and reverting to the muddled condition that had obtained before.

*The Bureau of Economy and Efficiency.** In order to place the general work of the administration upon a sound basis, the Council also set up a Bureau of Economy and Efficiency. The Director of the Bureau was John R. Commons,† who before taking up this post had been a professor at the University of Wisconsin at Madison. The staff of the Bureau was composed as follows: –

M. Cerf, Accountant.
Formerly with Ernest Reckitt & Co., Chicago.

John E. Treleven, Organisation.
Formerly with Wisconsin Tax Commission.

---

* Officially, the Bureau of Efficiency and Economy (as opposed to Bureau of Economy and Efficiency as Sylvia titles it throughout).

† John Rogers Commons (1862–1945), a radical economist and labour historian.

R. E. Goodell, Cost Accountant.
Formerly with Marwick, Mitchell & Co., Chicago.

Fayette H. Elwell, Accountant.
Formerly Professor of Accounting, Marquette University.

Percy H. Myers,
Accountant and Editor.

Ray Palmer.
Consulting Engineer, Chicago.

J. B. Tanner,
Certified Public Accountant, Cleveland.

S. M. Gunn, Sanitarian.
Asst. Prof. Public Health, Mass. Inst. of Technology.

J. C. Duncan, Accountant.
Asst. Prof. Accounting, University of Illinois.

George E. Frazer, Accountant.
Instructor in Accounting, The University of Wisconsin.

E. B. Norris, Engineer.
Asst. Prof. Mechanical Engineering, The University of Wisconsin.

W. R. Brown.
Sanitary Engineer, Chicago.

C. R. Sexton, Accountant.

The following were engaged as Consulting Experts to the Bureau: –

On Organization.

Major Charles Hine.
Organization Expert Harriman Lines, Chicago.

Harrington Emerson.
Consulting Efficiency Engineer, New York.

On Engineering.

F. E. Turneaure.
Dean College of Engineering, The University of Wisconsin.

Louis E. Reber.
> The University of Wisconsin.
> Formerly Dean College of Engineering, Pennsylvania State College.

On Accounting.

S. W. Gilman.
> The University of Wisconsin.
> Consulting Accountant President Taft's Inquiry into Economy and Efficiency.

Peter White.
> Accounting and Finance Counsel, Chicago Bureau of Public Efficiency.

On Health and Sanitation.

H. L. Russell.
> Dean College of Agriculture, The University of Wisconsin.

W. T. Sedgwick.
> Head Department Public Health and Biology, Massachusetts Institute of Technology.

On Finance and Taxation.

T. S. Adams.
> Member of Wisconsin Tax Commission.

H. R. Sands.
> Director Chicago Bureau Public Efficiency.

On Social Survey.

H. H. Jacobs.
> University Settlement, Milwaukee.

It will be seen that out of a staff of thirteen persons, eight were accountants and a ninth was formerly with the Wisconsin Tax Commission, there were engineers, and one was a professor of public health. Of the eleven consulting experts, six advised on finance, taxation, accounting and organisation, two on engineering, two on health and sanitation, and one only on social survey. Ten out of the eleven experts were either University professors or business men. They were many of them men of national reputation, but only one of them was put forward as having any special knowledge of social conditions or of working lives. A number of men and women of greater social experience were, however, called in from time to time to undertake special investigations.

The functions of the Bureau of Economy and Efficiency were to study actual social conditions, in order to find out how far the City Government was able to meet social needs. It had to discover whether the City's laws were enforced, and, if not, how they might be made effective. Also whether the existing laws were sufficient and, if not, what other laws were necessary. The Bureau was also obliged to make a thorough survey of all the Municipal departments from the business standpoint, and where necessary, to reorganise them with a view to economy and efficiency on a business basis.

It will be seen, therefore, that this Bureau was a most powerful force in the Socialist Administration, for every other department of the City Government was subject to its reorganisation, provided, of course, that the Council should agree to the recommendations made.

The social side of the Bureau's work had not progressed very far as yet, though various investigations were being made. An inquiry had been held into the possibility of setting up a free Municipal legal aid bureau, as had already been done in Kansas City, Missouri, but the bill which had been drafted as a result of this had been defeated by the Wisconsin State Legislature. A number of reports by outside organisations were republished by the Bureau. One of these reports, by the 'Consumers' League' of Wisconsin, dealt with women's wages in Milwaukee.* It contained the result of an investigation by Miss Ruby Stewart into the wages and conditions of women factory and home workers, which revealed very terrible poverty and sweating, and the text of a Bill before the Wisconsin Legislature to set up wages boards similar to those of Australia. Another republished report was that of an Industrial Commission on the newsboys of Milwaukee.† This was poor throughout and exceedingly weak in its conclusions, for, whilst it urged that paper selling on the city streets by little boys between the ages of ten and fourteen should be prohibited, it stated that the prohibition need not extend to boys, even of these tender years, who were employed to deliver papers from

---

* *Women's Wages in Milwaukee*, Bulletin No. 4 (Milwaukee, WI: Bureau of Efficiency and Economy, June 1911).

† Alexander Fleisher, *The Newsboys of Milwaukee*, Bulletin No. 8 (Milwaukee, WI: Bureau of Efficiency and Economy, November 1911).

house to house on given routes. It then added provisions for mitigating the evil, 'in case,' as it said, 'the passage of a law prohibiting newspaper selling by children is not practicable.' The report concluded with the following grotesquely harsh and ignorant sentence: – 'It will not be long before women and young girls will use the streets as a cover for begging, and it would be advisable, looking forward to this contingency, to keep girls out of the streets entirely. Twenty-one years should be the minimum age for girls. The danger to morals in the narrower sense is much exaggerated between the ages of sixteen and twenty-one, and after arriving at maturity, girls should be able to take care of themselves and our ordinances against "street walking" would protect the community.' Protecting 'the community' in this case of course meant protecting the men. But the Socialist Council are only responsible for this paper in so far as they, very properly, republished it, because of its being the report of a State Industrial Commission on an important subject. It may therefore be dismissed with the hope that the speedy enfranchisement of women, both in America and in England, will bring in its train equality of treatment for men and women on questions of sexual morality by law, custom and popular opinion.

It was into the business reorganisation of the City Government that the principal activities of the Bureau of Economy and Efficiency had been thrown.

Finding that there existed no accessible collection of the law affecting the powers, duties, and responsibilities of the Milwaukee Council and that to determine any legal point necessitated a long and difficult search, they at once began to make an exhaustive survey of the laws and ordinances of which they compiled a digest and furnished a copy of this to every municipal department. Then they proceeded with the work of reorganisation.

The rooms in the City Hall set apart for the Bureau of Economy and Efficiency were all hung with charts showing how the various Municipal departments were organised and how they were affected by charitable societies, labour organisations and other outside influences. Detailed charts, showing the relation of every city official and employee to his department, had also been prepared, to secure general thoroughness of organisation and in order that newcomers might gain at a glance a general knowledge of their duties and position.

The various economies and improvements introduced by the Bureau included the consolidation of the police and fire telegraphic alarm systems, by means of which a saving of 10,000 dollars (£2,000) a year had been effected and the preparation of reorganisation plans by which it was estimated that 64,000 dollars (£12,000) a year could be saved on the working of the refuse incinerator, 6,000 dollars (£1,200) a year on the inspection of house drains and plumbing and 9,648 dollars (£1,929) a year in the collection of garbage.*

I carefully read the detailed reports published by the Bureau on these and kindred matters and in each of them I found evidence of order, honesty, integrity and the desire to cut down expenses and to obtain the greatest possible return for the money of the ratepayers. I have heard it charged against the Socialist administrators of Milwaukee that their discipline was lax and that they were over generous in finding jobs for workless men, but these reports of their Bureau of Economy and Efficiency formed infinitely more pleasant reading for the com-mercially minded economist than for the tender hearted humanitarian and the Socialist. A report of twenty-eight pages was devoted to an exhaustive inquiry into the garbage collection system.† It explained that the Bureau had sent Inspectors out to keep a watch upon the collectors. The Inspectors reported that many of the men wasted time in talking by the way and in visiting saloons and that many of the horses provided by them were too old and feeble to draw the garbage wagons as they should. Yet, though this was a report prepared by a Socialist Bureau for a Socialist town council, there was no attempt to connect these reasons for complaint with the fact that the garbage collectors were very poorly paid.

As was stated in the report, each collector received three dollars (12/-) a day both for his own services and for those of his horse and running gear, half of this sum being considered the wages of the man and half the payment for the horse and gear. One and a half dollars a day is not a fair wage for an American workman owing to the high cost of living in the

---

* Sylvia evidently obtained these figures from the following Bulletins: J.E. Treleven, *Proposed Consolidation of Fire and Police Alarm Telegraph Systems*, Bulletin No. 2 (June 1911) on the plans though not inclusive of the savings figure cited; M. Cerf, Louis Reber et al., *The Refuse Incinerator*, Bulletin No. 5 (June 1911), p. 2; Fayette H. Elwell, *Plumbing and House Drain Inspection*, Bulletin No. 10 (December 1911), p. 2; Robert E. Goodell, *Reorganization of the System of Garbage Collection*, Bulletin No. 12 (January 1911), p. 24.

† Goodell, *Reorganization of the System of Garbage Collection*.

United States,* especially, as in this case, the men were only employed on five days a week during thirty weeks in the year.

The Bureau originated various precautions for insuring that a full eight hours work a day (or, as was actually the case, a night), should be got out of the garbage men, in order to reduce their numbers from 98 in summer and 95 in winter, to 76 all the year round. It was left to a supplementary report, dated three months later, to mention the fact that three dollars and a half, and not three dollars, as in the garbage department, was the price paid for a horse and man in all other city work. In suggesting that larger wagons, to be drawn by two horses, should be employed in future, it was therefore urged that, when this was done, the collectors should be paid five dollars a day.

As for the horses, of whose wretched condition the Inspectors had complained, the report merely stated that they were provided by the collectors. It did not say whether they belonged to the men, or were hired by them. If they were owned by those ill-paid men, it was not surprising that many of the horses should be old and feeble, for their owners could not afford to set them free and buy others to take their place. If, on the other hand, the men hired the horses individually from some Company, they could not so powerfully insist that the horses supplied to them should be fit for work, as could a Municipal Government employing a large number of horses. Surely every Municipality should own the horses that it needs and should make itself responsible for their care. The raising of the collectors' wages and the Municipalization of the horses used for garbage collection, seemed to me infinitely more urgent than the building of larger wagons!

But so it was in all these reports. Careful and conscientious as they were, they contained few really radical changes affecting the wages and well-being of the Council's employees and of the poorer members of the community in general. Almost every proposal was for the prevention of some leakage through carelessness or dishonesty, or for the saving of expense by lengthening the hours of labour, or by keeping the workpeople more rigidly to their tasks during the working hours, in order that it might be possible to dispense with a number of those hitherto employed. Nowhere did I find a suggestion that wages should be raised, except in the case of the garbage collectors already mentioned, and in that of the

---

* {SP} See Appendix B, Chapter 2.

Chief Plumbing Inspector whose salary was recommended to be raised from 1,500 to 1,800 dollars a year.*

Perhaps it had to be, but the Bureau of Economy and Efficiency certainly seemed to consider the methods and machinery before the human beings. When the official, who most kindly and thoroughly explained to me all the charts and diagrams, was showing me various sub-divisions of the police department, and the improvements in organisation effected by the Bureau, I asked what experiments had been made in regard to the more human side of the work. For instance, had they engaged police detectives to be called for whenever women were arrested or were found homeless and destitute? 'No', was the reply, 'as yet we have only been able to make purely administrative changes in the direction of placing everything on an efficient and economical basis'. He added that in the State of New York a woman had been appointed a Deputy Sheriff but she had been found to be disqualified, as such appointments could only be held by persons entitled to exercise the franchise. The same objection he said would apply to the women of Milwaukee and would bar out women police constables and detectives. I suppose that a special Act of the State Legislature would have been needed to circumvent the difficulty. I also asked whether in the construction of schools, bridges and other buildings direct labour was employed by the Milwaukee City Council, as is done by many English public bodies, but again the reply was, 'No, we have not been able to do that yet'. Indeed in most directions it was impossible for the Milwaukee Council to make any reform hastily. Even the consolidation of the police and fire alarms had necessitated the passage of a Bill through the State Legislature, and the consequent waste of much valuable time.

But in spite of its being handicapped by such checks and of the fact that it is easy to criticise, difficult to perform, its work seemed to me to show that the Bureau of Economy and Efficiency was too heavily weighted with accountants, business men and University professors, who had no practical knowledge of the hardship, toil and struggle of poorer working lives. I hoped that the Bureau's influence was not tending to divert the time and energies of the whole administration too much into purely mechanical and 'business' channels.

I felt this over-emphasising of the 'business' aspect, even in regard to what I learnt of the Bureau's reconstructive arrangements. I strongly

---

* Elwell, *Plumbing*, p. 14.

feel that, as far as possible, all action by the Municipal Government should be debated and voted upon in the City Council itself, or in one of its committees or sub-committees, that the Mayor should occupy the position of chairman of the Council, and that he should only act for the Council when empowered by them to do so and in accordance with the spirit of their decisions. Also that at all meetings of the Council and its committees, both Press and Public may be present to hear the debate and see the voting. It seems to me that only thus can the busy populace be kept closely informed as to the doings of their city government and induced to take a vital and constant interest in them.

In Milwaukee, as I gather is the case in many other American municipalities, the heads of the various departments (who are popularly elected) received their authority from the Mayor, the City Council acting as an advisory body, to whom reports on the work of Municipal departments were made from time to time, and who frequently did not even know of problems that had arisen, until after they had been disposed of – when of course they might criticise if they pleased. This system seems to me to concentrate too much power and responsibility in the hands of the Mayor, and to place him too much in the hands of the officials, for how can one man keep in touch with every detail of our complicated modern civic life? Moreover the system leaves the unofficial member of the Council with too little work and too little power.

This plan of relegating the City Council to the position of a mere advisory body is rather analogous to our British Parliamentary system than to that of our own local governing bodies. The heads of American Local Government Departments are, however, elected by popular vote, not appointed by the leader of the administration, like Cabinet Ministers. Moreover they are not members of the City Council, though they have very great administrative power.

It is now generally admitted that the British Cabinet system tends to make the Party machinery all-powerful and to crush out the initiative of the private Member. For this reason many of those who have had experience of the working of the larger English County and Town Councils, as well as of Parliament itself, wish to bring the Parliamentary system more into line with that of the Municipalities.

The American Local Government method of electing the heads of departments by popular vote, seems to me very much better than to allow the Prime Minister to choose his colleagues. Our Cabinet Ministers usually obtain their places by reason of their value as party men.* Generous donations to party funds, loyalty to the party machine, or leadership of a faction which the Prime Minister wishes to draw to his standard, together with a good platform manner, are the qualifications most likely to secure Cabinet rank in this country.

Though, as is the case in America, Party feeing would still undoubtedly exercise great influence in the election of British Ministers for a long time to come, it is quite certain that candidates standing for popular election to headships of Government Departments would be obliged to show some special qualifications for the office and some technical knowledge of the work. A change in the personnel, if not always in the politics, of Cabinet Ministers would immediately result, and non-party men who were recognized experts in various fields would begin to occupy Cabinet posts. If, for instance, the Presidency of the Local Government Board were to be thrown open to popular election, I think there is no doubt that Mr Sidney Webb (or Mrs Webb, if women were eligible) would receive the votes of the majority of the people of this country.[†] But Mr Sidney Webb is not a party man and so we have in that office Mr John Burns,[‡]

---

* {SP} This appears to be less true of American Cabinet Ministers, though they are chosen by the President of the United States and not by popular vote, because they act merely as heads of the various departments, are not members of the legislative assembly, and have no power to dictate the legislative programme, as our Cabinet Ministers have. I am sure those of them who really desire reforms must often wish that they had the power of the popular vote behind them.

† Sidney Webb (1859–1947) and Beatrice Webb, née Potter (1858–1943), were early members of the Fabian Society and founders of the London School of Economics. From 1905 to 1909, Beatrice Webb headed the Minority Report to the Royal Commission on the Poor Laws. The report, to which Sidney Webb also contributed, emphasised the structural causes of poverty and advocated increased state provision. This took place in close proximity to the London suffragettes: The National Committee to Promote the Break-Up of the Poor Law, which published the report, was based at 5–6 Clement's Inn while the WSPU was at number 4. Although rejected by the Royal Commission in favour of the more conservative Majority Report, it was widely influential and seen as one of the intellectual precursors of the welfare state. Sidney Webb would later hold Cabinet posts in the Labour governments of 1924 and 1929–31.

‡ John Burns (1858–1943) had formerly been a leading socialist. In 1886, he was tried and acquitted on charges of conspiracy and sedition for his part in a demonstration protesting against rising unemployment in the course of which windows of fashionable London clubs were smashed. On 13 November 1887, Burns joined a demonstration against government inaction over unemployment and repression in Ireland. The demonstration, which had been banned by the

who does not possess one-hundredth part of Mr Webb's technical knowledge and executive ability.

At the same time, even if some such expert as Mr Sidney Webb were to be placed at the head of the Local Government Board, I should consider it infinitely more satisfactory that he should preside as Chairman of a committee – a Local Government Board of Members of Parliament – than that he should be given, as at present, practically absolute autocratic power over his department. Though there is little danger that he would become, as Mr Burns has done, a mere tool of the permanent officials, I for one, should want to have Mr Webb's theories checked by the experience of men and women of the class that, when faced with want and misfortune, has been rebuffed and flouted by the Local Government Board these many many years.*

It is true, no doubt, that if a thoroughly able and honest administration can be guaranteed in every case, great speed, regularity, and business economy of working, can be secured by concentrating executive power in the hands of a small group of experts. But unless the majority of the ordinary busy people take a very lively interest in the government of their city, unless every department of that government is brought

---

Police Commissioner, was dubbed 'Bloody Sunday' as it was attacked by mounted police resulting in hundreds of arrests, multiple injuries and two deaths. Burns was again put on trial and this time jailed; Sylvia's father Dr Richard Pankhurst was among those on the platform of the meeting held to celebrate Burns's release from imprisonment six weeks later: *The Link*, 25 February 1888. In 1889, Burns played a leading role in the Great Dock Strike in London, often regarded as the birth of 'New Unionism'. While many of those involved in these struggles became involved in the early Labour Party, Burns became the Liberal MP for Battersea and was appointed to the Cabinet after the Liberals won the 1906 general election. In their high-profile trial in 1908, Emmeline and Christabel Pankhurst sought to undermine the prosecution by equating the suffragettes' actions with those of John Burns, the Cabinet Minister: 'he incited people to violence, and you know, of course, that he is in the Government to-day, and from being a law-breaker he is now a law-maker? Does it occur to you that we may follow the same course?': Christabel Pankhurst, quoted in Emmeline Pankhurst, *The Trial of the Suffragette Leaders* (London: The Woman's Press, 1908), p. 32. Sylvia later explained that Burns was a particular target of the suffragettes because '[a]s the assumed special representative of Labour and democracy in the Government, he was selected for attack by way of exposing the hollowness of the Government's professions, since it would not practise them towards women': Pankhurst, *The Suffragette Movement*, p. 220.

* The Local Government Board was responsible for administering poor relief.

before them, they cannot gain the experience that will fit them either to choose their administrators or to act as a check upon those whom they have chosen. Moreover the very basis of representative government is surely the principle that only the interplay of minds and wills, variously reflecting the interests of every section of the community, can secure justice and fair dealing for all. With the more perfect application of the representative idea, and the consequent development of the view that all forms of labour must receive due representation, one may look forward to the time when the garbage collectors, the scrub women,* and the other city employees, will be powerfully represented by those who will be able to speak for them with direct knowledge of their lives and work, when plans for the reconstruction of the departments employing them are underway. Who can doubt that, apart from its value to the workers to whom the community is indebted, a system which would give them a share of the decisive power when matters affecting their work were under consideration, must lead to many a useful practical result.

I understood, that in their reorganisation schemes, the tendency of the Milwaukee Bureau of Economy and Efficiency was to accentuate the custom of placing the chief executive power in the hands of the Mayor, and to provide that this power should pass direct through him, and not through the Council itself, to the heads of departments. This leaning towards the methods of private business undertakings, rather than to the further extension of the democratic ideal, seemed to me unfortunate and probably due to the very large preponderance of business men in the Bureau. Nevertheless I am aware that the Milwaukee Bureau was acting in accordance with the prevailing ideals of Municipal Reformers throughout the United States, and that they were in close touch with all the most progressive Councils in the country.

So strongly is the desire developing that Municipal power and responsibility shall be handed over to an expert few, that many advocate what is called the commission form of government. Under the commission system each Municipal Department is placed in the hands of a single popularly elected official. It is like the Cabinet without Parliament!

But however one might criticise certain features of the work of the Bureau of Economy and Efficiency, one could not fail to admire the

---

* {SP} If these have not been emancipated by mechanical inventions and opportunities of more congenial employment.

keenly enthusiastic desire to perfect the administration which was apparent amongst the officers of every department.

Municipal Library.   The Municipal Library, which the Socialist Council had established to keep its officials in touch with Municipal activities all over the world, was but one of the many evidences of this spirit.

Child Welfare Bureau.   The Bureau of Child Welfare, another department established by the Socialist administration, was set up with the object of co-ordinating the management of all the children's institutions for which the Municipality was already responsible and of adding many further activities for the benefit of the city's children. The Secretaries, Mr and Mrs Wilbur Phillips,* the clerks, probation officers and others in the Children's Bureau, all seemed eager, vigorous and essentially young – certainly all were young in spirit, if some few were no longer so in years. Only Americans would confide work so momentous to youthful hands, but they have faith in youth and in what is fresh enthusiasms can accomplish. I found everyone in this department preparing to leave at the close of the busy day, and have ever since regretted that circumstances prevented my finding other opportunities of seeing their work.

Free Labour Employment Bureau.   Passing to the Labour Employment Bureau, established by the Socialists in March 1911, I found the Superintendent, Mr Fred King, weighed down by the knowledge that his office gave him no power to strike at the root problems of unemployment, but only to tinker a little with the evil on the surface, by helping a few cases here and there. The record of the Bureau was depressing, as those of such institutions always are. Out of 3,850 persons who registered, work was found for 1,100, or 28 per cent, and only in the case of 497, or 12 per cent of the applicants, was the work of permanent character. Record cards were kept in the case of 915 of those for whom work was found. Of these 915, only 267 registered as labourers and 80 as farm hands, yet 815 of the applicants were obliged to accept employment as ordinary labourers and 174 as farm hands. Thus very few persons actually obtained permanent employment at their own trade.

---

* Socialist couple Wilbur C. Phillips (1880–1967) and Elsie Cole Phillips (1879–1961). Sylvia was the guest of Elsie Phillips and Crystal Eastman in Milwaukee on 31 January 1912.

Only four women applied for work to the Bureau, probably because there was no woman official and no separate room for women applicants. The maintenance of the Bureau cost 340 dollars (£68). That is to say 31 cents (1/ 3 ½d) for every person who obtained work. This cost was born by the Merchants' and Manufacturers' Association, representatives from whom and from the City City [sic] Council, the County Board of Supervisors, the Federated Trades Council, the Chamber of Commerce and the Press Club, formed a general committee on unemployment.*

THE HEALTH DEPARTMENT

The Director of the Health Department was Dr Kraft, a dark active man, with a black beard and sparkling eyes, full of vitality and talk. Dr Kraft and his Department felt that an important part of their mission was to teach the citizens of Milwaukee the laws of healthful living. With this object, they organised a Bureau of 'Education and Publications', which was opened on June 23rd, 1911. From this Bureau they issued large numbers of leaflets on hygiene, sanitation, milk, tuberculosis and the prevention of infectious and contagious diseases, and replied to correspondents asking advice on health matters. They also organised health exhibits in shop windows in two of the principal thoroughfares and in connection with various exhibitions that were held in the town. One of these exhibits represented a clean well-managed 'store', or as we should say, shop, placed side by side with a dirty neglected shop, kept by a dishonest man. Once an hour the insanitary shop was visited by an Inspector, who rated the shopkeeper for his various misdeeds and shortcomings for the information of all who might stop to hear.

A monthly magazine, called the *Healthologist*, was also published, and sent regularly to any who made application for it.† Its circulation quickly rose to between 7,000 and 8,000. Beside endeavouring to spread general hygienic knowledge amongst the citizens, the *Healthologist* gave statistical tables of births, marriages and deaths, the growth of population and the incidence of disease. It reported the work of the Sanitary

---

* These figures are evidently derived from Fred A. King, *Citizens' Free Employment Bureau*, Bulletin No. 6 (September 1911), pp. 4, 8, 10, 4, 3–4.

† Sylvia was impressed with the *Healthologist*. She sent some pages from the January 1912 edition of its exposure of insanitary conditions to Keir Hardie in her letter of 5 February 1912.

Inspectors, giving descriptions and photographs of slum property and dilapidated tenement dwellings, manufacturers' chimneys whose smoke was a nuisance to the neighbourhood, and defective lavatory accommodation in schools and factories, all of which had been, or were about to be condemned. Very drastic steps were taken to secure pure air for the citizens of Milwaukee, for whilst in 1908 and 1909 there were only respectively 9 and 21 prosecutions for excessive discharge of black smoke, in 1910, the Socialists having come into power in the autumn, there were 29 prosecutions and in 1911 there were 55 prosecutions before November 1st. In response to complaints of inhabitants in regard to the terrible smells arising during the rendering of animal matter, which was extensively practised in Milwaukee, the Socialist Council, after a number of abortive attempts to secure that it should be done under proper conditions, prohibited all the rendering of animal matter, except that intended for human food, within the corporate boundaries of the city.

Lists were published in the *Healthologist* of the Milwaukee Dairies and Bakeries, with an analysis showing how the Inspector had reported upon them, in order that the citizens might know where they could buy pure and clean milk and bread. An analysis was also given of various so-called 'soothing syrups' for babies, which showed that every one contained morphine, chloroform, opium, or some other drug highly dangerous to infant life.

By its fearless exposures of the corrupt practices which everywhere form so serious a menace to the public health, the *Healthologist* made for itself many enemies, and those who were interested in maintaining the evils against which it fought, described it as 'mental garbage'.

The Socialist Health Department did not content itself with giving advice and administering punishment. Amongst other things it issued freely on the written order of any Milwaukee physician, silver nitrate, for prevention of blindness in babies, to those who could not afford to pay for it. It also administered the Pasteur treatment without charge to the poor.

The Isolation Hospital. Shortly after the Socialists took office, an agitation arose for a new isolation hospital. The city had never hitherto undertaken such an effort, the two existing hospitals having been built originally by private enterprise and handed over to the city, because their promoters lacked the money for their support. These institutions had never been entirely satisfactory and with the growth of the town had become too small. The Council had therefore responded to the popular demand and had proceeded to build an isolation hospital, which was now nearing completion and would be one of the most well equipped in the United States.

*　*　*

THE PRISON FARM

Before my first visit to the City Hall, I had been taken to see the House of Correction – a prison, dingy and monotonous for men, a shade more dreary and monotonous for women. A reporter from the Socialist daily newspaper, *The Milwaukee Leader*, had met me at the door of the place as I came out and had asked my opinion of it. Some of what I said appeared in the *Milwaukee Leader* next morning,* and whilst I was at the City Hall that afternoon I was accosted by the Inspector of Prisons and a big strongly built man of the people with a German accent, – Mr Martin Mies, a member of the Milwaukee Prisons Board. Mr Mies told me, and his words were corroborated by the Inspector, that all my criticisms of the House of Correction would react against the Socialist administration and that the Socialists would be blamed for every fault that I had mentioned, though these faults had continued for more than a generation, and though many of them could never be eradicated until the building itself was pulled down. But though he opened the conversation as though he were angry with me, it soon appeared that Mr Mies – an enthusiast beneath his rather gruff exterior – was anxious to unfold to me – as anyone who would care for them – the plans that he and his friends were cherishing for the thing that was to supersede the dismal House of Correction before many months were gone. At once we agreed that Mr Mies, the Inspector and I should go together to visit the site of the future institution, and within half an hour we were starting off in a little open red motor car which belonged to the Municipality.

---

* Sylvia's comments appeared under the title 'Sylvia Pankhurst Thinks Prison Here Is Not as Bad as England's'. However, the text explained that she 'says that the Milwaukee prison is very bad indeed, compared with many other institutions which she has visited in this country' and that 'she shuddered perceptibly when shown the punishment cells': *Milwaukee Leader*, 31 January 1912, p. 5.

We rushed away, leaving behind the city streets and the scattered houses on the outskirts of the town, into the open country. The branches of the trees seemed quite black against the broad fields of snow. The road was terribly rough, with deep ruts and holes through which the car went jolting, but the sky was very bright and the air was fresh and keen.

Suddenly we dipped down into a hollow and stopped beside some overhanging trees. To the left of us was a little farm house. A tall man came to the farmyard gate and opened it for us, as we jumped out of the car. As we climbed the high steps leading to the front door a buxom rosy-faced woman came smiling out to us. The door opened into a little kitchen where there was a fine big fire. She took us through the kitchen into her parlour which was lined with homely* country furniture and ornaments, and where also there was a blazing fire. A bedroom opened out of the parlour, and this completed her own and her husband's home.

I went with her into the bedroom to tidy my hair, now all blown about by our speedy drive. I asked her how she liked the place and how she thought she should like the Institution. She laughed and said that the place was healthy, that, though she had never before had anything to do with an Institution, she thought she could 'get used to it', and that, so far, she had seen nothing to complain of in 'them'.

When we joined Mr Mies and the Inspector, her husband was saying: 'Why, yes, of course, they are all right.'

Then we went out to explore. In the lower part of the little farm house was a sort of granary, where there were many filled sacks and tools of all kinds. A carrot top that had sent out long pale green shoots hung against the wall. A middle-aged man came in as we stood there and took a spade from amongst a pile of them that were leaning against the wall. He was dressed in the shabby, ill-fitting brown clothes of the House of Correction. The farmer spoke a cheery word to him and the man said 'good-day' to us all as we passed out.

We crossed the farmyard and made our way, by a narrow trodden path at the edge of a little wood, to the door of a shed which the farmer opened for us. It was dusky and warm inside, with straw on the ground and a pile of some kind of tall dried grass in one corner and big sleek horses standing in their stalls. A dark skinned American Indian was rubbing down one of the horses and another man was cleaning out one of the

---

* {SP}'Homely' in the English sense, as it is used, here, means 'homelike'. To Americans it means ugly.

stalls. Both wore the House of Correction clothing. For a few moments we stayed to talk with them about the weather, the late snow and the possibility of another fall, crop prospects and other things connected with the farm.

Close to the stable was a little old house partly furnished. One of its rooms was used for storing beans and household cereals, and a man in whitish cotton overalls, was pouring some beans into a sieve. We were told that he had been chosen to help with the cooking and that this was considered a special privilege. There were two or three beds in each of the upstairs rooms, and altogether they could accommodate about a dozen men, who were sent down here from the House of Correction, to help with the farming as required, until the new Institution should be built, when both the existing houses would be pulled down.

'Then you do not find it necessary for someone to be always in charge of the men, to see that they work and to prevent them running away?' I asked the farmer. 'Why, no,' he answered. 'There's no trouble with them. They like being here.' 'If they were to run away,' the Inspector said, 'I should soon find them out and bring them back. I know them all.'

On a little eminence flanked by dark pine woods, was the proposed site of the Institution. The plans were not yet drawn, but Mr Mies kindly lent to me the instructions laid down for the guidance of the architects who were to send in competing designs. From these instructions I learnt that the Institution was to consist of the following buildings: –

A 12-roomed house for the Inspector and his family and a 12-roomed house for the Deputy Inspector, four rooms of which were to be set apart for other officers and approached by a separate entrance.

An administration building, consisting of a reception room, library, business office, Inspector's office, Deputy Inspector's office, guard room, measuring room, housekeeper's closet, store closet, surgery, operating theatre, drug room, special sick wards and so on, the total ground floor area not to exceed 6,000 square feet.

A hospital of two wings, one of which was to be used for tubercular patients.

A Refectory Building, to contain accommodation for the preparation and distribution of food for 600 inmates, and to include a kitchen; pantry; cold storage, with separate rooms for meat, meat cutting, milk, butter, cheese, scraps and two cold storage rooms for vegetables; a bakery, with flour room having capacity for 400 barrels, bake room and bread room; a serving room, two dining rooms, each to accommodate 100 inmates.

A chapel to accommodate 600 inmates.

An unspecified number of punishment cells were to be attached to the administration building.

There were to be 160 cells for 'hardened criminals'. These cells were to be built up in two separate cell houses of two storeys high, each cell house to contain 80 cells. One cell house was to be arranged on the interior cell block plan, the other to have the cells built against the outer walls. Each cell was to contain not less than 60 square feet. There was to be a bathroom for the alternate use of the inmates of the two cell houses.

There were also to be erected two buildings, each containing ten special cells to be used as 'living and occupation rooms' for persons in solitary confinement.

Arrangements to accommodate one hundred and sixty 'hardened criminals' and to keep twenty persons in close solitary confinement, seemed out of harmony with the farm as I had seen it. I hoped that, in practice, it would be found unnecessary to keep either in sleeping cells or close confinement 30 per cent of the 600 inmates as here suggested. Happily America more readily 'tears down' unsuitable buildings and starts afresh than we in England do.

The remaining four hundred and twenty inmates were to be housed in cottages. These were to be built in three distinct groups, two cottages to be at first erected in each group and others to be added as required.

Two of the groups were to have one cottage for sixty inmates and one for forty. The cottages for sixty inmates were to contain officers' quarters, ample housekeeper's closets, and clothes airing rooms, pantry and sewing room, inmates' coat rooms and bath rooms with showers, and barber's shop. The inmates were to sleep in dormitories, 45 square feet of floor space being allowed for each one. There was to be a dining room, a day room (2,000 square feet) and a reading room (400 square feet).

The cottages for forty inmates were to be much the same, except that in addition to the dining room, day room and reading room, there was also to be a workroom.

In the third group both the cottages were to accommodate forty inmates. One of these was to be exactly like those in the other groups, but the other was to have separate bedrooms instead of dormitories, and a shoemaker's shop and tailor's shop were to be attached to it.

Two separate workshops for varied trades were to be provided for the men whose cottages contained no workroom, and a third for the 'hardened criminals' of the cell houses. A laundry building was to be erected, to cope with the washing, sorting and mending for the 600 male inmates and the officers; also a Power House, containing boiler rooms, engine rooms, electric power and light generators, pump rooms and so on; and a tool repair shop and blacksmith's shop.

From the foregoing arrangements it will be seen that a very varied life and training was to be opened to the men.

The women's department was to accommodate thirty-five inmates. Twenty-five of these were to be housed in one cottage, which was to contain a reception room, matron's room, assistant matron's room, sitting room and dining room for matron and assistant matron, kitchen, pantry and serving room, housekeeper's closet, clean clothes room and clothes airing room. Also twenty-five single bedrooms, each containing 80 square feet, the bedrooms to be divided into two distinct groups, a sitting and bathroom to be provided for each group. Also three hospital bedrooms and a doctor's room.

Another cottage was to house the remaining ten inmates. It was to contain a sitting room, dining room and bedroom for one woman officer, ten bedrooms and a dining room, sitting room and bathroom for the inmates, a kitchen, pantry, store closet and so on as before.

A hand laundry was to be attached to each of these cottages.

These architectural instructions seemed to indicate that the women were to be taught domestic work alone, even the washing was to be done by hand as it would be in an ordinary home. The life that was being planned for them promised to be much less varied than that designed for the men, who, beside the work of the farm, would be able to learn boot-making, blacksmithing, tailoring and a variety of other trades. The fact that whilst the men inmates would number from 400 to 600, no more than 35 women were expected would to a certain extent account for this difference. But, for the individual woman prisoner, the fact that women are the more law-abiding half of the community and are therefore sent to prison in smaller numbers, does not make it less important that complete facilities should be provided to give her a new start in life, than if she were a man!

To secure for the women prisoners a variety of training suited to many temperaments, ages, and capabilities, it would probably be necessary for various localities to share a joint prison and to elect joint boards of management.

It is not always realized with sufficient clearness that women are no more 'all alike' than are men, and that if a human being has gone astray when engaged in one occupation, there is at least a strong probability that, either the occupation itself, or the sort of life that it entailed, has been unsuited to the character of the individual concerned. A change of work and surroundings may remove the cause of the trouble.

A striking example of this kind was the case of a toy-maker whose house I once visited in the Tyrol. This man was for many years a ne'er do well, who refused to work, drank heavily and was supported by his wife, who worked terribly hard to maintain the home and children by any odd jobs that she could get. By some chance, the man all at once discovered that he had a talent, and, which was infinitely more important, a desire to paint. He was soon hard at work painting quaint conventional ornaments on boxes, baskets and furniture, and wooden figures of people and animals cut out in silhouette. Before long he had developed a most profitable business and was employing several men and women to copy his designs. He had become a thoroughly respected member of the community – a reformed character in every way.*

From the raised site of the institution, a road between the fir trees led us down to a broad grassy opening and the sloping banks of a round pond. 'This is where the men will bathe,' said Mr Mies. 'I can see them all sitting together out here in the evening after the day's work is done. … We must not treat them as criminals, they are just men like ourselves, who are down and out and have had nothing but hard luck. … We want to give them a chance here to build up their health and their manhood and to start life again. …' So he talked on in his enthusiasm.

There was a glamour about the place with its dark trees and vastness of snow covered country, the keen sweet air, and the broad sky now flooded with evening gold. Such a strong fine contrast it was to that dismal prison in the town with the bowed listless men and the women always cooped in the same dreary house of cells. I could see the men, as he could, ploughing, sowing and reaping and working at all their many trades. I

---

* This refers to an episode in Partenkirchen during the holiday to Austria and Germany that Emmeline Pethick Lawrence invited Sylvia and Annie Kenney to join her on in the summer of 1910. Sylvia would also recall this individual in her suffragette memoirs, once again as a means of critiquing a prison system that denied prisoners productive activity and self-respect: 'the organizer of the industry [toy and furniture painting] had been the "black sheep" of his village till he discovered his aptitude for this craft. That took my thoughts back to the drear wastefulness of our English prisons, and my impatience to have the vote struggle over and done with that we might move on to constructive work caused an un- restful undercurrent in my mind': Pankhurst, *The Suffragette Movement*, p. 335.

could see the women too, milking the cows and feeding the chickens and tending the garden patch. I could see them out in the hayfields in the sunshine and working in the little cottages with the windows opened wide. And, as well as the men, who would bathe in the pond each morning and lie around it, telling stories perhaps, after their day's work was done, I could see the women playing too. Once or twice I asked him questions about the women and the plans that were being made for them, but though he answered kindly enough, it was easy to see that all his hopes and enthusiasms were for the men. And so, as I heard him talk, I prayed that some woman with heart and brain tuned to the task might have the power to plan and strive for the women and to toil to make a new future for them also, as this man was doing for the men.

Then we went back to the little house, where the farmer's wife gave us great glasses of rich milk and huge brawn sandwiches and cake, beside the kitchen fire. Afterwards she came out on the step with smiles and kind words to watch us go. The farmer and one of the prisoners held the gate open for us and helped us to settle our rugs in the car as we set off in the dusk. Mr Mies talked on still of the farm and its possibilities, but there was a weight on my heart, for I knew that those who had conceived this work of human regeneration would not be allowed to build it. This would either be done by other people, perhaps by people whose sympathies were alien to the task, or the whole scheme might be dropped for years to come.

*   *   *

THE WATER

When I had scarcely reached the borders of Wisconsin, on buying a newspaper in the train, I learnt that there was a typhoid scare in Milwaukee and that a hue and cry was being raised about the water. Typhoid had been rife in many other cities that I had visited and I was frequently warned not to drink the water anywhere, unless I could learn on good authority that it was pure. But in no town save Milwaukee, had the water question appeared to arouse excitement.

Milwaukee draws its water supply from Lake Michigan, on whose banks it stands, and it drains all its sewage into the Lake. Ever since the town began this has continued, and as the population has grown, the evil effects of the practice have naturally grown with it. Generations of administrators had come and gone from the City Hall and had done nothing to check the pollution of the Lake; but when, for the first time, the *Socialists* secured office, the Democratic, the 'Standpat' Republicans and the 'Progressive' Republican* Newspapers all found in this typhoid scare a weapon with which to flagellate the Socialist administration! In October 1911 there were 90 cases of typhoid fever, in November there were 77 new cases and including those who had not recovered since the last report, 136 cases in all; in December there were 139 cases, including 73 new cases. In these three months there were respectively two, thirteen and six deaths from typhoid.[†]

The following table gives the relative positions in regard to mortality from typhoid (enteric) of a number of European countries, and of Australia, New Zealand and Ontario, also the approximate typhoid death rate in Milwaukee, taking the months of October, November and December 1911 as one fourth of the year.

	Average death rate per 1,000 living in the years 1906–1910 from enteric.
Spain.	0.32
Hungary.	0.27
Austria.	0.14
Roumania.	0.20
Netherlands.	0.06
Prussia.	0.05
England and Wales.	0.07
Ireland.	0.08
Australia.	0.16
New Zealand.	0.07
Ontario.	0.31
Milwaukee. (population 383,000)	Annual death rate per 1,000 taking the months of October, November and December 1911 as one-fourth of the year. 0.21

---

* 'Standpat' Republicans were the more conservative faction; in context of Milwaukee, the 'Progressive' Republicans refers to the supporters of Robert LaFollette (1855–1925), who broke with the Republican Party to found the Progressive Party.

† Sylvia would have found these figures in the *Healthologist*, November 1911, p. 28; December 1911, p. 28 and January 1912, p. 28.

Counting the typhoid case rate per 100,000 of the Milwaukee population in the months of October, November and December, as though it were a quarter of that for the whole year, and comparing it with the case rates in the worst English districts, we see that Milwaukee, with great natural advantages, had at least during those three months a higher typhoid case rate than any of them,* as the following table shows:-

	Case rate.
Blaydon (Urban district) Durham.	311
Houghton le Spring (Rural District) Durham.	204
Ashton in Makerfield (Urban District) Lancashire.	237
Ashington (Urban District) Northumberland.	329
Milwaukee, (October, November and December taken as a quarter of year 1911).	357

The pollution of the city's water was undoubtedly a serious matter and as everyone was abusing Dr Kraft, I enquired of Dr Kraft about it. He told me that the water was less impure than that of many other cities, notably that of Cleveland, but he admitted, that from the hygienic point of view, to be merely less bad than others is no defence. I asked him whether it would not be possible for Milwaukee to cease turning its sewage into the Lake and, instead, to put it onto the land, where it might be converted into useful products for farming and other purposes. He replied that such a scheme would be very costly and would take perhaps ten years to accomplish. He considered that it would be more possible to sterilize the water by means of ozone, as is done in St. Petersburg. He and his colleagues had begun investigating the water question and consulting experts upon it, long before the typhoid scare had arisen. They had arranged for the public exhibition of an ozone apparatus during the summer and several articles on the properties of ozone had appeared in the *Healthologist*.

The ozone plan did not appeal to me, except as a temporary expedient for purifying the water, for it seemed to me fundamentally unwise to

---

* {SP} Even during the typhoid epidemic, tuberculosis was however a more serious menace to the citizens of Milwaukee, for whilst in October, November and December 1911 the cases of typhoid numbered 77, 136 and 139 respectively and the deaths 2, 13 and 6, the cases of tuberculosis during the same months numbered 1,406, 1,403 and 1,451, and the deaths 42, 15 and 31.

continue the pollution of the lake, even if afterwards the water could be rendered absolutely sterile. But as I talked to Dr Kraft, I felt that he, and probably his colleagues with him, had somewhat failed to realise the magnitude of the storm of feeling that was being raised against them and that Dr Kraft, at least, had failed to understand that some part of that feeling was not animated by mere party antagonism, but by the desire to safeguard the public health. I wished that the Socialist administration would immediately come forward with a big scheme for dealing with the sewage on the land in the most scientific manner possible, and that they would also adopt some immediate means of purifying the water supply. I was impatient at their delay. Yet I knew that they were faced with tremendous difficulties on every hand. Their critics, who were urging on the water outcry, confined themselves to vaguely charging the Health Department with inertia and to complaining that it was not giving sufficiently grave warning of the water's condition. Warnings, from any quarter, inclined to be superfluous at the time, for every newspaper was publishing long columns of warning and startling alarmist headlines. It was certain that whatever the Socialists might do to strike at the root of the water evil, critics would bitterly oppose on the score of its cost. The same sections that had clamoured for the isolation hospital were already making capital out of the money which the Socialist administration had been obliged to spend in building it. A reporter on one of the Republican newspapers said to me: 'The Socialists are not a bit better than other people, they were expected to reduce the rates and they have not done so and they only built the isolation hospital because they were forced to do it.' 'How can they reduce the rates when they are undertaking such schemes as the Isolation Hospital?' I asked.

The answer was: 'Well, they have not done so much as they might for housing. We are publishing the result of an investigation which shows how bad housing still is.'

I said: 'I suppose when they take up the housing question on an extensive scale you will attack them for raising the rates?'

'I suppose so,' was the cynical reply.

To abuse reformers for their expenditure is, naturally, a very powerful means of attack upon them. The very poor, whom their reforms were designed to help and by whom they are most needed, are prone to resent the raising of the rates to pay for reforms, because they can so ill afford to pay any rates at all. When a City Council raises the wages of its sweated employees, the even more sweated employees of private persons must help to pay for the increase.

There was little wonder, that with but two months left of their term of office, the Milwaukee Socialist administration should wish to see the Isolation Hospital, the prison farm and other half finished schemes fairly started before undertaking another big enterprise. Yet I wish they had plunged into a bold plan for dealing with the sewage and the purification of the water and had done as much as they could to get all the contracts settled, so that they could not be withdrawn from, however the coming election might result. To have done this – to have tried to do it – would probably have lost them the election –? The event proved it had been lost without.*

Sympathetic doubters of Socialism and Socialists frequently believe, as politicians of the old schools tell them, that Socialist legislators and administrators must be feared for their quixotic recklessness and hot headed zeal. And yet how circumstances combine to wear down the active fighting faculties of the legislative and administrative pioneer! All the atmosphere and tradition of politics, all the influence of politicians, make for inaction, compromise, delay. The earnest sense of responsibility, the very strength of the desire to act worthily in the pioneer's own breast often lead to hesitation. Caution whispers 'to act boldly is to lose your seat and with it all your opportunity for good.' Meanwhile political opponents magnify mild little acts and sayings into things of revolutionary import and so cause friends and foes, who are not conversant with practical details and do not realize that this is merely politicians' make-believe, to think that doughty and even reckless fights are taking place.

Already the rival Political Parties – the Democrats, the 'Standpat' Republicans and the Progressive Republicans, the Lafollette followers, were joining their forces to oust the Milwaukee Socialists.† The previous administration had been notoriously corrupt and the Socialists had been sent in on a wave of popular indignation to drive corruption out. They had succeeded. The Progressive Republicans who professed to specialise in purity of administration, were obliged to admit, 'Oh yes, they have

---

* Seidel's opponents united on the 'nonpartisan' candidature of former commissioner of health, Dr Gerhard Bading, to unseat the socialist mayor in the elections of 1912.

† See note above on p. 132.

given a clean administration', and as a matter of fact the Socialists had not, so far, introduced any reform that could be held to be out of harmony with the *professions* of the Progressive Party. Yet the Progressive Party was making common cause with the old reactionaries to secure the Socialists' defeat.

The defeat, which followed surely, was numerically overwhelming, but this much had been gained, – for the first time in the history of Milwaukee's Municipal politics, the Socialist administrators had set a high standard of integrity and endeavour, and once having known a genuinely honest and efficient administration, Milwaukee will expect more of its City Council in the future than it ever did before. It will not be long before the Socialists are given another chance.*

Meanwhile the Socialists elected to govern Schenectady in New York State, were able to carry on the work which their comrades of Milwaukee had been obliged, for the time being, to lay aside. Mayor Lunn and his colleagues on the Schenectady Council early discovered a means of surmounting the obstacles to municipal trading which had proved so formidable a handicap in Milwaukee.† When, during the summer of 1912, the price of ice was forced up by a Trust, until the poor could not afford to buy it, the Municipality began selling ice to the citizens on its own account and found that it could do so, without loss, at one third of the prevailing price. The Ice Trust of course obtained an injunction to restrain the Town Council's operations, but the Mayor and Councillors then formed themselves into a co-operative society and carried on their business as before. They afterwards commenced trading in both coal and groceries and whereas private companies were selling coal at 14 dollars, (£2-16-0), a ton, the Council was able to sell it, without loss, at 5 dollars (£1-0-0).

---

* Sylvia's prediction proved correct. The socialists were re-elected in 1916 with Daniel Hoan (1881–1961), the former City Attorney, becoming the city's second socialist mayor, a post he held until 1940. Frank P. Zeidler (1912–2006) became Milwaukee's third socialist mayor, holding the post from 1948 to 1960.

† George R. Lunn (1873–1948), socialist mayor of Schenectady, elected in 1911. Sylvia spoke in Schenectady's Red Men's Hall on 27 March 1912 as part of the WPU's tour of upstate New York. Her comments here on events in the summer of 1912 testify to her continued interest in socialism in America.

6. A Red Indian College

Sylvia's identity as an artist is most apparent in this chapter on Native Americans. The beginning of the chapter is drawn from another letter written to Keir Hardie from a train, this time the Union Pacific, which Sylvia took from Los Angeles in California to Lawrence in Kansas in mid-March 1911. As the train sped through New Mexico, Sylvia tried to capture the atmosphere, the colours and the figures as they sped past: 'We are going through [New] Mexico. Oh the strangest and most desolate country. What indeed possessed any body of people to settle here? The ground is all sandy a dull redish [*sic*] brown with faded shrubs some grey and dead looking.'[1]

These words, and those that followed, were then adapted for the descriptive opening of this chapter in which the flashes of colour and changes in tone suggest an artist craving her brushes. It is as an artist that Sylvia identifies with the Native Americans. Influenced by the Arts and Crafts movement in Britain, she is evidently impressed by the crafts-manship of Native American artists. The letter to Hardie informs us that at the railway station, where Sylvia admired Native American wares, she bought Hardie a gift: 'the blue stones that my Darling likes and so I found something for him.'[2] Sylvia was, however, acutely aware of the destructive effect of the commercialisation of Native American culture and writes passionately against the exploitation that she sees business-men, and not Native Americans themselves, profiting from. She mourns the way that the forcing of Native Americans into the labour market, and their low wages, results in a cultural impoverishment, as they can only afford to purchase 'cheap machine-made things'.

Sylvia demonstrated a sophisticated and multifaceted understanding of the relationship between the ideology of the modern American nation and the racism experienced by Native Americans. In this chapter, she notes the ubiquitous state representations of Native Americans among the wild beasts forced aside by white settlers. The dispossession of the Native Americans from their land runs throughout the chapter. In her letter to Hardie, she explained how the harsh conditions of the reservations that the Native Americans had been forced onto would provide the pretext for further racist representations: 'the whole land is barren and forlorn. It is here they have driven the poor Indians and now they will say they are lazy and will not work!'[3] Her discussion of this in her letter to Hardie underlines their shared concern to understand and challenge racist narratives.

Sylvia was evidently expected by her hosts to express her approval of Haskell Institute, a college for Native Americans in Lawrence; on 16 March, a luncheon was held in Sylvia's honour by Mrs H.H. Fiske, the wife of the college superintendent.[4] Again, Sylvia observed the destruction of indigenous skills, which was a stated intention of the college, and which was boasted of by the teacher Sylvia encountered.[5] Writing on the training that female students received, Sylvia noticed the similarity of their work to those of 'the jaded sweated factory wage slaves'. Myriam Vučković's study of Haskell demonstrates that in this period, the propagation of a 'scientific' racism which proclaimed racially proscribed differences, justified limiting education in Native American colleges to 'vocational training in order to prepare students for a working-class life on the margin of American society'.[6] Sylvia did not attempt to conceal her objections. In an interview with a Kansas reporter (a female whom Sylvia asked if she received equal pay), Sylvia provided 'an explanation that the Indian school at Haskell was so civilized as to give no adequate idea of the real Indian'.[7] Capitalist 'civilization', Sylvia identified, was obliterating a people and their culture not only in obvious but also in insidious and apparently enlightened ways. As an artist, she found the language to express her disgust at that process and her solidarity with its victims.

A RED INDIAN COLLEGE

The train passed on through New Mexico, on through the dreary desert. Far as the eye could reach, behind and before us, stretched the dull red sand and the withered-looking tufts of grey-green sage bush. On the horizon to right and left, great red stone ridges rose sheer out of the sand. There was something repellent and unnatural about them, perhaps because their sides seemed rather to have fallen away in slices, without cause, than as other hills and mountains, to have been worn away by waters, or to have been thrown up molten hot during some vast volcanic movement. No bird or beast or any living thing was in sight, but beside the occasional dried-up watercourses lay the whitening bones of cattle, and there were many little skeletons upon the sand. Under the leaden sky it seemed a land of death, forsaken of God and man.

Hour after hour went by thus as the train sped on. Then, suddenly, a figure in loose dark blue garments with a touch of brilliant scarlet, started out, ran half crouching along the ground, and disappeared behind a mound of sand. A few moments later was seen a tiny village of huts built of sun-dried bricks made from the red sand. Close to the huts were little patches of tilled land, some of which showed the tall dried-up stalks of last year's maize, whilst others were planted with tiny trees. We were passing through one of the 'reservations' which the American Government has set apart for the Indians.

Everywhere that one goes in the United States one meets a certain picture. It is chosen for the decoration of the State House and the theatre. Should the descendants of the pilgrim fathers, or the 'Sons' or 'Daughters' of the American Revolution, desire to present a work of statuary or painting to their native town, it is always the subject chosen. In it is represented the joyous entering of the white settlers into the rich blossoming country of America, whilst the lion and the tiger and the other beasts of prey, the Red Indian people, the original natives of the land, steal off into the darkness of the past. Here, in the midst of the dreary New Mexican desert, is one of the spots to which the Indians have been driven.

Some hours later the train stops at a small town. The passengers flock out to stretch their limbs, after many tedious days in the over-heated car. Several Indian men, with broad, brown faces and long coarse black hair, wearing loose blue cotton suits, with blankets about their shoulders, are selling little bits of turquoise matrix and smoky topaz. Women, with short red skirts and white felt leggings, are selling bead chains and earthenware pottery that they themselves have made.

But it is inside a wide-doored barbaric-looking building in the centre of the platform, that the best Indian work is to be seen. Here is an abundance of wrought silver, iron, and copper work, baskets woven with extraordinary fineness, and pottery decorated with simple harmonious pattern. Women and girls are weaving richly-coloured woollen rugs, but they are merely servants. The whole business is managed by loud-voiced Yankee hustlers, who demand high prices for the goods.

As the train starts off, and the passengers flock into the dining car, a man of the district talks freely of the trade in Indian wares. He is one of those who live by it, and he exports rugs and other things to Europe, as well as to New York and other eastern cities. He employs large numbers of the Indians. He says that a squaw can make a rug such as we have seen in a month's time. He sells the rug for many pounds; but he tells without hesitation the incredibly small sum he pays the woman for her work. When a word of protest is uttered, he excuses his meanness by saying that it is difficult to prevent the women wasting or stealing some of the wool that he doles out to them for weaving in their homes. When asked if the Indians still use for themselves rugs of their own making, he says, 'No', and explains that they cannot afford them, but must buy instead (out of what the white trader pays them for their own wares) cheap machine-made things.

Now that the red people well nigh have been exterminated, perhaps partly from pure pity and compunction, and partly perhaps because the aborigines are an interesting curiosity like the buffalo or any other rare wild thing, the American Government now wishes to save them from becoming extinct. They are called the 'wards' of the nation, and where the soil of the reservations is too poor, or the conditions are too unkindly to maintain them, rations are dealt out to them. Several Indian Colleges have been set up, where any young man or woman who has even a sixth part of Indian blood may be admitted, and the Government sends out into the reservations to collect free students for these institutions.

* * *

It was the mid-day hour for recreation at the Indian College of Haskell, at Lawrence, Kansas. A number of tall, strongly-built youths in ordinary modern clothes of navy blue were strolling about with arms around each other's necks. A group of dark-eyed girls with bright blue cotton pinafores, were skipping in the sun.

Later, we saw them at work in the various spacious buildings that make up the institution. In learning reading, writing, arithmetic, geography, history, drawing, and all the various things usually taught in schools, the boys and girls, whose ages seemed to range mostly between 15 and 20 years, worked side by side. They were graded, without distinction of sex, according to their progress. On the notice boards in the class-rooms and corridors were announcements of various debating and other societies run by the students. Amongst these was a pen and ink drawing showing Uncle Sam dressed in the Stars and Stripes, with President Taft and the 'stand-patters' and 'insurgents'. It had the hasty spirited look that one expects from the pen of a cartoonist and was very much better than many of the cartoons one sees in the Daily Press.

Many buildings are devoted to teaching the lads practical trades – blacksmithing, plumbing, carpentering, building, house painting, and numbers of others. The superintendent said that the manual work produced at Haskell was better than that done by the students at the Chicago University; also that the architects trained at Haskell frequently obtained Government posts. Everything seemed to be turned out with the accustomed modern finish, and, except for some specimens of engraved steel work and wood and metal inlay, there seemed nothing distinctively Indian. The architectural drawings were of buildings such as are to be seen by the mile in any American town.

Garment making played an important part in the women's side of the institution. One large room contained rows and rows of sewing machines; another was devoted to cutting out and fitting. Ordinary shirts, blouses and dresses, like those of any modern commercial factory, were being turned out by the score. The students were also taught to make 'fancy work', which consisted chiefly of mats, table centres, and antimacassars. Some of these were of white muslin, dotted over with foolish little pieces of green paper, cut to represent shamrock leaves. Others were embroidered with floral patterns, exactly like those which are designed, in the least possible time, by the jaded sweated factory wage slaves, who cannot pause to observe real flowers.

There was nothing to indicate that these things had been produced by Indians; no least hint of that unerring sense of fitness, proportion and harmony, that is invariably present in native Indian wares. There was nothing barbaric, inventive, fanciful – none of that joy in ornament and colour that characterizes primitive craft work. Though much of this was true of the men's side of the Institution alas, the fact jarred less tragically, for the teaching there was very much better of its kind and would develop a higher order of skill in the pupil. Moreover the very mechanical and structural nature of the things that the lads were making, necessitated their being useful and workmanlike, and there is always some beauty and interest in every really useful thing.

At the back of a show-case filled with tawdry artificial flowers, was one genuine native Indian rug – a harmonious commingling of brilliant colours grateful [*sic*] to the eye. Seeing it, I said to the teacher: 'the girls here still do some of their native weaving, pottery, and rug-making, then?' 'No', was the reply, and then, with evident scorn, 'Oh, that rug – that was made years ago. There is no weaving anything of that kind done here now'! 'Has the native work been given up because those who come here are expert in it already?' 'Oh, no', she said, 'most of the girls know nothing whatever when they come here. They do not even know what a needle is! Rug-making and all that sort of thing, is dying out amongst them as fast as it can!'

So the crafts and the decorative arts are dying out through poverty and disease in the reservations, and they are being stamped out, even more absolutely, by contact with commerce-made ugliness and false standards in schools and colleges. Soon, those sharp Yankee hustlers will have no more Indian wares to make their money with.

We watched her flitting in and out amongst her pupils – the little white woman, with her drawn, jaded face – doing her best, teaching them what she knew. There was rich blood in their veins. One saw it through their clear glowing skin, and in their strong, dark eyes, their firm full lips, their black abundant hair, and their well-nourished limbs. They were all, because of these things, comely; but while some had the squat forms and features characteristic of certain tribes, others were tall, and their faces possessed a strange dignity and beauty, immobile and statuesque.

What, with the passing of the ages, might the Red race have become had the white men not gone with fire and slaughter to make war on them? Were they in an early stage of a long development, or would they, if unmolested, have remained always simple and primitive as then? What is their future now? Will they die out altogether? They do not take kindly to the life that the white men have given them. 'I will not stay in one place', said the old chief, when the reservation was offered. 'I see that in one place my people die off from famine and sickness more quickly than by the sword. When I am dead you may put me in one place.'

When the spring comes, many boys break loose from Haskell College, and fly back to the tribal home.

'It is no use bothering about the Indians,' says the man in the street. 'Whatever you do for them, they nearly all go back to their old ways. They are too lazy to work!' 'They make very good house servants,' says his wife, 'but you can hardly ever get them to stay'.

'Onwards floweth the water, onward through meadows broad;

'"How happy," the meadows say, "art thou to be rippling onward."'

7. Universities and Legislatures

EDITOR'S INTRODUCTION

Incorporating much of Sylvia's public letter to Emmeline Pethick Lawrence about her address at the Iowa State House, this chapter contains the first references to her own lectures. The experiences relayed here all derive from the 1911 tour and convey the spontaneity that was often required of her. As she explains here, at neither Iowa, where she spoke on 1 February 1911, nor Michigan, where she spoke on 24 March 1911, did she arrive expecting to speak before the state government. When she reached Iowa, the strain of the tour had taken its toll: her throat was sore and her ability to speak was restored by the swift intervention of a local osteopath, Dr Nina Wilson Dewey. It is testament to the impact that Sylvia made in America that this would not be their only encounter. The following year, Sylvia left St Louis, Missouri (where this book ends) believing that Feakins had arranged for her to speak in Des Moines, when instead she was booked to speak at Streator, Illinois. Arriving unexpectedly in Des Moines on the morning of 23 February 1912, it was reported that Sylvia spent the day with Dr Dewey who sent the necessary telegrams. In fact, the reports referred to 'Lady Pankhurst', both the press and the minutes of the state government indicate that this was a shared misapprehension that had somehow taken hold locally (perhaps the evening gown Sylvia had been persuaded to wear for a daytime address helped cause confusion).[1] After Sylvia returned to England, she sent her account of force feeding to the American press (see Introduction, p. 51), but she also sent it in a letter to her 'Des Moines Friend' Dr Dewey who ensured extracts were published in the local press.[2]

Above all, this chapter confirms Sylvia's optimism that American society would see fundamental changes and that this would be effected by women's political emancipation. It was in her speech to the Michigan state government that Sylvia spoke of sweeping away the 'bridge, balls and dinners' women (see Introduction, p. 14), explaining that the suffragists would show the 'money spenders' that 'every woman owes a duty to her fellows and that every woman must do her share of the world's work.'[3]

Sylvia found her view confirmed by her experiences in Colorado where women had the right to vote and where she sat in the State House beside a female elected representative, Alma Lafferty, an energetic reformer described by contemporaries as 'the woman who does things'.[4] Whereas elsewhere Sylvia had observed 'graft' and resultant political cynicism, she felt that there was a marked difference in Colorado:

> I was at once impressed by the fact that, whereas all over America most of the people whom one met appeared to take very scant interest in legislative affairs [...] here in Colorado every woman appeared to understand politics, and almost all were interested in some particular measure or measures of social reform. Instead of the usual buzz of small talk about the weather, dress, and one's neighbour, at the receptions at which I was present here everyone was talking of legislation.[5]

The antithesis of bridge, balls and dinners, Sylvia was also impressed that this sense of social responsibility was combined with an atmosphere of jovial informality in the State House. Sylvia twins the Legislatures here with Universities which she likewise characterised as youthfully exuberant and lacking in oppressive, conservative stuffiness. She placed great hope in the women studying at university in America; the day before speaking at the college in Lawrence, Kansas, on 16 March, about which she writes here, she stated:

> The movement for woman suffrage in the United States will depend largely upon the college women in politics. To these young women who have received the benefits of courses in economics, civics and kindred subjects will fall the task of spreading the doctrine of justice to the women throughout the country.[6]

One of those college women was Doris Stevens who was sat in the sociology class at Oberlin in which Sylvia Pankhurst spoke and with which this chapter opens.[7] Inspired to become involved in the suffrage struggle, Stevens joined that year and was to become one of the American 'militants' when she was imprisoned in Occoquan Workhouse for picketing the White House in 1917.[8]

UNIVERSITIES AND LEGISLATURES

In January 1911 on my visit to the United States I spoke at Oberlin University in the State of Ohio. I arrived at Oberlin in the morning and spent the day with the students.

They were delightfully and spontaneously young and gay. On the whole they seemed to be younger and more buoyant than the students of the English Universities. They rose very early and their meals were spartan in their simplicity.

After my meeting in the evening some of the young men and women students surprised me by asking me to take the 'Social Problems Class' next morning, saying that if I would do so, they were sure that the Professor would agree. I said that *I* felt sure the Professor would not approve of their suggestion and begged them not to mention the matter to him.

However, when morning came, I was conducted to the 'Social Problems Class Room', where an unusually large number of students had assembled. Professor Wolf, who had vacated his chair for me, introduced me to his class and at his request, I discussed women's suffrage in some of its historical aspects, explained the technicalities of the English Parliamentary and Local Government franchises and answered questions put to me by the students.

This incident made me feel very decidedly that I had come to a country where red tape was very much less in evidence than in my own.

Oberlin was the first of the American colleges that I saw, but I soon became quite familiar with the college 'yells'. Waiting at the door of the University chapel of Lawrence Kansas, I heard a most formidable uproar, produced by the commingling of the local yells with other cries and shouts of laughter and occasionally my own christian name. Knowing the boisterous ways of the young men students of British Universities, I wondered, as I stood listening to the din, what sort of reception I was to get and whether I should be able to make myself heard. But as soon as I reached the platform, absolute quiet reigned and the gathering was as generous and attentive as could be. From letters which some of the students sent home to their parents and which found their way into the Press, I learnt that many of those present had expected to see a very old lady, instead of someone who looked not so very much older than themselves. But I am certain that whoever had come to speak to the students would have received the uniformly courteous hearing, which, in America, the students always give.

* * *

On the following first of February, wearied with much travelling and many meetings and with my throat so sore that I could hardly speak, I arrived, after a night journey, at Des Moines, Iowa, where I had to change trains, on my way to a little place called Boone. As I climbed down the high steps of the train, a group of newspaper reporters and others came running towards me and told me that I was to speak at the State House in Des Moines that day. I thought that there must be some mistake, for my itinerary stated that I must go straight on to Boone by the first train, but just as I saw insisting that I must go and trying vainly to learn from what station my train was to start, someone came up behind me, and putting her hand upon my arm, said in a deep voice: 'I am Mrs Stevens of Boone'.*

Her words relieved my anxiety, for I knew that, being at hand, Mrs Stevens would see that I did not risk missing the meeting that she had arranged. In that unknown country of vast distances and tremendous snowfalls, which cause the trains to be frequently hours, sometimes days, behind time, the fear of not being able to keep one's engagements was an ever present one. Then Dr Nina Dewey,† a clever Osteopath, said that she would cure my throat, a promise that she faithfully and most marvellously kept, before an hour had passed.

Soon after Dr Dewey, Mrs Stevens and Mrs Coggeshall,‡ a little old lady, since dead, who had given the best years of her life to the suffrage cause, drove with me to the State House.

The Iowa State House is a big modern building, finely placed on the top of a hill. On reaching it we went up in a lift to the first floor and found ourselves in a large hall decorated with mural paintings.

---

* Rowena Edna Stevens (1852–1918) was president of the Boone Equality Club.

† Dr Nina Wilson Dewey, member of the executive committee of the Iowa Equal Suffrage Association.

‡ Mary Jane Whitley Coggeshall (1836–1911), described by Carrie Chapman Catt as 'the mother of woman suffrage in Iowa', she was a long-standing suffrage campaigner. At the time Sylvia met her, she was the honorary president of the Iowa Woman Suffrage Association. She died in December 1911.

Then, piloted by one of the Members, we passed through a wide corridor and entered the Assembly Chamber. It was a large circular hall surrounded by a wide gallery, with seats sloping upward, which was thrown open to visitors and which I judged would accommodate at least a thousand people. Seats on the floor, under the gallery, were also provided for visitors. Right opposite to us as we entered, was a raised platform and on the wall behind was an engraved portrait of Abraham Lincoln with the stars and stripes draped around it.

As this was a Joint Convention of the Senate and the Assembly, the President of the Senate and the speaker of the Assembly both sat on the platform, surrounded by a number of officials.

The Legislators occupied the centre of the floor. Each one had his own revolving office chair and his own separate desk, placed a foot or two apart from its neighbour's and fitted with little drawers down either side. On every desk were a number of substantial looking volumes which I took to be the local equivalent of our Hansard, containing the Parliamentary debates.

Many of the Legislators sat with their feet upon their desks. There was a constant buzz of talk from the visitors' seats and [the] sound of people coming and going. An official walked about, raising his hand and snapping his fingers, when the noise grew specially loud. The Speaker tapped with a wooden hammer on his desk when he wished to make any announcement.

Presently began the business of electing a United States Senator, for which object the members of the Upper House had come to sit with the Assemblymen. The Clerk in a monotonous voice called in turn the name of each Legislator, who replied with the name of a candidate. The Clerk then repeated the name of the Legislator and of the candidate for whom he had voted and passed on to the name of the next Legislator. It sounded like this: –

'Jackson'

'Johnson'

'Jackson votes Johnson - - - Jameson?'

'Thompson'

'Jameson votes Thompson - - - Jefferson?'

And so on for a time that seemed as though it would never end.

Again and again had this question been voted upon, but it had remained unsettled for many weeks. No candidate could be elected unless he polled a clear majority of the votes of the House. So far no candidate had done this and, as the supporters of the rival claimants stubbornly refused to give way, and successive roll calls left the figures practically stationery, there seemed no reason why the dead lock should ever be brought to an end.

But at last the voting was over for that day, the President announced that I was present to address the House and, following Mrs Stevens, I passed down the central aisle to the Speaker's seat. The President and the Speaker received me graciously and the former briefly introduced me to the House.

It seemed to me a very solemn occasion. I had learnt that the only woman who had ever before addressed the Iowa Legislature was Susan B. Anthony, who had pleaded for the Married Woman's Property Bill a generation before. A Bill for the enfranchisement of the women of the State was to be laid before the House that very afternoon and I felt most seriously the responsibility of speaking for these women to the elected representatives of the men of Iowa, many of whom probably never had been and perhaps would never go to a suffrage meeting, and yet would be called upon to say aye, or nay, to the Women's Bill. I also knew, that by what I might say to them and by the impression I might produce in their minds, those present would very largely judge our British militant struggle, of which the majority had heard only through newspaper reports. I strove to properly interpret the spirit of that struggle and of the brave women who have so eagerly and selflessly given and sacrificed for its sake. I longed to feel with greater intensity the strength and beauty of the ideal, which is at the root of the world wide woman's movement, the ideal of the boundless value of human life and the human spirit, and of the comradeship of men and women, as equal guardians of the human family, in the cherishing and ordering of the nation's home and in the uplifting of the race. I longed to feel this with every fibre and to be as a window through which all those present might see it too, but who is there that can find words to tell of things so great? Nevertheless it seemed to me that the whole hall was with me. Two old men in the front seats shed tears and afterwards the Legislators and visitors flocked round to wish God-speed to the suffragettes at home.

I asked many Legislators if they would vote for the Iowa Women's Bill and all whom I asked said 'Yes'. I said 'will it pass' and they answered: 'It needs the incentive of the women's work'.*

---

* {SP} A majority of the Legislators voted for the Bill but not the two-thirds majority necessary to carry it.

* * *

Sometime afterwards, on arriving at Grand Rapids, Michigan, I learnt, as unexpectedly as at Iowa, that I was to speak to the Michigan Legislature at Lansing. This had been arranged by Mrs Huntley Russell,* one of the ablest and hardest workers for women's suffrage in the State. Mrs Russell herself introduced me to the Legislators, to whom she was well known, having lobbied them assiduously. She and I were the first women to speak in the Michigan Legislative Chamber.

The suffrage Bill had been defeated some weeks previously and it was expected that before it could be brought up again, a General election, probably resulting in considerable changes in the Legislative personnel, would have taken place and that two years would have elapsed, for as a rule, the Michigan Legislature only sits in alternate years. Early in 1912, however, a Special Session was called to discuss a Bill for the 'Presidential Primaries' and in that Session, the Governor having included votes for women in his message to them, the Legislators reversed their earlier unfavourable decision and passed the Women's Bill. When the question was submitted to a referendum vote of the men electors, as everyone knows, it was first declared that the women had won and afterwards that they had lost by a few hundred votes. Whatever may be the result of a closer inquiry, there can be little doubt that success is not far distant.

* * *

On paying a flying visit, to Denver, Colorado, I was invited by the five women members of the Legislature to visit the State House, and was asked to sit amongst the Legislators at the desk next to that of Mrs Alma Lafferty.† Boys with baskets of large rosy apples were threading their way in and out amongst the seats and handing two or three of the apples, which had been sent by the Colorado growers, to each of the members of the House. Though I was not a member, I also received two apples.

A roll call was meanwhile being taken and when it was over the Sergeant-at-Arms brought in two of the members, whom he had arrested for not being in their places. It was proposed that by way of fine they

---

*   Clara Comstock Russell (1866–1935), the first vice-president of Michigan Equal Suffrage Association.

†   Alma V. Lafferty (1854–1928), elected to the Colorado House of Representatives in 1908 and 1910.

should present cigars to the men members and chocolates to the women. One of the women urged that the culprits should be excused, but it was decided that the cigar and chocolate fine must be paid. All this seemed wonderfully unlike the House of Commons.

Afterwards, at the Speaker's invitation, I addressed the House on the English Militant Suffrage Movement.

It was a regret to be obliged to leave Denver next day, without having seen the working of the Juvenile Court and many other excellent institutions, in the promotion of which the women voters of Colorado have played an active part.

8. The South

EDITOR'S INTRODUCTION

Determined to go to the South to investigate the working conditions of women and children, Sylvia accepted the invitation of the Nashville Equal Suffrage League and, on 13 February, boarded a sleeper train from Chicago to Nashville, Tennessee.

Accommodated in the plush Hermitage Hotel on Nashville's 6th Avenue, Sylvia was not immediately able to avoid the imposition of social functions; a day after her arrival, the local newspaper reported approvingly that, for the visiting suffragette, 'today is quite filled in with many charming engagements.'[1] One of these, wearily recorded towards the beginning of this chapter, was the 'Eligibles Ball' – presumably one of the many Valentine's Day parties that coincided with Sylvia's arrival.[2]

Billed as an 'Artist, Historian, Agitator, Educator Direct from London', Sylvia's first meeting in Nashville, held at the Ryman Auditorium on the evening of 15 February before 2,000 people, was by all accounts a great success.[3] Consistent with the political radicalism she expressed in the rest of her 1912 tour, at the Ryman Auditorium Sylvia associated the struggle for women's political equality with working women's struggles for economic equality. She therefore championed 'equal pay for equal work', and she was almost certainly referring, once again, to the 1911 women's strike in Bermondsey when

> speaking of the under payment of working women, Miss Pankhurst said that men hold that women need less to live on, but she declared they overlooked the fact that many of them have children to take care of. She gave a pitiful illustration of a women's strike in London, which included women in all sorts of trades, not one of whom earned more than six shillings a week.[4]

It seems that she went even further in defying the WSPU's proscription to separate the women's movement from the labour movement and its parliamentary party when she unabashedly declared '[t]he labor party is now coming out for us.'⁵

Invitations to speak poured in, especially from colleges. Sylvia recalls here travelling to speak to the students at Cumberland University, in Lebanon, Tennessee, and the Nashville press reported her appearances at Belmont College, a Methodist training school and Ward Seminary, prompting one 'Out-of-Town-Mother' to protest 'that these girls should have been allowed to listen to a woman who holds lightly all the virtues our southern girls are taught to cherish'.⁶ This chapter also demonstrates that Sylvia was able to explore the labour conditions of working women in the South as she had intended, always taking care to note, as in her observation of the factories in Lebanon, how women's inferior status, embodied in their political disenfranchisement, enabled their greater exploitation in the workplace.

Sylvia's tour of Tennessee not only involved a rebellion against the leadership of the WSPU in Britain, she also challenged that of the National American Woman Suffrage Association (NAWSA). In Britain, the WSPU's insistence on keeping the women's suffrage movement 'separate' from the labour movement had precluded co-operation and eventually facilitated a reactionary hostility towards it, while in America, NAWSA's policy of 'neutrality' towards racism, resulted in the marginalisation and exclusion of black women activists, with some campaigners raising openly racist arguments which promised (white) women's suffrage as a bulwark against black voters.⁷ Sylvia's refusal to collude in the construction of an elitist suffragette movement corresponded to a like refusal to turn a blind eye to racism.

An understanding of racism as a means of securing the domination of a white elite is apparent throughout this manuscript. In the first chapter, she noted a laundry in New York that paid immigrant Italian workers less than their counterparts born in the United States, while Chapter 6 explored the extermination and exploitation of Native Americans. In Tennessee, Sylvia encountered the violence of a society racially segregated by the Jim Crow laws. The recent history of slavery haunts the text: rich white people 'talk glibly of the "slavery days"' while their black servants wait on them. As one of the 'charming engagements', Sylvia was taken to the Hermitage, the plantation mansion of President Andrew Jackson preserved then, as now, as a museum. All the features Sylvia describes remain there still on display, from the wallpaper that so offended Sylvia's artistic sensibilities, the steps up to the beds – and 'the cabins in which the slaves were housed'. In her discussion of past and present, Sylvia's text bears witness to the continuity of racist exploitation.

In the same way that Sylvia repeatedly recorded the inequalities between men and women, she also recorded the unequal treatment meted out to black people. Although Sylvia's descriptions at times draw upon racial stereotypes, there is no ambiguity in her indictment of systemic racism. This is outlined most extensively in her harrowing account of her visit to the prisons in Nashville. In this nightmare reality, Sylvia, a passionate advocate of penal reform who had herself experienced imprisonment, attempts to identify with the prisoners, speak with them and take up their complaints. The moment when she finds herself too afraid to enter a cell is a desperately painful, vulnerably honest and self-reflective piece of writing. There is no hero in this narrative and Sylvia's most active resistance to racism is concealed in the section titled 'A Negro University', which details her attendance at a service and speaking at Fisk University, a college for black students. She would only later recall that, when it was announced she would speak at the college, 'I was astonished to find every newspaper I opened on my journey thither, protesting against my action.'[8] Addressing a black audience in Tennessee represented an explicit rejection of the racist, elitist arguments for women's suffrage that some activists espoused and, indeed, one newspaper in Missouri confidently asserted that Sylvia would be prohibited from attending: 'The Nashville suffragettes would not let Sylvia Pankhurst even look at the Fiske [sic] University students, and Sylvia, being mindful of the loaves and fishes, meekly obeyed.'[9] The account in The Crisis, the organ of the National Association for the Advancement of Coloured People, suggests that the local suffragists made strenuous efforts to exert the pressure of the national organisation to prevent Sylvia's attendance:

> It has leaked out that when Sylvia Pankhurst went to Nashville at the invitation of the local suffrage association, the Nashville League learned that she had accepted an invitation to address the students of Fisk University. They 'kept the wires hot between that city and New York,' but Miss Pankhurst kept her engagement.[10]

Accordingly, on 16 February, Sylvia spoke to an audience of black students in the chapel of Fisk University, an experience warmly recalled here.[11] Her determination reflected her understanding that the women's movement could not benefit from selling itself as a tool to maintain elite privilege, but had instead a common interest with the labour movement and the struggle for racial equality in wresting power from those elites by seizing democratic control of society.

It is fitting, in this incomplete manuscript, that the last chapter deals so extensively with the racist oppression of black people. Sylvia Pankhurst would later be prominently associated with the anti-racist movements of the twentieth century; this manuscript testifies to the importance that she afforded to challenging racism throughout a lifetime's struggle for democracy and emancipation.

THE SOUTH

In the bitter cold one evening I left Chicago, on the Dixie Flyer, for Nashville, Tennessee, and awoke to find the snow all vanished and a feeling of genial warmness in the air.

In the hurry of dressing and getting together my luggage, I had not a moment to look around, and the first sight I had of Tennessee, was as I stood in the space between the two coaches, where the negro porter, ever kindly solicitous for the comfort of the passenger, and especially the passenger travelling alone, had already put my bags. He had thrown the door open and was already leaning far out with one foot on the second step, though we had not yet reached the station.

Suddenly I saw a deep pit down below us, we were passing close along its edge. The sides of the pit were covered with rock and shale and rubbish, and there were heaps of this all around the brow. Crouching and picking amongst the rubbish were a number of negro women.

They were lost to sight in a moment, for our train had entered the dark and smoky station.

They say that Nashville is a typical Southern City. It is a smoky little town that has grown up gradually, as English towns do, instead of being built on a fixed plan as typical North American cities are. Its narrow roughly paved streets wind about unexpectedly, all up and down hill. Its architecture is a curious jumble of buildings. There are some few big shops and warehouses, faced with stone in the usual, brand new, tremendous-fronted, American style, and close beside them are many low, old-fashioned, often tumble-down looking structures, built of brick, or even of wood. Everything, be it new or old, is rapidly begrimed by the smoke from the tall factory chimneys, that pours itself forth right in the centre of the town, unchecked, and scatters large smuts everywhere.

Driving over the steep cobbles are many little hooded vehicles, perched high on a pair of slender, spidery looking wheels. These conveyances, like almost everything else in Nashville, appear, as a rule, to be several coats of paint lacking. It often happens that their occupants are negroes, and indeed one of the first things one notices is the very great number of negroes in the streets, amongst whom are types rarely seen further North.

On the outskirts of the town one finds the negro dwellings, poor miserable little hovels most of them. One wonders how all the dark skinned people with gleaming white teeth, that one sees at the open doors, can find room to eat and sleep inside. As a rule they smile cheerfully when a carriage drives past, whilst the members of the old Nashville families, who boast of their pure English descent, talk glibly of the 'slavery days' as they sit behind the Negro coachman, or are waited on at table by the Negro women servants.

*　　*　　*

On the afternoon of my arrival, I was driven some miles from the town to see 'The Hermitage', the old home of President General Jackson.* Our road lay through a beautiful country of hills and dales and rocky bedded swiftly running streams. The grass was a rich brown colour, there were quantities of deep green firs and cedars and there were patches of brilliant emerald moss upon the stones. These things were infinitely welcome to eyes tired with the vast stretches of flat land, and the monotonous wastes of still ice and snow of the Middle West. Even the hardiest Northern evergreens were withered and brown this bitter winter in the North; but here the leaf buds were near to bursting and one could feel the Springtime in the air.

'The Hermitage' is reached through an avenue of cedars, and in its garden are trees that they call hollies there, but the berries of those trees

---

*　　Andrew Jackson (1767–1845) served as a general in the war of 1812 against the British, in the course of which he also led campaigns against Native American and Spanish forces. He was, from 1829 until 1837, the seventh president of the United States. The Hermitage was Jackson's mansion and plantation which profited from the labour of enslaved black people. It remains, as it was when Sylvia visited, a museum open to the public.

are smaller and fewer than the berries of English hollies, whilst the leaves, beside being smaller, are differently grown, and though they possess, as holly should, a certain spikiness, they lack the high glossy polish and sharp cut edge that, to us, are so characteristic of the holly tree.

The house itself is built in a style which, I am told, was a very favourite one in the old colonial days. It is a dignified, comfortable looking structure of red brick, with a row of massive fluted columns of white stone along the front, reaching from floor to roof and topped by a low obtuse angled pediment.

The glow of the old well-burned brick makes the place look warm and attractive from without, but within it is cold and dreary. The walls of the entrance hall are covered with a hideous hand-painted paper, specially procured from Paris in General Jackson's time, which shows innumerable little six inch gods and goddesses passing through a series of meaningless adventures. It seems impossible that nineteenth century Paris could ever have produced anything more ugly.

The rooms are crowded with dark heavy furniture, loaded with tasteless ornaments, and there are many stiff, awkward looking portraits upon the walls. Beside the great four post beds are still placed the steps by which the family were obliged to climb up to them at night. It all looks stuffily artificial and conventional, and yet it was the home of a romance.

We are told that one day General Jackson rode out of this house and returned with the wife of another prominent officer. This lady stayed with the General as 'Mrs Jackson' for the rest of her life, and no one appears to have questioned her right to the title.* Thereafter, as far as mutual love, respect, and constancy can do so, these people seem to have justified the breaking of society's conventions and, as no children were born to them, he adopted her young relations to be his sons and daughters.

Two rooms alone are pleasing and restful, the dining room and the kitchen. In the dining room are hung the best portraits in the house, and there is a quaint old hickory mantel piece and a long dining table, beautifully shaped and perfectly polished.

The Kitchen is a separate building, which stands some four or five yards away from the house. On one side of its great fireplace is a large

---

* Rachel Jackson, née Donelson (1767–1828). Sylvia's claim that the two lived together unmarried is mistaken; Rachel was separated from, but still married to, Captain Lewis Robards when she married Andrew Jackson in 1791. Once the divorce was obtained, they married again in 1794.

old spinning wheel, and on the other are hung the ripe heads of black, red, white, and yellow Indian corn. It seems miles away from the dull ugly rooms so near to it, and though long deserted, it seems kindly and homelike still. What an enduring charm there is in a place built for work! Next to the Kitchen is the coach house where are the two old carriages in which General Jackson used to ride, and in one of which he made his long journeys to the White House at Washington to attend Congress.

At the end of the garden to the left of the house, is the little grave yard where lie the General's adopted family, and the tomb with its glowing tribute to her memory which he shares with his stolen love.

Just across the field from here, still standing in a row, are the cabins in which the slaves were housed.

* * *

That evening I was prevailed upon, by the kindest of invitations, to visit a function arranged by one of Nashville's fashionable clubs, which was called the 'Eligibles Ball' and was given for a group of unmarried young people all of whom were supposed to be under thirty years of age. In the entrance hall the chaperons, a crowd of tall well-groomed men and women in evening dress, sauntered up and down, groups of them stopping occasionally, with whispering and laughter, to peer through an open doorway, into the room where the 'eligibles' were dining together at a round table decorated with red flowers.

The 'eligible' young men all wore ordinary black evening dress, but their ladies had disguised themselves as musical comedy heroines. There were Pink Ladies, Quaker Girls, Spring Maids with sunbonnets and very short skirts, and numbers of others whom I could not name. Some of the 'eligibles' were obviously very young, but others, especially the men, looked far far older than one ought to at thirty years.

Just as we old fogies* stood clustering around the door, snapdragon was brought in, the lights in the dining room suddenly went out, and we could see nothing but the tiny blue flames flickering, to a chorus of noisy laughter and little screams.

The chaperons turned away to talk amongst themselves, skimming all sorts of subjects lightly in bantering tones.

---

* Despite describing herself as one of the 'old fogies', Pankhurst was within the age-range of the 'Eligibles' themselves: her thirtieth birthday was on 5 May 1912.

'Prohibition? Why what's the use of that?', said a young German who had spent much time in England, 'It would be unthinkable in London, and don't you know that in Kansas City the street that runs between the State of Kansas, that is dry, and the State of Missouri, that is wet, has a row of saloons all along the Missouri side?' 'Yes,' someone else interrupted 'and you're just settling down to a drink, and a game of cards in the Pullman, when the porter rushes in and makes you put your cards up and your glasses down, because you've passed into the next State!' 'When I heard that the Women of California had voted against Prohibition, I began to think I might give them the Suffrage after all – "Oh! votes for women – "'. So it went on.

Presently the 'eligibles' came trooping from dinner, wearing little hearts and tiny cupids, cut out of red paper and pinned to their chests, not hidden away under their coats like the Jewish Secretary's Frithian dove of peace and goodwill in Mr. Zangwill's War-God, but openly displayed.*

At midnight the dance began and in it joined all the 'eligibles' and many of the chaperons. Mark Twain says that the soul and spirit of a people cannot be understood except by a process of 'absorption', by 'years and years of intercourse with the life concerned'.† Therefore I, who am ever an outsider in matters of this kind, whether at home or abroad, could only look on as a foreigner, with curious amaze. I saw young men and women dancing together with slow jerky prancing steps, bodies leaning very much backwards, knees very much bent, arms held out very

---

* *The War God*, an anti-war play by Israel Zangwill, a prominent supporter of the militant suffragettes, was first performed at His Majesty's Theatre in London in November 1911, shortly before Sylvia set out for her second trip to North America.

† 'A foreigner can photograph the exteriors of a nation, but I think that that is as far as he can get. I think that no foreigner can report its interior – its soul, its life, its speech, its thought. I think that a knowledge of these things is acquirable in only one way; not two or four or six – *absorption*; years and years of unconscious absorption; years and years of intercourse with the life concerned; of living it, indeed; sharing personally in its shames and prides, its joys and griefs, its loves and hates, its propensities and reverses, its shows and shabbinesses, its deep patriotisms, its whirlwinds of political passion, its adorations – of flag, and heroic deed, and the glory of the national name. Observation? Of what real value is it? One learns people through the heart, not the eyes or the intellect': Mark Twain, 'What Paul Bourget Thinks of Us', *The North American Review*, Vol. 160, No. 458, (January, 1895), pp. 50–51.

stiff and wagged jerkily up and down. 'I am sorry' said my hostess, 'that they are dancing the new dances'.

I slipped away then and left them dancing on till the sun shone.

* * *

At the meeting in the Auditorium next evening, which I was told was the first public meeting on Women's Suffrage ever held in Nashville, though I think that Susan B. Anthony and her Colleagues must surely have been there in the old days, between 2,000 and 3,000 persons were present.* I thought that I had never had a more sympathetic audience. Before the proceedings began I was told that the Governor's little nine year old daughter was present, and as she declared herself to be an enthusiastic believer in the cause, it was suggested that she should make a speech. I said that I could not agree to this, as I considered her to be many years too young, and so the matter dropped. I fear that if the young lady heard of my veto, she must have felt as much mortified and wounded as I did, when, at an even earlier age, I was turned away from the doors of a Medical Museum, where I earnestly wished to examine the human skeleton, on the ground that children were not admitted.

A few weeks after I had left Nashville, I learnt that the Governor's little daughter had actually mounted the Speaker's rostrum in the State House and had addressed a plea for Votes for Women to the Legislators of Tennessee.†

A NEGRO UNIVERSITY

On a piece of waste ground beside a church on the outskirts of Tennessee, there stands a pathetic little one-roomed building, in which, a year after

---

* Sylvia spoke at the Ryman Auditorium in Nashville on 15 February 1912. The local press estimated 2,000 people attended: *Nashville Tennessean*, 16 February 1912, p. 7.

† Nine-year-old Anna B. Hooper, the daughter of Tennessee governor, Ben W. Hooper, did indeed deliver a speech in favour of women's suffrage at the State House. She is reported to have said: 'My fellow citizens: – I come pleading for you men to let the women vote. Do you believe in the way Mrs. Pankhurst is trying to get votes? No, I do not. I do not believe in smashing up the windows, but I do think you ought to let us vote. Why should we not help to make the laws of our country? The ignorant men are allowed to vote, but the educated women are denied this privilege. This is not right, and every sensible man knows it': *Woman's Journal*, 16 March 1912, p. 82.

the Civil War of emancipation, a Negro university was started. One passes this little place on one's way out to the imposing buildings which now form Fisk University.*

We were late. Already the service had started. In a moment I found myself on the platform looking down upon hundreds of dark earnest faces and steady lustrous eyes, eyes that for all their darkness, seemed to glow with inward light, as do rich wine and precious stones, or as a deep well with the sun glancing through it.

An aisle down the centre of the hall separated the rows of men and women students who were about equal in number. Sitting in the front row on the women's side was a little soft dark woodland creature, her head, broad above and small and delicate below, poised on a slender neck, her hair a mass of curling rings, and her eyes wide and gentle as a fawn's. There were others of her type, but she it was, in her dark crimson woollen jacket, who first caught my sight.

Here and there on the benches were women with rather flat yellow faces and black hair, straight and coarse as an American Indian's.

One man's face, long and strange to a European, was so absolutely jet black and immobile that he might have been carved of ebony, and in his stiff college mortar board, he made one think of some ancient idol. In common with many other students, he had come straight from Africa to attend the college. Near him sat a youth with pale skin and head of classically European type.

A tall dark skinned student on the platform stood up to lead a Negro hymn. In a voice sweet, wonderfully almost incredibly sweet, he sang: 'Oh that I had the wings of the dove, oh that I had the wings of the dove!' Again and again those same words, to a melody that rose and fell and changed in growing. Gradually hundreds of other voices joined him, echoing and re-echoing in many toned chorus. Now a single woman's voice sang of the gushing of the waters, or the waving of green palm branches, and each time the chorus hushed, to return after a space, to their longing for the dove's wings, and to break forth with many many

---

* {SP} Fisk University is, I understand, the only Negro institution for higher education, the other Negro colleges being rather manual and technical training schools in which the academic work is not very advanced. The Fisk entrance examination, I am told, is similar to those of Harvard, Yale and other well known American Universities, and though there is a tendency for the Fisk students to fall behind in the five years course, this is said to be chiefly due to the fact that most of them are obliged to earn their daily bread during their time of study.

voices, rising and falling as the doves might soar, now in a cadence of scattered units, now in a simultaneous onward sweep of sound, free and spontaneous, always and ever marvellously sweet.

Surely there was never such singing. Who could find words to speak to them of things material after this?

I only know that I felt their earnest gaze upon me. They seemed to listen more intently than other audiences.

LEBANON

I was considering by what train I should leave Nashville, when I received by the long distance telephone, an invitation to speak for the Socialist Society of Cumberland University, one of the oldest and most noted law schools of the South.

Lebanon, a little town of 2,600 inhabitants, is about two hours' journey from Nashville. I was met at the dingy, unfinished-looking station, by a crowd of young men – the Socialists of Cumberland University. They all shook hands solemnly, and stood around, whilst Mr. C–, with whom I had spoken on the telephone, helped me into the rickety old hotel bus. Mr. C–, was tall and thin, probably about thirty years of age, with kindly cheerful blue eyes and very pink cheeks. It was he who had determined that I should come, and had carried through all the arrangements for my meeting. He seemed very enthusiastic and excited about it and exceedingly anxious to help me up or down every available step, and over every possible difficulty.

The hotel was a curious shabby place, long and low, and built of two storeys.* We entered a large bare room, clouded with tobacco smoke, some men were lounging in wicker chairs, others were standing drinking at a bar, at which I registered my name. Whilst I was doing so, another band of university students were brought up to be introduced. Then I was taken to my room by a shabby, almost ragged Negro, whom one might describe as a huge dwarf, for though he was as tall as an ordinary man, he was shaped like a dwarf, with ungainly stooping figure and enormously long arms. He seized my luggage and went on before me, dragging his feet and catching them dangerously in the holes of the worn oil cloth.

The staircase was in the centre of the house, and on the upper storey it opened on to a broad landing, furnished with four settees. This

---

* Sylvia stayed at the West Side Hotel, which burnt down in 1982.

landing was called the 'parlour', and except the bar room, where I had registered, it was the only sitting-room in the hotel. This so-called 'parlour' was intersected at right angles to the stairs, by a long narrow passage, running from one end of the house to the other, from either side of which opened the bedrooms. My bedroom was at the far end of the passage on the right hand, and I learnt that the bathroom was at the extreme end of the passage on the left, so that to reach it, one must pass each time through the 'parlour' and traverse the whole length of the house. Everything about the house seemed to have been made originally of the very cheapest possible material and then to have been altogether neglected. Everything presented the most striking contrast to the smart Hermitage Hotel in Nashville, and others of its kind in the big cities, where all the furniture looks as though just sent in from the maker's and every visitor has his, or her, own private bathroom, with porcelain bath and gleaming taps.

Lunch was served in a large dingy room on the ground floor, where there were three long tables. It was pouring hard outside, and there was no glimmer of sun, but the wooden shutters were only partly open. The table cloths and napkins were of coarse calico, roughly hemmed at the edge, and badly washed. A plate for each visitor was laid face downwards on the table, possibly to keep the dust off until the person for whom it was intended should arrive to turn it up and use it. The two-course meal was brought in by negroes, in soiled white coats with frayed cuffs, and a general air of untidiness. First there was soup, then fried mutton, hard and overcooked, potatoes, two or three kinds of dried beans in separate little dishes, ice cream, sponge cake, corn cake, rolls and black and white bread, – all placed on the table together, as well as iced water, tea and coffee.

The tables were crowded with the delegates to a Methodist Conference that was taking place in the town. In appearance, the ladies of the party seemed to me to be very much more English than American. I could not make up my mind quite why, but came to the conclusion at last, that it was because their clothes were less awe-inspiringly fashionable in cut than most of the others that I had seen.

Shortly after lunch, a troop of the law students and two ladies came to call on me, and shortly afterwards, five of us packed ourselves into a small cab, and set off in the rain to visit the two factories of Lebanon.

We went first to the 'pencil factory' in which, not pencils, but the wood for covering pencils, is prepared from the cedars, because of whose abundance here, this Lebanon was named.

The factory is a roughly built wooden structure with an outside staircase. We climbed the stairs, and entered a place that might well serve as a representation of Hell. The noise was deafeningly tremendous. At first one could see only a cloud of dust, and a confusion of machinery and human beings covered with dull red powder. Gradually, as one became accustomed to the relatively dim light and the stupefying roar, one began to disentangle the crowded scene. On a raised platform in the centre of the room was a huge negro, working at a great circular revolving saw that cut up big logs of wood with lightning speed. These pieces of log fell from the saw, then passed into receivers, and were carried automatically in different directions to several relays of men who cut up the logs with smaller and smaller revolving saws, till they had been subdivided again and again, and finally were reduced to thin little oblong pieces of wood, out of which the casing of two, four, or six lead pencils might be cut. Then the little pieces of wood slid away out of sight, down shafts that carried them into a room below. All this was going on constantly. The giant negro cutting up the big logs in the centre, always kept busy the relays of men extending to the four corners of the room, who subdivided the logs into smaller and smaller pieces.

Negroes and white men were working side by side together, and except by their build and the shape of their features, were indistinguishable, because of the cedar dust which covered them and filled the air. Absolutely nothing was done to carry off the dust, yet to preserve anything like decent conditions for the workers, every saw ought to have been fitted with an exhaust fan.

In the room below, girls and women were sorting, according to size and quality, the little pieces of wood that came down on to their benches through the shafts. Here too the air was heavily charged with dust, and whilst the women wore newspaper caps to protect their hair, nothing whatsoever was done to protect their lungs. They worked with breathless haste – one marvelled that they could keep up that extraordinary rate of speed for more than a few moments, but they never paused from their clap, clap, clapping of one little piece of wood upon another.

The women and girls were paid by the piece, some earned three dollars a week, some four or five, or even six. One child who had only been there a short time, told me that she had earned one and a half dollars the week before. These were all white girls, presumably of English extraction. I did not see any negresses amongst them. I do not know how their wages compared with those of the men, with whom, owing to the noise, it would have been impossible to talk without stopping the machinery.

Carrying away on little wheeled carts the piles of wood that had been sorted out by the women and girls, were a number of boys. Many of these were quite little fellows, others must have been fifteen or sixteen years of age. Some few of the boys were sorting wood like the girls, but in a much more leisurely way. The boys were all paid by time, at the rate of a dollar a day. One might easily have guessed that the boys were not paid by the piece, for, of all the workers in the factory, they alone seemed to have time to take life comfortably. It could not be said that they were idling, but they smiled and spoke a word to each other as they passed, and one little lad rushed up to Mr. C – , who seemed to be an old friend, and pinched his arm in a playful way.

Before we left the 'pencil' factory we stopped in the little office, to see the machine that marks the exact moment of each worker's arrival, and to have the clinging red cedar dust brushed from our clothes.

I wondered what could be the average number of years during which people could continue to work at the terribly high rate of speed that I had witnessed, and amid the nerve racking noise of machinery, and the injurious dust. I wondered how long it could be, on the average, before the workers were worn out.

The virtual impossibility of manufacturing under the fierce competitive system in which we live, except at a financial loss, or at an infinitely more serious loss of health and happiness to the workers, is everywhere apparent. How long will it be, one wonders, before some community of free men and women sets itself steadily to build up a true Republican brother and sisterhood in which this odious system shall find no place?

At the blanket factory, where work seemed scarce, for many looms were standing idle, the wages of women employed on full time, varied from three dollars, to five and a half, or six dollars a week. A widow with several children dependent on her, told me that she was a new comer to the factory, and had earned less than two dollars the preceding week.

Just as I was getting ready for the Lebanon meeting another lady visitor was announced. She soon disclosed the fact that she was a journalist and an anti-suffragist. She told me that somewhere in the neighbouring hills, the women writers of Tennessee had a bungalow club house of their own. The men writers had built it of wood for them, and in a certain hollow log, each woman had placed one of her own compositions to be read in future times. My visitor had wished to put in an anti-suffrage article that she had written, but one of her colleagues had prevented her saying: 'you will disgrace us all!'

The meeting hall was well filled.* The general public were admitted, but the young men of the law school formed at least half the audience. I was introduced by the President of the University, a genial old man, who said, raising both hands above his head, that the men of Tennessee kept their women 'up in the gallery' away from the strife and turmoil of life, and that he thought that this was best.

The audience were in a lively frame of mind, and clapped him vigorously, but they cheered me when I referred to the women of Lebanon, whom I had seen working in the dust of the pencil factory. They agreed with me also, when I reminded them that in the State of Tennessee a married woman has no legal existence, that she has no right to her own property or earnings, that she cannot bring an action in a court of law, and that a husband, even if he has not yet reached the age of twenty-one, is in life, the sole guardian of the children, and at death, may will them all, even the unborn child, away from their mother.

When question time came, an old man stood up slowly, and asked: 'If we give women the vote, *will you get out and work the roads?*' At that, all the young men clapped and shouted, because Tennessee is one of the States where the voters are supposed to work a certain length of the public road. I replied by asking every man voter in the audience, who had ever worked the road, to hold up his hand. The hand of my questioner and three others went up. There was a roar of laughter, and the students yelled and whistled. I saw that I had guessed rightly in thinking that the law is not now enforced. Everyone applauded cordially when I pointed out, that the rule which stipulated that every voter must work a certain length of road, was not a law of God, but had merely been set up by men law makers, as a provision suited to themselves. If women alone had been enfranchised they might have decided that every voter must be able to cook a dinner, make a suit of clothes, or manage a household.

* * *

---

* Sylvia spoke at Caruthers Hall, Lebanon, on 20 February 1912.

THE NASHVILLE PRISONS

Next day, with a dreadful blizzard blowing and occasional fine snow in the gusts of wind, which seemed unpleasantly ominous of what I might expect in the North, I went back to Nashville. Having some hours to spare before leaving, I agreed to visit the prisons with Mrs T – , a woman lawyer in the town.

There are three prisons situated in Nashville, the Town Gaol, the County Gaol, and the Workhouse. Both the County & Town Gaols are intended primarily for the detention of persons awaiting trial, but gaol sentences, up to one year, are given for minor offences. Prisoners awaiting trial, frequently remain in gaol for many months, for American trials, as everyone knows, are often terribly delayed.

The workhouses are intended for the punishment of petty offenders, and their name suggests that they were originally intended as reformatories, where the more promising of the petty offenders might be set to work, whilst the more hardened cases were relegated to the gaols. On the whole the workhouses seemed to me to be better than the gaols, but prison is certainly a much more suitable name for them than workhouse.

The Town and County Gaols of Nashville, both heavy, gloomy looking structures, are situated quite close together on opposite sides of the same street.

After the great door had been opened, we passed across the dimly lighted entrance hall to an office, where sat two unkempt, dejected looking men. One of these was the Superintendent of the gaol, and with him we passed through the office into the cell house beyond.

The air within was foul and heavy, and the pitch darkness hardly relieved by a few feeble little electric lights that hung from the ceiling.

Two groups of cells were built up in the cell house. Each group was three stories high and each storey consisted of two long rows of cells built back to back. Each cell had three walls only, the front being covered with iron bars. A caged-in passage way, about a yard in width and entered by a gate at one end, connected each row of cells. The windows on one side of the cell house gave very inadequate light to the cells facing them, but on the side by which we entered, there were no windows, only the faint glimmer of the small electric bulbs that hung from the cell house ceiling.

We stood peering through the double rows of bars into the black recesses of the cells before us, unable to descry anything within, until the Superintendent led us up the first flight of stairs to the floor above, where the light was a little stronger. As we reached the top of the steps he called out: 'Hi you yellow boy, come here!' At once a pale half-caste negro broke away from a group of men, whom we could see laughing and talking together in front of some of the dark ground floor cells* in the further cell group, and came running up the stairs towards us. The Superintendent explained that he was what is called a 'trusty', that is to say, a prisoner who can be relied on to obey orders, and not attempt to break out of prison and is treated as a sort of assistant warder.

We stood by a row of empty cells. At the word of command, the trusty drew back a lever that opened the barred front of every cell and the Superintendent opened the gate of the caged passage for us to enter. We then saw that each cell was about six feet deep, by eight or nine feet wide, and contained an open water-closet, and four bunks, two of which, placed one above the other, were on either side of the door.

Having examined the empty cells, we passed on to those that were tenanted. Many of the prisoners were in bed, and in the dim light, we could see dark round heads and gleaming eyeballs against the greyish bed covering. Where the cell fronts were open, the men stood out in the caged passage way, generally huddled together in a group at one end, and leaning against the bars. Sometimes it was a group of pale shiftless anaemic looking white men, unwashed and unshaven, sometimes of negroes, in ragged greyish clothes, seeming for the most part, to have grown fleshy and gross looking from the lack of exercise. All appeared ill, miserable and degenerate.

At the back of the space between the two cell groups, were two cells, like cages, with bars all round. One of these cells, which was empty, except for the water closet, was reserved for persons condemned to death or suspected of insanity. The other cell differed only in that it contained a bed. It belonged to the trusty, and he was locked into it at night.

If he happened to be awake, he could hear all, and through the bars could see a part of what took place in the cell house, and if anything went wrong, his duty was to alarm the officials by shouting. No one else was in charge during the night.

There was light enough on this side of the cell house to see the long-standing dirt of years upon the stone floors, and the horrible

---

* {SP} Too late to see them we learnt that these were the negro women cells. They were, the Superintendent told us, exactly like the neighbouring cells occupied by men.

filthiness of the trusty's bed. The mattress had no covering but the original ticking, and this was coated with greasy black, in parts so thick that one could have scraped it off on the blade of a knife. Two dark rugs that served as bed clothes were also dirty in the extreme.

I was filled with an overwhelming horror of the place, and though I was there of my own free will, it seemed as though something in my breast fought to get away. The Superintendent was just opening another of those gates that led to the narrow cage-like passage ways in front of the rows of cells. Inside were a number of huge, degenerate-looking negroes, half-dressed in shabby garments, their figures showed hopeless misery in every line. I thought that the Superintendent was motioning us to go in amongst them, and though my heart was torn with pity, and shame that we should degrade them so, I could not overcome a wave of terror and repulsion that swept over me. It seemed to me that these prisoners must hate the whole white race! This one man, our guide, would be powerless against them, if they seized me, – they could crush me to death, like a sparrow in the grip of some huge loose-bodied creature with fierce jaws. I knew that all this was foolishness, but I felt that if one of them even brushed my dress, I should die of fear and horror. Half suffocated, I touched Mrs T –'s arm. 'I can't go in there' I said. She laughed. 'Oh he was only opening the gate for us to see', she answered.

The gate was shut and the dumb pain in their eyes made me ashamed of my fears.

One shuddered to think that human beings could be kept shut up for a year in this awful prison. Who is there that could properly defend himself in a court of law and appear, sane, upright, and respectable after a long confinement here? To be remanded to this prison must indeed be a long march on the road to conviction!

As for those who are convicted and sent here for punishment, one may well wonder if any of them are able to climb back to the ranks of self-supporting, self-respecting citizens. The dehumanizing atmosphere of the place has fastened upon the Superintendent also; he too is debili-tated and degraded by the defiance of all rules of healthful living under which the prisoners are kept.

Leaving the cell house we passed across to the other side of the prison, which was of entirely different construction, its walls being plastered and its floors of wood. Much of it appeared to be unused. In one large bare room, containing two beds, a table, and a couple of chairs, we saw a white woman who was awaiting her trial. She was heavily built and probably about forty years of age. She sat still and listless, her chin sunk upon her breast, and her arms hanging limply across her knees, gazing dismally out of the window at the prison wall across the quadrangle. She did not turn to look at us as we stood beside her, but when we spoke to her, she said that she was glad to see us. When Mrs T – asked why she was there, she answered bluntly that she had been arrested for drunkenness in the street. She said that she had never been arrested before, and that her drink had been 'fixed' by the man who had given it to her. She told us that she had been imprisoned in that room for four days, and that she had been refused leave to communicate either with a lawyer, or with her mother who would have helped her. She also complained that during those four days she had been kept without soap, towels, brush or comb. She mentioned this several times, and evidently spoke the truth, for when I turned to the Superintendent, who stood by, and heard her, and asked whether she would be allowed to have these necessaries if I sent them in to her, he agreed without comment. When we left the room he excused himself for not having sent for the woman's mother by telling Mrs T – that her sister's divorced husband had refused to do anything for her. We were also shown, as one of the curiosities of the prison, another large and scantily furnished room with two beds in it, in which two men who had shot and killed a prominent politician, had been confined a short time before. After a few days they had been allowed to go free, as it was suggested to me, for political considerations.

Opening out of this room was another containing three pitch dark cells, two of which were padded.

The Superintendent opened a small panel in the door of one of the padded cells, to show us how absolutely pitch dark it was within. The place seemed almost airless, and from it there came a heavy musty smell. 'That is the sweat shop,' he said with a grim chuckle, 'We put people in there when we want them to tell things. Four or five days of it always settles them! We had a little nigger in there the other day. She had been stealing and wouldn't tell – she soon coughed it up!'

He laughed. Poor 'little nigger', poor little woman, there is no pity in this hard place – her misery and her terror, her cries, as they dug their fingers into her soft flesh were a joke to this man and his assistants, an incident to relieve the horrid monotony of their lives. Not for an instant did they hesitate to thrust her mercilessly into this dark stifling dungeon, where, half mad with fear, she would confess anything they wished, whether it were true or no. Oh awful prison, your very walls whisper of nameless cruelties!

We left the County gaol and crossed to the Town gaol opposite. The office through which we passed had a cleanly scrubbed floor and the cell house itself was fairly well lighted, but there was little else to be said in its favour.

The cell group comprised only one storey, but this was terribly crowded. It consisted of two long rows of cells, with a narrow passage way of about eighteen inches, extending from end to end between them, a somewhat wider passage way being left between the entire group of cells and the walls of the cell house all round. Each cell was divided from its neighbour on either side by a stone party wall, but both the front and back of the cell were there enclosed by iron bars, so that the prisoners could never hide themselves for a moment, either from the inmates of the cells behind, or from the officials moving about in the cell house. Some of the prisoners were allowed to come out into the narrow passage way between the two rows of cells, which was closed by a gate at either end, and they of course could look into every cell in turn.

Each cell was about six feet deep and between three and four feet wide. It contained an open W.C. and two wooden shelves for sleeping upon. No mattresses or other bedding were provided, for it was said that it would be impossible to keep them clean. The cells were occupied indiscriminately by white men, or by negroes.

There was a most horrible smell, and whilst many of the closets were choked with paper, they were all literally caked with filth.* I wanted to think that what I saw was rust, but I knew it could not be, because the closets were of white earthenware. When I asked our guide, an old man who looked after the prisoners, what arrangements were made for cleaning the cells, he replied: 'All these cells are flushed every day'. 'Every day!' I said looking at the piles of dust in the corners, but he went on 'We do it like this, once a day, when the closets become too offensive'. As he spoke he pulled a lever outside the cell group, and set running the water in all the closets! Could anyone have imagined such unnecessary, indecent and dangerous cruelty as not [to] allow the poor wretches to flush those closets for themselves as soon as they had been used? Bad

---

* {SP} Such details are not pleasant to dwell upon, but publicity will speedily put an end to them.

enough the horrid lack of privacy and space to move about in, without that!

As we walked along the rows of cells, we came to one in which there was an old man standing propped up, with his elbows upon the topmost bunk, his hands crossed upon his breast, and his head bowed upon them. His hair and beard were long and grey. His face, beautiful as that of a saint, white and fragile, with features exquisitely chiselled. I gazed upon it fascinated, and moved on with reluctance. Presently we heard a loud heavy thud. 'It is that old man falling' said our guide, and immediately afterwards a prisoner called out: 'An old man here has had a dreadful fall'. 'Oh he's all right' was the official answer, but we rushed back to see, and our guide followed. It was true, the old man had fallen. He was lying now with his back propped up against the wall, and his legs stretched out under the bottom bunk. His head was still bowed upon his breast. He was alive, for one could see him breathing. That was all I knew. They assured us that he was drunk, and that he was an habitual drunkard. They had found him lying unconscious in the snow, and had brought him in just before we arrived. I could only hope that this was true – that it was not some horrible mistake!

There were no women prisoners at the time, but we saw the place set apart for them – a room opening out of the cell house with a wooden seat around the wall.

Until recently, both European women and Negresses had been kept here together. But [up]on a white woman, whose case had created a sensation, being imprisoned here for shooting a Negro who had assaulted her, an outcry was raised which resulted in the erection of a partition to divide the races.

In this Town Gaol, as in the State Gaol over the way, there were no women attendants to take charge of the women prisoners. In fact I was told that there were only two prison Matrons in the whole State of Tennessee.

When I commented on this, the old man, whose duty it was to care for all the prisoners, loudly protested that no woman could possibly tolerate the women prisoners because, he said, they were so 'tough'. In illustrating this he spoke of two little white girls in their early teens who had been confined in that very room, and whose language he considered unfit for women to hear.

As we came out, Mrs T – whispered to me that it was said that the women, especially the white women, met with terrible experiences when imprisoned in these matronless gaols.

* * *

By this time I felt absolutely miserable. I had seen more than enough of gaols for one day. But there was a burly red-faced policeman waiting to take us to yet another prison – the workhouse. I spurred myself on to go there, in the hope that it might be a great improvement upon the gaols.

Whilst conducting us to the Workhouse, the burly policeman explained to us that the men prisoners there were taken out to work on the road in gangs with heavy fetters upon their legs, and that the women after scrubbing the Workhouse itself, and [sic] were taken over to scrub the floors in the Town Gaol every day. This accounted for the cleanly appearance of the floors in the office and entrance passages, and the flagged space around the cell group, but it was obvious that the cells themselves had not been scrubbed for a long time.

On reaching the Workhouse we found the men prisoners in a sort of huge cage, divided by bars into three tiers of many small cells. Negroes were kept in one half of the cage, and white men in the other. White men were in the majority at that time.

There were no white women in the Workhouse just then, but about a dozen negresses. They were housed in two rooms, one opening out of the other, with a locked gate between. Some wooden benches against the wall could accommodate about four of the prisoners, the others must sleep upon the floor. All the women were obviously wearing their own clothes.

In the outer room two girls were huddled on the floor as though asleep. Another was stretched out on a bench, lying on her back with arms folded. She was quite young, a big well-developed girl, with a small head and very dark skin. I bent over and asked: 'How did you come here?' She opened her eyes and gave me a weird mocking smile. Her face had a strange, almost snake-like look, uncanny and repellent, and yet beautiful in a strange inhuman way. I imagined that I saw her gliding about amid dark tropical foliage, peering through the leaves at me with that smile – but she called out startlingly loud in answer to my question: 'I don't know, I don't know' in a high-pitched sing-song voice, and began tossing her arms about. I thought that she was probably insane, and fearing to disturb her further, I abruptly turned away.

Mrs T – and the policeman were standing at the gate leading to the inner room, and close to the bars on the other side was a very black, very plain, and very tidily dressed negro woman in a spotless white apron, who was talking to them in excited tones. She said that she had been imprisoned for being found intoxicated in the railway station, but declared that the charge was false, that she had merely gone to the station to meet some friends, and that after waiting many hours for the train, she had fallen asleep and had been awakened by her arrest. This was an exceedingly plausible story, as the trains are frequently from six to twelve hours late, or even more. 'Oh yes, of course' interrupted our guide, the fat red-faced policeman, chuckling, 'you jest went to meet your friends, you never was drunk was you? Oh you're a great girl you are!' He kept teasing and laughing at her and she continued arguing and protesting. 'The policeman slapped me – he slapped me on the head right here!' she cried, growing more and more angry and distressed. 'I never hit you', he jeered. 'No *you* didn't,' she agreed, 'it was the one who brought me here!'

After a time he appeared to think that the thing had gone far enough, and he tried to draw us away, whispering to us that she was 'not right', and tapping his forehead, but at that moment she caught sight of me and cried out: 'Oh there's the lady that was speaking at the Auditorium, I know her from the picture, you *are* Miss Pankhurst, aren't you? I believe in votes'for women too, lady, I read about you'. Then, seeing that I had some newspapers under my arm, 'Please Miss Pankhurst could you spare me one of those papers now?' I handed a paper to her and she thanked me eagerly.

All this time a number of young women were lying or sitting silent and unheeding on the floor in the room beside her. One of these sat with her knees drawn up and her head bent down upon them, vigorously running her fingers through her long black hair (perhaps because she had no comb.) Occasionally she looked up at us, with pale young face and wild tragic eyes. For days after her figure haunted me. She seemed to remind me of someone, but of whom I could not tell. At last I remembered – she was like Lydia Yavorska as the unfortunate in Maxim Gorki's 'Lowest Depths'.*

---

* The second time that Sylvia refers to a play performed in London in late 1911 (the other being Zangwill's *The War God*, see note above on p. 159). Lydia Yavorska played Nastya in *The Lower Depths*, first performed at the Kingsway Theatre, London, 2 December 1911.

As we left, the voluble negress began reading from the newspaper I had given her in a very loud voice that echoed through the place, but the other women did not seem to listen.

* * *

It was a relief to find ourselves out again in the fresh air, and to look up into the quiet evening sky, but the burly policeman came with us and poured horrible stories into our ears. In the midst of his tales of wholesale, official, clubbing and shooting and of unofficial murders of the most revolting kind, he declared that the present treatment of negroes was too lenient, 'We ought to burn them!' he said.

As we turned up one street he told us of an encounter he had had there with two white drunkards. He had arrested them for disorderly conduct, but suddenly they had pinioned his arms. 'Then', he said, 'they took my club and beat my head to a jelly. I got out my revolver and shot at them. I killed one, and wounded the other, but he got away. I knew who he was but I wouldn't prosecute him. I don't believe in beating people up and shooting them, and then putting them in gaol!'

I was glad to find that the old ruffian possessed some sort of code of honour, and hoped that all his stories were as much exaggerated as that regarding his own head.

* * *

Soon I was in the Sleeper speeding away North to Des Moines Iowa, and all night long, as I tossed and turned in my berth, I kept seeing those black noisome cells with their miserable inmates, the whites, pale, shiftless, degraded, and weary with despair, the negroes, their black faces blending with the surrounding darkness, their gleaming eyeballs, and their bodies grown gross and degenerate from lack of exercise, the women huddled on the floor, and the pale tragic face of the young coloured girl; and after these, with pain and shame, at the bitter contrast, and the awful responsibility of our race, there would come before my eyes the Chapel of Fisk University, with its sweet, its wonderfully sweet singers, their vivid faces and lustrous yearning eyes.

* * *

In the morning I awoke to find that the snow I had feared in Nashville, had swept down upon us during the night time, and had caused us several hours delay. I had missed my connection and had eleven hours to wait in St. Louis, Missouri, 'the gateway to the South'.

It was dreary waiting in the station, so I walked out to see the town.

As soon as I got outside I found myself in a strange and dingy neighbourhood. The snow, which was beginning to melt, had been shovelled from the tram lines and was piled high on either side of the road, and the pavements were covered with dirty slush. The buildings beside the way were, for the most part, dismal and dilapidated, with windows long unwashed. Every third or fourth shop was devoted to the sale of intoxicating liquors. Some of these drink shops broke the prevailing rule of dinginess, and were smartly and flashily decorated outside. Many of them displayed announcements offering free* lunches, of which, to testify to their value, the three or four course bill of fare was frequently shown outside. Other drinking saloons gave lunches for five cents.

The spaces between the saloons were filled up largely by barbers who, in lieu of the historic pole, called attention to their whereabouts by means of two fat striped pillars, which were placed, one on each side of the door, and either had a lamp on top, or were lit up from within at night. In the windows one saw the men who were being shaved, lying stretched out upon long chairs. There were many tobacconists' shops also, with carved wooden American Indians in feathers and war-paint standing on the pavement outside. There were several freak and monstrosity shows and a number of 'Anatomical Museums' which as men stationed at the door loudly proclaimed, were free all day to men only.

Scattered amongst the other shops, were a few where women's and children's clothing was on sale. There I gazed in amazement to see, in this country of high prices, ready made garments as cheap, or cheaper, than one could find in England! Amongst other things was a little boy's overall suit with tunic, belt, and knickerbockers made of blue cotton stuff and trimmed with white braid for 25 cents (one shilling). I knew without possibility of doubt that only the most awful sweating had produced these things.

---

* {SP} I am told that these lunches are highly flavoured with pepper and hot spices to create thirst, and that the saloon keepers consider that they gain by them more than enough custom to pay for serving them gratuitously.

I walked on and on along this Market street till I was tired, but the scene did not change. I wondered how one city could possibly support all these saloons. There was scarcely a woman in the street, but there were many men and their faces were not good to see.

Weary and despondent I retraced my steps and so I saw my last of the South. How many a thousand of my own country people have left home and kindred to build up a new life in this new world and have found here a grave for their hopes – and perhaps their souls!

Notes

1. INTRODUCTION

1. *New York Times*, 13 January 1912, p. 7.
2. Elizabeth Gurley Flynn, 'Women in American Socialist Struggles' (1960), in Elizabeth Gurley Flynn, *Words on Fire: The Life and Writings of Elizabeth Gurley Flynn*, compiled by Rosalyn Fraad Baxandall (New Brunswick, NJ and London: Rutgers University Press, 1987), p. 171; see also the report in *New York Call*, 13 January 1912, p. 3.
3. *New York Times*, 13 January 1912, p. 7; see also *Woman's Journal*, 22 January 1912, p. 23.
4. In Britain, Sylvia kept quiet about this activity until a year later, publishing her account in *Votes for Women* in October 1912 when her sister Christabel was out of the country, in exile in Paris. Once again, this appears to be an example of Sylvia feeling freer in America to express the links she was drawing between the labour and suffrage movements, before gaining the confidence to do so in Britain. On Sylvia's role in Bermondsey, see my *Sylvia Pankhurst*, p. 45.
5. *New York Times*, 13 January 1912, p. 7.
6. See Mary E. Dreier, 'To Wash or Not to Wash: Ay, There's the Rub: The New York Laundry Strike', *Life and Labour*, Vol. 2, No. 3 (March 1912), pp. 68–72.
7. Arwen P. Mohun's study of steam laundries cites overheated, damp conditions and a lack of additional rooms to change clothes and eat food as typical of the industry in this period: *Steam Laundries: Gender, Technology, and Work in the United States and Great Britain, 1880–1940* (Baltimore, MD and London: Johns Hopkins University Press, 1999), p. 74.
8. *New York Times*, 13 January 1912, p. 7.
9. On the defeat of the strike see Sandra Adickes, *To Be Young Was Very Heaven: Women in New York Before the Great War* (Basingstoke: Macmillan Press Ltd., 1997), p. 117.

2. INTRODUCTION

1. *Evening Wisconsin*, 29 January 1912, p. 1.
2. Pankhurst to Hardie, 5 February 1912, ESP Papers, 9.
3. Sylvia described Miss Miller to Keir Hardie as a 'young girl' (she estimated between 20 and 30 years old) who might benefit from viewing factories: 'I guessed seeing those conditions would be good for her'; Pankhurst to Hardie, 5 February 1912, ESP Papers, 9.

4. For contrasting feminist visions of the workplace in this period, see Sheila Rowbotham, *Dreamers of a New Day: Women Who Invented the Twentieth Century* (London: Verso, 2011), Chapter 9.

5. *Milwaukee Journal*, 31 January 1912, p. 3.

6. Ibid.

7. *Milwaukee Free Press*, 3 February 1912, p. 1.

8. Ibid.

9. Ibid.; see also *Evening Wisconsin*, 3 February 1912, p. 4.

10. Ruby Stewart, 'Women's Wages in Milwaukee', in *Women's Wages in Milwaukee*, Bulletin No. 4 (Milwaukee, WI: Bureau of Efficiency and Economy, June 1911), pp. 6–11.

11. *Milwaukee Free Press*, 3 February 1912, p. 1.

12. Ibid.

13. Ibid. Although neither Australia or New Zealand had legislated for equal pay it is likely that Sylvia was referring to the wage boards both countries had established to regulate against low wages.

3. INTRODUCTION

1. Dates established from Pankhurst to Hardie, 22 January [year not recorded but the content demonstrates it is 1912], ESP Papers, 9; *Akron Beacon Journal*, 15 March 1912, p. 1; *News-Herald*, 15 March 1912, p. 1; *New York Times*, 6 April 1912, p. 1.

2. Pankhurst, *The Suffragette Movement*, p. 349.

3. Text Sleeping Beauty in Neighborhood Playhouse 8-MWEZ + n.c. 10,290, Billy Rose Theatre Division, NYPL.

4. Ibid.

5. Ibid., and 'Program for Midwinter Pantomime' (two versions) in Neighborhood Playhouse folder, Billy Rose Theatre Division, NYPL.

6. Melanie Nelda Blood, 'The Neighborhood Playhouse 1915–1927: A History and Analysis', PhD thesis, Northwestern University, 1994, Appendix A, p. 393.

7. *Daily Oregon Statesman*, 7 August 1914, p. 3.

8. Pankhurst to Hardie, 22 January [1912], ESP Papers, 9.

9. Mabel Pollen to Mrs Myers, undated, NYPL (transcript available at http://archives.nypl.org/uploads/documents/transcript/collection_10602_virginia_myers_letters.pdf).

10. Pankhurst to Hardie, 22 January [1912], ESP Papers, 9.

11. See the chronology of productions in Blood, 'The Neighborhood Playhouse', p. 393.

12. *New York Times*, 5 April 1912, p. 1.

13. *Times-Democrat*, 2 April 1912, p. 16.

14. Lillian D. Wald, *Windows on Henry Street* (Boston, MA: Little, Brown, and Company, 1936), p. 22.

15. Alice Lewisohn Crowley, *The Neighborhood Playhouse: Leaves from a Theatre Scrapbook* (New York: Theatre Arts and Books, 1959), p. 11.

16. Pankhurst to Wald, 30 April 1912, Lillian D. Wald Papers, NYPL.
17. Untitled typescript in Neighbourhood Playhouse, Billy Rose Theatre Division, NYPL; see also Crowley, *The Neighborhood Playhouse*, p. 16.

4. INTRODUCTION

1. Pankhurst, *The Suffragette Movement*, p. 255.
2. *New York Times*, 7 January 1911, p. 3.
3. *Ottawa Citizen*, 11 February 1911, p. 1.
4. *Chicago Sunday Tribune*, 22 January 1911, p. 7.
5. *Ottawa Citizen*, 11 February 1911, p. 1.
6. Charles Dickens, *American Notes*, p. 113; see also Mark Colvin, *Penitentiaries, Reformatories, and Chain Gangs: Social Theory and the History of Punishment in Nineteenth-Century America* (Basingstoke and London: Macmillan Press Ltd., 1997), pp. 85–106. The building still exists as a museum.
7. *Altoona Tribune*, 5 April 1911, p. 8.
8. *Topeka State Journal*, 6 May 1911, p. 14.
9. *Evening Wisconsin*, 31 January 1912, p. 2.
10. See Colvin, *Penitentiaries, Reformatories and Chain Gangs*, pp. 171–179; Larry E. Sullivan, *The Prison Reform Movement: Forlorn Hope* (Boston, MA: Twayne Publishers, 1990), pp. 36–37.

5. INTRODUCTION

1. Pankhurst to Hardie, 5 February 1912, ESP Papers, 9.
2. Ibid.
3. Ibid.
4. Ibid.
5. Ibid. As a guest of Eastman and Phillips – see *Milwaukee Leader*, 1 February 1912, p. 3. Crystal Eastman was known as Crystal Eastman Benedict at this point as she had married Wallace Benedict in 1911. However the marriage was short-lived and she soon reverted back to her maiden name by which she is better known.
6. *Evening Wisconsin*, 1 February 1912, p. 8.
7. *Woman's Dreadnought*, 8 March 1914, p. 3.

6. INTRODUCTION

1. Pankhurst to Hardie, undated letter [March 1911], ESP Papers, 9.
2. Ibid.
3. Ibid.
4. *Jeffersonian Gazette*, 15 March 1911, p. 5; *Daily Gazette* (Lawrence, KS), 15 March 1911, p. 2.

5. See Myriam Vučković, *Voices from Haskell: Indian Students between Two Worlds, 1884–1928* (Lawrence, KS: University Press of Kansas: 2008), pp. 11–29.
6. Ibid., p. 16.
7. *Hutchinson Gazette*, 21 March 1911, p. 8.

7. INTRODUCTION

1. *Des Moines Register*, 24 February 1912, p. 5; the Journals of both the House and Senate of Iowa record that 'Lady Pankhurst ... addressed the Joint Convention' in 1911, *Journal of the House of Representatives of the Thirty-Fourth General Assembly of the State of Iowa*, 1 February 1911, p. 331; *Journal of the Senate of the Thirty-Fourth General Assembly of the State of Iowa*, 1 February 1911, p. 301.
2. *Des Moines Register*, 20 April 1913, p. 5.
3. *Detroit Free Press*, 25 March 1911, p. 6.
4. James Alexander Semple, *Representative Women of Colorado: A Pictorial Collection of the Women of Colorado who have Attained Prominence in the Social, Political, Professional, Pioneer and Club Life of the State* (Denver, CO: The Alexander Art Publishing Co., 1911), p. 57.
5. Pankhurst, 'Some American Impressions', *Votes for Women*, 28 April 1911, p. 495.
6. *Kansas City Times*, 16 March 1911, p. 1.
7. Doris Stevens entry in *Dictionary of American Biography*, Vol. 17 (New York: Scribner, 1981), p. 717.
8. For her own account of this, see Doris Stevens, *Jailed for Freedom* (New York: Schocken, 1976).

8. INTRODUCTION

1. *Nashville Tennessean*, 15 February 1912, p. 5.
2. For the advertisements of the Valentine's Day parties, see *Nashville Tennessean*, 16 February 1912, p. 5.
3. *Nashville Tennessean*, 6 February 1912, p. 7, and 16 February 1912, pp. 1, 7.
4. *Nashville Tennessean*, 16 February 1912, p. 7.
5. Ibid.
6. Quoted in A. Elizabeth Taylor, *The Woman Suffrage Movement in Tennessee* (New York: Octagon Books, 1978), p. 40.
7. For a very useful analysis of this process, see Davis, *Women, Race & Class*, especially Chapter 7.
8. Pankhurst, *The Suffragette Movement*, p. 348.
9. *St. Louis Star and Times*, 25 February 1912, p. 12.
10. *The Crisis*, Vol. 3, No. 6 (April 1912), p. 228.
11. *Fisk University News*, Nashville, TN, Vol. 3, No. 2 (March 1912), p. 4.

Index

Printed and bound by PG in the USA

USA2019PGIL